James Merrick, William Dechair Tattersall

A Version or Paraphrase of the Psalms

James Merrick, William Dechair Tattersall

A Version or Paraphrase of the Psalms

ISBN/EAN: 9783337002695

Printed in Europe, USA, Canada, Australia, Japan

Cover: Foto ©Lupo / pixelio.de

More available books at **www.hansebooks.com**

A

VERSION or PARAPHRASE.

OF THE

PSALMS,

ORIGINALLY WRITTEN

BY THE

REV. *JAMES MERRICK*, A. M.

DIVIDED INTO STANZAS,

AND

ADAPTED TO THE PURPOSES

OF

PUBLIC OR PRIVATE DEVOTION,

By the Rev. W. D. TATTERSALL, A.M.
Vicar of Wotton under Edge, GLOUCESTERSHIRE,
and Chaplain to the Hon. Mr. Juſtice BULLER.

LONDON:

Printed for THOMAS PAYNE and SON, at the Mews Gate;
BENJAMIN WHITE and SON, Fleet Street; ROBSON
and CLARKE, New Bond Street; G. G. J. and J.
ROBINSON, Paternoſter Row; Mr. FLETCHER and
M. PRINCE, Oxford; Mr. MERRILL, Cambridge;
and JOSEPH BENCE, Wotton under Edge.
M.DCC.LXXXIX.

THE KING.

SIR,

THE following work, the refult of much application, was at firft undertaken, and has been completed folely from a defire to promote the caufe of Religion, and the credit of the Eftablifhed Church.

In this point of view, I truft, it may not appear unworthy the regard of a Monarch, who has uniformly fhewn himfelf the firm fupporter of that Church, and gracioufly expreffed his conviction of its intrinfic purity,

§ and

and infeparable connection with our excellent Conftitution.

That the Church of England may continue to flourifh, and preferve its accuftomed mildnefs and moderation, under the happy government of Your Majefty and Your illuftrious defcendants, to the lateft ages, is the earneft. prayer of,

SIR,

YOUR MAJESTY'S

Moft dutiful, and

moft obedient Servant,

W. D. TATTERSALL.

ADVERTISEMENT.

THIS alteration of Mr. MERRICK's learned and truly Poetical Verſion of the Pſalms would have been too preſumptuous an undertaking, if its aim had not been to improve that part of our Church Service which has long been the ſubject of the moſt ſevere animadverſions. Although it has been printed nearly two years, the Editor was unwilling to offer it to the Public, till he had collected the ſentiments of the Rulers of our Church, and of thoſe friends whoſe abilities are well known, and on whoſe judgment he could ſafely rely. He has the greateſt pleaſure to perceive that the principal objection to its admiſſion into pariſh churches appears to be the difficulty of adapting ſeveral of our beſt old tunes to a metre differing from the ancient verſion. Some tunes have been varied in his muſical collection *, whence an opinion may be formed of farther improvements : and if this objection ſhould be done away, the Editor will have reaſon to entertain hopes that his undertaking may, at ſome future period, obtain a proper ſanction for

* To be had at BLAND's Muſic-Warehouſe, N° 45, Holborn ; and of all Bookſellers in town and country.

its

ADVERTISEMENT.

its general introduction into churches. He has therefore taken some pains to select a number of tunes more than sufficient to answer the design of having one to each psalm, and intends to submit them to the inspection of the best judges of music, that he may retain those only which shall be esteemed most likely to do credit to the service, and which he intends publishing hereafter, in addition to the present work. Dr. COOKE, Dr. HAYES, Dr. PARSONS, Mr. CALLCOTT, the Rev. OSBORNE WIGHT, Mr. WEBBE, Mr. SHIELD, Mr. STEVENS, and many other persons of musical skill and eminence, have kindly promised him their assistance; and, as it is his earnest wish to bring forward such a work as may be an ornament to our Liturgy, he solicits the like assistance from the Professors of Music in general, and will think himself extremely obliged to any gentlemen, who will favour him with tunes, either of their own composition, or selected from old melodies, that may be adapted to the purposes of Psalmody, or calculated to employ the leisure hours of a Sunday evening.

Wotton under Edge,
May 1791.

THE AUTHOR's

PREFACE.

THE following attempt on the Pſalms, though a mixture of Tranſlation and Paraphraſe, will, I hope, be found to contain little more of the latter kind than what may be uſeful either in opening the ſenſe, or in pointing out the connexion, of the Original. The defects of it, great as they muſt be, would probably have been much greater, had it not been favoured with a reviſal by a gentleman, whoſe various and well-known abilities, together with his ſingular acquaintance with the Hebrew Poetry, rendered him peculiarly qualified for the office. The Re-

A 2   verend

verend Doctor Lowth, Prebendary of Durham, having read a part of the work, was pleased to express a desire of seeing the whole: The Author of it was too sensible of the advantage which was likely to result from his inspection of it, to decline such an offer; and takes this opportunity of publicly acknowledging the very great service which he has received from this gentleman's assistance; who, after having in a most friendly and candid manner proposed his objections where he judged them necessary, was pleased to encourage and advise the publication of the work. My thanks are also particularly due to my very worthy and learned neighbour John Loveday, Esq; to whose perusal the several parts of the work were submitted, almost as soon as composed, and whose accurate criticisms have rendered it less unworthy of the public light; to which, without consulting such judicious friends as himself and the gentleman abovementioned, it had been presumption to expose it: As the latter of these gentlemen (whose son Mr. John Loveday, of

Magdalen

Magdalen College, Oxford, a young gentleman of diftinguifhed abilities and learning,
has feconded him in every office of friendfhip
and humanity towards me) has moft readily
affifted me in confidering the fenfe of the
Original whenever I have applied to him, fo
the former has favoured me with a great
number of obfervations on the Hebrew Text;
which I may hereafter (if God give me
health) commit to the prefs, together with
many others communicated to me by perfons
of very great learning and eminence, and
with fuch remarks as have occurred to
myfelf in comparing my Verfion or Paraphrafe with the Original. Though the annotations which I have received from Dr.
Lowth were written in a very expeditious
manner, without confulting many commen-
tators, yet the fingular attention which that
learned gentleman appears (in his admirable
lectures on the Hebrew Poetry) to have paid
to the Pfalms, as well as to the other poetical parts of Holy Scripture, had fo prepared
him for the work which he has thus obligingly
taken upon him, that they will, I am per-

fuaded,

fuaded, be found worthy of their author. As those annotations which have been put into my hands are (many of them at leaft) fuch as will not be underftood by any perfons who have not applied themfelves to the ftudy of the learned languages, I have rather chofen to referve them for a feparate volume than to fubjoin them to the Verfion or Paraphrafe which is here prefented to the reader. The inconveniences arifing from my fituation, remote from any of the moft public libraries, have been in a great meafure remedied by my acccefs to the large and well-chofen libraries of a gentleman before mentioned, and of my late pious, learned, and ingenious friend, the Reverend Doctor BOLTON Dean of Carlifle, as alfo by the favour of the moft Reverend the Lord Archbifhop of CANTERBURY ; who has (in addition to the many other inftances, which I have experienced, of his Grace's goodnefs and condefcenfion) been pleafed to honour me, on this occafion, with the voluntary offer, and the ufe, of fome of the moft confiderable expofitions of the Pfalms ;

fuch

such as those of Geierus, Michaelis, and Houbigant; together with Celsius's Hie-robotanicon, Hillerus's Hierophyticon, and several new Versions of the Psalter in different languages. As the communication of these valuable helps demands my humblest gratitude, so it likewise encourages me to hope (though my own incapacity and a long course of ill health will scarce allow me to think of attempting a regular Comment on the Psalms) that it may be in my power, in some instances, to confirm by sufficient authorities such interpretations of several difficult texts as I have followed, and, in others, to discover the errors which I have committed.

It may be proper to advertise the reader, that The Version or Paraphrase of the Psalms now put into his hands has not been calculated for the uses of public Worship. The translator knew not how, without neglecting the Poetry, to write in such language as the common sort of people would be likely to understand: For the same reason he could not confine himself

in

in general to ftanzas, nor, confequently, adopt the meafures to which the tunes ufed in our Churches correfpond. How- ever, as his meafures are all of the Lyric kind, his work may, he hopes, anfwer the purpofes of private devotion. Two of the Pfalms, the hundred and eleventh and the hundred and twelfth, have indeed been purpofely tranflated or paraphrafed in the meafure which anfwers to the tune of the hundredth Pfalm, as it is fung in the Church, on account of its known excel- lence.

The judicious reader will not, it is hoped, be offended, if he finds the fame phrafes, and even the fame lines, fome- times occur in different Pfalms, when he confiders what liberty of repetition the He- brew Poetry admits in one and the fame Poem, and, confequently, how often the fame expreffions are likely to be found in a collection of many Hebrew Poems com- pofed on fimilar fubjects. The candid Critic may the better judge what degree of indulgence the tranflator of fuch a work

may

may ſtand in need of, if he knows to how great difficulties no leſs able a writer than CORNEILLE was reduced on a like occaſion : whoſe words, in the Preface to his poetical Verſion and Paraphraſe of Thomas a Kempis, are as follows:——*Sur tout les redites y ſont ſi fréquentes, que quand noſtre Langue ſeroit dix fois plus abondante qu' elle n' eſt, je l' aurois épuiſée fort aiſement, et j' avoüe que je n' ay pû trouver le ſecret de diverſifier mes expreſſions, toutes les fois que j' ay eu la meſme choſe à exprimer.*

Whatever imperfections may be diſcovered in the following performance, when examined with a critical view, I ſhall by no means think my labour either uſeleſs or unrecompenſed, if any pious perſons ſhall find their devotion aſſiſted and improved by it, or their love more ſtrongly excited towards the great Author of our Salvation, ſo evidently pointed out in the courſe of theſe divine Compoſitions.

June 5, 1765.

THE

THE EDITOR's

PREFACE.

THE Liturgy of the Church of England is allowed, by the most learned and devout of the reformed churches abroad, as well as by the most candid and liberal of all religious sects among ourselves, to contain a judicious compilation of sublime and admirable compositions. Probably it is altogether the best that ever was formed for the use of any Christian community, except perhaps in the apostolic age. It has, therefore, been often lamented, that the poetical version of the Psalms, by Sternhold and Hopkins, should be, on the whole, so unsuitable to it; that the part of the service, which consists in singing the praises of our Creator, has consequently suffered a shameful neglect; and that, from the same cause, various abuses have gradually arisen, which it requires a very careful interference to correct. For the removal of these complaints, it appeared to the Editor, that the

version

version compofed by the late Mr. Merrick
was peculiarly fitted, excepting only that it
was not divided into ftanzas throughout; an
objection which it has coft him fome time
and attention to obviate. Frequent endea-
vours have indeed been ufed to render the
old verfion lefs objectionable, by felecting
from it certain portions of the Pfalms; but
thefe well-meant defigns, from fome defect
or other, have generally failed of producing
the defired effect. As a more complete re-
medy, Brady and Tate employed themfelves
in forming an entire new verfion, which
they obtained permiffion to introduce among
thofe congregations who were inclined to
receive it. This performance did indeed
deferve confiderable approbation when pro-
duced, but appears to come far fhort of
that fince made by Mr. Merrick, both
in perfpicuity and fublimity of expreffion.
Yet the utmoft hope of this excellent
Author, refpecting the practical ufe of his
verfion, feems to have been that it might be
found to ferve the purpofes of private devotion. He has even affigned a reafon why
he could not make it fit for public worfhip;
namely, " that he knew not how, without
" neglecting the poetry, to write in fuch lan-
" guage as the common fort of people would
" be likely to underftand. And for the fame
" reafon,"

" reafon," he adds, " he could not confine " himfelf in general to ftanzas, nor confe- " quently adopt the meafures to which the " tunes ufed in our churches correfpond." He has, however, with a view to the former purpofe, compofed Doxologies adapted to his own metres, and that even where he has not divided the Pfalm into ftanzas : a circum- ftance very favourable to the defign of intro- ducing his verfion into general ufe.

Many perfons indeed have thought with the Author himfelf, that Mr. Merrick's ver- fion is entirely above the capacity of the loweft clafs of people; and perhaps it is hardly poffible to write any thing, which, to perfons fo uninftructed, fhall be in all refpects intelli- gible : but whoever compares it with the verfion of Sternhold and Hopkins, or the later production of Brady and Tate, will cer- tainly difcover that this objection holds not lefs ftrongly againft them : and that, in the work before us, the expreffions which convey the fentiments of the Royal Prophet, are for the moft part clear, as well as poetical and fublime.   But though the Author found it not convenient to divide the Pfalms in gene- ral into ftanzas, a difficulty has arifen to fome readers from that very circumftance : for in long-continued fentences they have feemed to

want, notwithstanding the punctuation, some
guide to direct and fix their attention, and to
shew them where to rest. In the form now
given to these compositions, besides that they
are thereby fitted for parochial use, the reader
will be enabled to dwell upon each verse at
pleasure, and digest the sense, without fear of
error, as he proceeds.

The two former versions, allowing for
the times in which they were made, may
certainly be regarded as efforts greatly laud-
able; but when we consider to what degree of perfection our language has now ar-
rived, and with what propriety and elegance
Mr. Merrick has expressed, and often ex-
plained the sense of his inspired Author, it is
no unfair derogation from them to point out
where the preference must unavoidably be given. The lustre of Mr. Merrick's performance
will perhaps be found in some measure di-
minished in those places where the Editor
has been obliged to make a few alterations :
but when his motive for the undertaking
shall be fairly considered, he flatters himself
that not many will censure him for the liberty, which, through necessity, he has taken.
As Mr. Merrick has declared that he was
particularly attentive to the poetry in his
version, and as the success of that atten-

tion is univerſally allowed, the Editor has
been always on his guard to vary from him
as little, and as ſeldom as poſſible: and, to
render the performance free from all ma-
terial exceptions, whenever an addition was
neceſſary, he has preferred, almoſt conſtantly,
the introduction of lines written by Mr.
Merrick himſelf, in ſome other part of the
verſion, to ſupplying the deficience by his
own pen. Where this could not conveniently
be done, he has carefully endeavoured to
imitate Mr. Merrick's ſtyle. He has alſo paid
great attention to the Bible tranſlation, and
has been guided and directed by the beſt com-
mentators.

Some perſons, on being conſulted, have ſug-
geſted, that by leaving out certain lines which
appear rather redundant, the neceſſary alterations would frequently have been made with
greater eaſe. The aſſertion perhaps is juſt;
but, unwilling to omit any part of compoſitions ſo deſervedly admired, the Editor
has generally put himſelf to difficulties to
preſerve as many as poſſible of the original
lines. In ſome paſſages however he found omiſ-
ſion altogether unavoidable: he was neceſſi-
tated alſo in a few inſtances to alter the tenſes,
the perſons, and the ſtops, that the ſenſe in
each verſe might be clear and diſtinct. This
liberty

liberty he thought himself fully warranted to take, upon the authority of that very worthy and judicious critic, Dr. Lowth, the late Bishop of London, who, in one of his remarks on the eighteenth Pfalm, has delivered his fentiments to Mr. Merrick in this manner: " You feem in doubt here about the Time. " You fee the Paft and the Future are all " along very much confounded in the He- " brew; and, I believe, the beft direction will " be, to fuit the Time as well as you can to " the context and courfe of your verfion."

The Pfalms are divided into ftanzas of from four to twelve lines, by which means the purpofe of variety is fully anfwered. The fhorteft ftanza has been in general preferred. The Editor, fome few years fince, formed a portion of Mr. Merrick's Pfalms into ftanzas for the ufe of his own church; and at the fame time, with the aid of feveral ingenious profeffors of mufic, adapted to the words fome of the choiceft tunes he could obtain, which he has now publifhed as a fpecimen of what may be effected: from that partial attempt he has been led on imperceptibly through the whole work. It is certain he met with many difficulties at the firft, in removing the prejudices of his congregation, who were ftrongly attached to the verfion they had been

fo

fo long accuftomed to ufe, and were little
difpofed to admit of any innovation: yet he
has the fatisfaction to obferve, that, by per-
feverance, every obftacle has been overcome;
that his parifhioners now, fo far from object-
ing to the change, are highly pleafed with it,
and give it every encouragement. It is, indeed, the general remark, that there are few
churches, where the pfalmody is more de-
cently and folemnly performed, and, on the
whole, more juftly admired.

There can be little occafion further to detain the reader with remarks, either on the
prefent imperfections of our pfalmody, fince
they are very generally acknowledged, or
on the means of removing them, among
which, the prefent publications, affifted by
the attention of the clergy and others, will,
it is hoped, be found efficacious. Should any
thing further be thought neceffary to illuf-
trate either of thefe points, it may be given
under the authority of names that carry
with them the utmoft weight. Dr. Brown,
in his Differtation on the Rife, &c. of Poetry
and Mufic, obferves, that " in the Pfalms as
" they are verfified by Sternhold and Hopkins,
" there are few ftanzas which do not prefent
" expreffions to excite the ridicule of fome

" part

" part of every congregation." " This ver-
" fion," he adds, " might well be abolifhed,
" as it expofeth one of the nobleft parts of
" divine fervice to contempt. Efpecially as
" there is another verfion already privileged,
" which, though not excellent, is not intole-
" rable. The parochial Mufic feems to need
" no reform: its fimplicity and folemnity fuit
" well its general deftination, and it is of
" power, when properly performed, to raife
" affections of the nobleft nature." And
Dr. Vincent *, in his excellent treatife, inti-
tled, " Confiderations on Parochial Mufic,"
after citing the above obfervations, declares,
that " if from the improvement of our lan-
" guage, or the refinement of our knowledge,
" the whole is become unfit for its office;
" the dictates of reafon, and the fervice of re-
" ligion, require that it fhould now be dif-
" carded, and fome fubftitute prepared to fup-
" ply its place." He further remarks, that
" if pfalmody were once reftored to its origi-
" nal rank and eftimation, it would become
" an object of regard to the ruling powers to
" have this whole matter re-confidered and
" revifed. In that cafe it would not be diffi-

* Head Mafter of Weftminfter School, Sub-almoner and
Chaplain to the King, and Rector of Allhallows the Great
and Lefs, London.

a 3.　　　　" cult

" cult to form a collection from different au-
" thors, which might carry this point as near
" perfection as is requisite. There is a ver-
" sion by King James the First, which Mr.
" Pope commends, and is worthy his com-
" mendation; there is another by Sandys;
" an excellent one by Mr. Merrick; there
" are detached psalms in Milton, and other
" authors; all which might be examined and
" appreciated, and a whole formed which
" would do honour to our own or any other
" church; and if such a selection were once
" sanctioned by Episcopal and Royal Autho-
" rity, it would come to the people with every
" prospect of producing all the reformation
" that is desired. Such a work as this, would
" contribute to form a national taste, as well
" as promote the national religion, nor is it
" impossible, that, with suitable encourage-
" ment, religious music should again enter
" into the recreation of domestic leisure, and
" revive the sentiments of primitive religion.
" Then also an opportunity might offer for
" once more calling in the aid of fresh mu-
" sical composition, which new metres might
" require, or the simplicity of the present
" metres could admit; but nothing of this
" sort can be attempted till many of the pre-
" vious points are established."

It

It appears indeed highly defirable, that the poetical verfion of the Pfalms fhould be rendered as pleafing as poffible to every perfon who is a member of the church, whether he be employed as a performer, or only as a reader and hearer ; for it frequently happens that many in our congregations, without being much attracted by the mufic, will take up their prayer-books to follow the fingers in the words. But fuch perfons, though ferioufly difpofed, have feldom been able, where the old verfion was ufed, to forbear fmiling at the quaint and injudicious expreffions which there continually prefent themfelves : nor can it be expected that many readers of this age will be induced to look more than once into the verfion of Sternhold and Hopkins, with the view of deriving any rational fatisfaction from the perufal. This, it may fafely be afferted, can never be the cafe with the work of Mr. Merrick, which, on a variety of accounts, muft, to every judicious mind, afford the trueft fatisfaction and delight. The following quotation from the poetical Prelections of the late Bifhop of London, would be alone fufficient to recommend that verfion to public notice:—" *Vir doctiffi-* " *mus* JACOBUS MERRICK, *Verfionem Pfalmo-* " *rum carmine vernaculo jam abfolvit* ; *opus*

† " *eximium,*

" *eximium, multis eruditionis, artis, ingenii lu-*
" *minibus diſtinctum*.*"

Should the ſtanzas in this Edition appear to be arranged with ſufficient ſkill and
judgment to deſerve the ſuffrage of the public ; and ſhould Mr. Merrick's work, in this
form, be conſequently annexed, by permiſſion
or authority, to our book of common prayer,
it might ſoon, inſtead of lying hid in the libraries of the learned, become a very pleaſing
and improving help to religious meditation
and praiſe. The devout member of the
church, having poured out his ſoul in prayer
with zeal and fervency, would naturally be
inclined to cloſe his addreſs with the pious
effuſions of the inſpired Pſalmiſt ; which,
when expreſſed as they are in this verſion,
with a dignity and energy proportioned to
their original excellence, would be found to
ſupply a variety of hymns, the moſt animating
that religion can employ, and adapted to every
poſſible ſtate and condition of human life.

---

* " Mr. James Merrick, a man of great learning, has
" lately finiſhed a verſion of the Pſalms in Engliſh ; an
" admirable work, diſtinguiſhed by many ſplendid marks
" of learning, art, and genius."—Lowth Prel. 26. p. 347.
Not.

INDEX.

I N D E X.

My

b   Thou

PSALM,	Verse.	Line.	ERRATA.
IV	7	5	*for* shall *read* shalt
X	15	4	*for* vengance *read* vengeance
XXII	17	4	at the end, *for* ? *put* .
XXIV	3	3	*for* Then *read* There.
XXXI	24	3	*dele* the two ( )
XXXVII	15	1	at the end, *for* . *put* ,
LXXIV	20	2	*for* his *read* its
LXXV	5	4	at the end, *for* : *put* ?
CI	3	1	*for* O come *read* Come
——	—	2	at the end, *for* ? *put* ;
——	—	4	at the end, *for* ? *put* .
CII	6	1	*for* its *read* the
CXXXV	8	3	*for* Thy *read* His

A VER.

A
VERSION or PARAPHRASE
OF THE
PSALMS.

PSALM I.

1.

O How bleſt the Man, whoſe ear
Impious counſel ſhuns to hear,
Who nor loves to tread the way
Where the Sons of Folly ſtray,
Nor their frantic mirth to ſhare,
Seated in Deriſion's chair;
But, to Virtue's path confin'd,
Spurns the men of ſinful mind,
And, poſſeſs'd with ſacred awe,
Meditates, great God, thy Law;
This by day his fix'd employ,
This by night his conſtant joy.

2.

Like the Tree that, taught to grow
Where the ſtreams irriguous flow,
Oft as the revolving Sun
Through the deſtin'd Months has run,
Regular, its ſeaſon knows,
Bending low its loaded boughs,

B

He

He his verdant branch shall spread,
Nor his sick'ning leaves shall shed;
He, whate'er his thoughts devise,
Joyful to the work applies,
Sure to find the wish'd success
Crown his hope, his labour bless.

3.

See, ah! see a diff'rent fate
God's obdurate foes await;
See them, to his wrath consign'd,
Fly like chaff before the wind.
When thy Judge, O Earth, shall come,
And to Each assign their doom,
Say, shall then the impious Band
With the Just assembled stand?
These th' Almighty, These alone,
Objects of his Love shall own,
While his vengeance who defy
Whelm'd in endless ruin lie.

P S A L M   II.

1.

WHY thus enrag'd, ye Tribes profane?
Why strive the Gentiles thus in vain?
Why, rouz'd by Discord's fierce Alarms,
Do headlong Nations rush to Arms?

2.

Earth's scepter'd Lords rebellious rise
Against the Ruler of the Skies,
And Him on whose distinguish'd head
His hand the sacred oil has shed.

3. In

3:

In factious Counfels thus they join,
And vaunting brave the Pow'r divine;
" Quick let us each renounce their Sway,
" And caft their hated bands away."

4.

God from on high their threats fhall hear,
Laugh, as the tumult meets his ear,
And, arm'd with vengeance, thus aloud
Superior quell the frantic Croud:

5.

" Yet, Mortals, yet your Monarch fee,
" And bow to Him the humble knee;
" His throne on *Sion*'s hill my hand
" Has built, and what I build fhall ftand."

6.

Thy Will, great Father, I obey;
Pleas'd I accept the offer'd Sway,
And through the Earth's extended frame
The Counfels of thy Love proclaim.

7.

" Thou art my Son, on this bleft Day
" Begotten; (thus I hear thee fay;)
" Prefer thy wifh, and to thy hand
" Lo! I confign each heathen Land.

8.

" I bid thee rule the Nations round,
" Far as to Earth's remoteft bound;
" Though join'd in firmeft league, thy foes
" With vain attempt thy pow'r oppofe.

9. " Thy

9.

" Thy arm the iron rod extends;
" Behold them, as the ſtroke deſcends,
" Cruſh'd like the potter's brittle ſtore,
" And ſcatter'd, to unite no more."

10.

Ye Kings, from Error's ſleep ariſe,
Ye Judges of the Earth, be wiſe;
And, warm'd with duteous zeal, conſpire
To ſerve with joy th' eternal Sire.

11.

O, leſt Ye periſh from the way
That leads to realms of endleſs day,
With awful love, with holy fear,
His Son, the World's great Hope, revere.

12.

If yet but kindling in his hand
The vengeful bolt uplifted ſtand,
Thrice happy, who on Him depend,
And thankful own th' almighty Friend.

P S A L M III.

1.

BEHOLD, my God, what num'rous foes
With dire intent my ſteps incloſe,
While, fluſh'd with hope, the impious Band
In haughty triumph round me ſtand:
" Lo! there," they cry, " our obvious prey,
" The wretch whom God has caſt away."

2. But

2.

But fee Omnipotence my fhield !
My head aloft by Thee upheld,
Thy fav'ring beams around me fhine ;
Thou, Lord, from *Sion*'s hallow'd fhrine
With kind regard fhalt hear my cry,
And inftant grant the wifh'd reply.

3.

Opprefs'd with toil, I fought repofe,
I laid me down, I flept, I rofe ;
For Thou, my God, wert waking ftill,
To guard my flumb'ring head from ill :
Though Myriads, leagu'd, againft me rife,
My heart fecure their rage defies.

4.

Thy aid, bleft Lord, indulgent yield :
Oft, as I trod the doubtful field,
Each hoftile cheek has felt thy ftroke ;
Thy rod their teeth vindictive broke ;
O yield (nor fhall I afk in vain,)
That oft experienc'd aid again.

5.

Th' impending ftorm, my God, affwage,
'Tis thine to quell their impious Rage,
'Tis thine, great God, 'tis thine to fave
Thy Servants from th' expecting grave,
'Tis thine to blefs them from above,
And crown them with eternal Love.

1.

DEFENDER of my rightful caufe,
    While anguifh from my bofom draws
The deep-felt figh, the ceafelefs pray'r,
O make thy fervant ftill thy care;
That aid, which oft my griefs has heal'd,
That aid again, intreated, yield.

2.

How long, ye fons of pride, how long
Shall falfhood arm your impious tongue?
How long fhall fecret love of ill
To wretched malice urge your will,
And erring rage your breaft inflame,
My pow'r to thwart, my acts defame?

3.

To God my heart fhall vent its woe,
Who, prompt his bleffings to beftow
On each whofe breaft has learn'd his fear,
Bows to my plaint the willing ear:
Him wouldft thou pleafe? With rev'rent awe
Obferve the dictates of his Law.

4.

In fecret on thy couch reclin'd
Search to its depth thy reftlefs mind,
Till hufh'd to peace the tumult lie,
And wrath and ftrife within thee die:
With pureft gifts approach his fhrine,
And fafe to Him thy care refign.

5. I

5.

I hear a hopeleſs train demand,
" Where's now the wiſh'd Deliv'rer's hand ?"
Do Thou, my God, do Thou reply,
And let thy preſence from on high
In full effuſion o'er our head
Its all-enliv'ning influence ſhed.

6.

What joy my conſcious heart o'erflows !
Not ſuch th' exulting lab'rer knows,
When to his long-expecting eyes
The vintage and the harveſts riſe,
And, ſhadowing wide the cultur'd ſoil,
With full requital crown his toil.

7.

My weary eyes in ſleep I cloſe,
My limbs, ſecure, to reſt compoſe ;
For Thou, great God, ſhalt ſcreen my head,
And plant a guard around my bed,
Thy choiceſt Gifts ſhall bid me ſhare,
And make my ſafety ſtill thy care.

P S A L M V.

1.

THE words that from my lips proceed,
My thoughts (for Thou thoſe thoughts
canſt read,)
My God, my King, attentive weigh,
And hear, O hear me, when I pray.

2.

With earlieſt zeal, with wakeful care,
To Thee my ſoul ſhall pour its pray'r,

And,

And, ere the dawn has ftreak'd the fky,
To Thee direct its longing eye :—

3.

To Thee, whom nought obfcur'd by ftain
Can pleafe ; whofe doors to feet profane
Inexorable ftand ; whofe Law
Offenders from thy fight fhall awe.

4.

Let each whofe tongue to lies is turn'd,
Who leffons of deceit has learn'd,
Or thirfts a brother's blood to fhed,
Thy hate and heavieft vengeance dread.

5.

But I, whofe hope thy Love fupports,
(How great that Love !) will tread thy Courts,
My knees in lowlieft rev'rence bend,
And tow'rd thy fhrine my hands extend.

6.

Do Thou, juft God, my path prepare,
And guard me from each hoftile fnare ;
O lend me thy conducting ray,
And level to my fteps thy way.

7.

Behold me by a troop inclos'd,
Of hatred and of guilt compos'd,
Nurs'd in deceit, in fin allied,
Nor faith nor truth their actions guide :

8.

Their throat a fepulchre difplays,
Deep, wide, infatiate ; in their praife
Lurks flatt'ry, and with fpecious art
Belies the purpofe of their heart.

9. O

9.

O let the mifchiefs they intend
Retorted on themfelves defcend,
And let thy wrath correct their fin,
Whofe hearts thy mercy fails to win.

10.

May All who truft in Thee, employ
Their grateful voice in fongs of joy,
And fhare the gifts on thofe beftow'd,
Who love the name of *Jacob*'s God.

11.

To each, who bears a guiltlefs heart,
Thy grace its blefling fhall impart;
Strong as the brazen fhield, thy aid
Around him cafts its cov'ring fhade.

PSALM VI.

1.

O Spare me, Lord, nor o'er my head
    The fulnefs of thy vengeance fhed;
With pitying eye my weaknefs view,
Heal my vex'd Soul, my ftrength renew,
And O, if yet my fins demand
The wife corrections of thy hand,
Yet give my pains their bounds to know,
And fix a period to my woe.
    Return, great God, return, and fave
    Thy fervant from the greedy grave.

2.

Shall Death's long-filent tongue, O fay,
The records of thy pow'r difplay,

Or

Or pale Corruption's ſtartled ear
Thy praiſe within its priſon hear?
By languor, grief, and care, oppreſs'd,
With groans perpetual heaves my breaſt,
And tears, in large profuſion ſhed,
Inceſſant lave my ſleepleſs bed.
　　Return, great God, return, and ſave
　　Thy ſervant from the greedy grave.

3.

While clouds of grief around me roll,
And hoſtile ſtorms invade my ſoul,
My life, though yet in mid career,
Beholds the winter of its year
Relentleſs from my cheek each trace
Of youth and blooming health eraſe,
And ſpread before my waſting fight
The ſhades of all-obſcuring night.
　　Return, great God, return, and ſave
　　Thy ſervant from the greedy grave.

4.

Hence, ye profane: My Saviour hears;
While yet I ſpeak, he wipes my tears,
Accepts my pray'r, and bids each foe
With ſhame their vain attempts forego,
His vengeance whelms their ſouls in dread,
And burſts in tempeſts o'er their head,
While, ſtruck with horror from on high,
In wild amaze they backward fly.
　　My Saviour hears; and 'deigns to ſave
　　His ſervant from the greedy grave.

P S A L M

PSALM VII.

1.

O Save me, Lord, and to my foes
Do Thou (in Thee I truſt) oppoſe
Thy pow'r, and let the arm divine,
Stretch'd in my cauſe, beſpeak me thine:

2.

Left, while I mourn thy abſent aid,
The Lion fierce my ſoul invade,
Pleas'd, with my blood his thirſt allay,
And rend the unreſiſting prey.

3.

My God, if truth their cenſure guide,
If guilt be in my facts deſcried,
If e'er from my diſſembling heart
My Friend has found the hoſtile part,—

4.

If, gracious Lord, with ſtubborn mind
To wrathful violence inclin'd,
Impell'd by wrongs, I taught my Foe
The terrors of my hand to know,—

5.

That Foe's worſt vengeance let me meet,
Till trampled underneath his feet
Low in the duſt my life be laid,
And Earth's dark womb my glory ſhade.

6.

Riſe, mightieſt Lord, triumphant riſe
O'er each whoſe hand thy pow'r defies;
O let thy wrath chaſtiſe my Foes,
Hear, and relieve thy Servant's woes.

7. Judge-

7.

Judgement is thine: In awful ftate,
While circling crouds the doom await,
Afcend thy throne, great God, again,
And juftify thy ways to Men.

8.

O Thou, on whom our fates depend,
My caufe, my guiltlefs caufe, defend;
Awake, thy aiding ftrength excite,
Awake and vindicate my right.

9.

Sin's baneful growth do Thou controul,
And guard from ill the upright foul;
For Thou, juft Lord, with fearching eye
The heart and inmoft reins canft try.

10.

To God, my Soul, for help repair,
Who makes the faithful heart his care,
Th' impartial Judge! whofe eyes each day,
Indignant, fcenes of guilt furvey.

11.

If Man his Law refufe to know,
He whets his fword, he bends his bow,
He tips with fire the fatal dart,
Ordain'd to pierce th' Oppreffor's heart.

12.

With mifchief teem their breafts, but woe
And fruftrate hope attend the throe;
They dig, and with exacteft care
A pit, but for themfelves, prepare.

13. They

They toil, and each, condemn'd to gain
The luckless harveſt of his pain,
Ills for a brother's head deſign'd
Retorted on his own ſhall find.

14.

Thy juſtice, Lord, ſhall on my breaſt
In ſure remembrance ſtand impreſs'd,
With grateful joy my heart inſpire,
And wake to ceaſeleſs praiſe my lyre.

PSALM VIII.

1.

IMmortal King! Thro' Earth's wide frame
How great thy honour, praiſe, and name!
Whoſe reign o'er diſtant worlds extends,
Whoſe glory heav'n's vaſt height tranſcends.

2.

From infants Thou canſt ſtrength upraiſe,
And form their liſping tongues to praiſe,
That ſtruck with awe, each wrathful band
In mute aſtoniſhment may ſtand.

3.

When, rapt in thought, with wakeful eye
I view the wonders of the ſky,
Whoſe frame thy fingers o'er our head
In rich magnificence have ſpread,—

4.

The ſilent Moon, with waxing horn
Along th' ethereal region borne,
The Stars with vivid luſtre crown'd,
That nightly walk their deſtin'd round,—

C   5. ‗ord!

5.

Lord! What is Man, that in thy care
His humble lot fhould find a fhare,
Or what the Son of Man, that THOU
Thus to his wants thy ear fhouldft bow?

6.

His rank awhile, by thy decree,
Th' Angelic Tribes beneath them fee,
Till round him thy imparted rays
With unextinguifh'd glory blaze.

7.

Subjected to his feet by Thee
To Him all Nature bows the knee;
The beafts in Him their Lord behold,
The grazing herd, the bleating fold,—

8.

The fowls, of various wing, that fly
O'er the vaft defert of the fky,
And all the watry tribes, that glide
Through paths to human fight denied.

9.

Immortal King! Thro' Earth's wide frame
How great thy honour, praife, and name!
Thy reign o'er diftant worlds extends,
Thy glory Heav'n's vaft height tranfcends.

P S A L M IX.

1.

WARM'D to its inmoft depth my breaft
Thanks, not by words to be exprefs'd,
Conceives, nor fhall my grateful tongue
E'er leave thy wondrous acts unfung.

2. Thee,

2.

Thee, Lord, I boaſt my blifs ſupreme,
'Thy praiſe my ſong's exhauſtlefs theme;
O higher than the higheſt, hail !
Thou, Thou haſt bid my cauſe prevail.

3.

Lo ! from the terror of thine eye
My foes with ſtumbling ſtep ſhall fly,
Or, ſtruck by thy refiſtlefs hand,
In heaps promifcuous ſtrew the Land.

4.

Strict Juſtice, Lord, ſupports thy throne,
And Her decrees and Thine are one ;
Thy ſtern rebuke the Heathen feel,
Their name Oblivion's ſhades conceal.

5.

See, o'er their guilt-polluted plain
Deſtruction, Death, and Horror reign ;
While, where the rural waſte extends,
No more the village ſmoke afcends:

6.

No more their cities brave the ſky,
But (ras'd by Thee,) forgotten lie,
Scarce ev'n in ſhapelefs ruins view'd,
That mark where once the Wonder ſtood.

7.

But Thou, when Time ſhall reach its end,
Unchang'd the ſcepter ſhalt extend ;
Then fill thy Throne in awful State,
While Man's whole Race thy Judgment wait.

C 2　　　　8. Come

8.

Come Ye, who in the dang'rous hour
Wifh for your guard the ftrong-built tow'r;
Each terror to the winds refign'd,
In God a furer refuge find.

9.

The fouls, that erft opprefs'd with woe
Have learn'd thy name, great God, to know,
Their hope on Thee fhall ftill fuftain,
Whom none has fought, and fought in vain.

10.

In *Sion* God has fix'd his reft;
O be his praife aloud confeft;
His Acts through ev'ry clime refound,
Far as to Earth's extremeft bound.

11.

He from the proud Oppreffor's hands
The poor man's guiltlefs blood demands,
And (nor with unregarding ear,)
His juft complaint from heav'n fhall hear.

12.

O Thou, whofe care prolongs my breath,
And lifts me from the gates of death,
Thy fervant's woes attentive view,
While impious men my fteps purfue:

13.

So fhall thy praife employ my tongue,
And *Sion's* portals hear my fong,
While with experienc'd heart I fhow
What joys from thy Salvation flow.

14. Low

14.

Low in the pit for others made
Th' artificers of death are laid,
And, ſtruck with dire amazement, find
Their nets around themſelves intwin'd.

15.

His juſtice thus our God diſplays,
And miſchief with itſelf repays
On thóſe who thus their Arts prepare,
And for the guiltleſs plant the Snare.

16.

Behold the grave its jaws extend,
While to its depths the crouds deſcend,
Who dare in lawleſs counſels join,
Forgetful of the will divine.

17.

For think not, O ye Good diſtreſt,
That in the all-remembring breaſt
Your woes and wrongs unnotic'd riſe,
That Virtue's hope for ever dies.

18.

Up, Lord, nor let the impious ſoul
Build ſin on ſin without controul ;
Thy balance, mightieſt Judge, aſſume,
Paſs on the heathen race their doom.

19.

O let thy terrors, ſcatter'd wide,
Correct them, till each ſon of pride,
By Thee convinc'd, his weakneſs ſcan,
And humbled own himſelf but Man.

PSALM X.

1.

SAY, Lord, why thus thy aiding pow'r
Deserts us in the needful hour,
Why clouds impervious, round thee roll'd,
Thy presence from our sight withhold.

2.

Shall impious men escape thy view,
While thus the guiltless they pursue?
O let them, by themselves chastis'd,
The ills sustain for Him devis'd,—

3.

No longer boast their mad desires,
And acts which headlong rage inspires,
Or joyous grasp their lawless gain,
And Thee, the soul's best wealth, disdain.

4.

Proud Wretch! who shuns o'er Nature's face
The footsteps of thy care to trace,
And Thee, th' all-potent Monarch, Thee
Denies, who gav'st himself to be.

5.

Behold, while, high above all height,
Thy Judgements, Lord, his distant sight
Elude, this Minister of woe
Blast with his breath each obvious foe;

6.

" See, proof to each assault I stand:
" What pow'r shall e'er my fear demand?
" What ill, to life's remotest day,
" Obstruct the tenour of my way?"

7. His

7.

His venom'd lips, with curſes fraught,
Words ill according to his thought
Have utter'd, and beneath his tongue
Lurk fraud, and violence, and wrong.

8.

Beſide the ſolitary way,
Intent the helpleſs poor to ſlay,
He waits, and with malignant eye
Inſidious marks each paſſer by.

9.

As, couch'd within his buſhy lair,
The lion fierce with hideous glare
Around him caſts his wide ſurvey,
And meditates the future prey,—

10.

So longs the man of blood to ſeize
The Souls that own thy juſt Decrees;
When planted with ſucceſsful care,
His nets their captive feet inſnare:

11.

What, Lord, his fury ſhall withſtand,
Or ſave them from the murth'rous Band,
That, leagu'd in ſin, aſſiſt his toil,
And ſhare with him the guilty ſpoil?

12.

" Shall Heav'n's high Lord, he cries, deſcend
" The human actions to attend?
" The paths by Me at will purſu'd
" His mem'ry and his thought elude."

13. Riſe,

· 13 ·

Rife, mightieft Lord, and lift thy hand,
Nor let the injur'd poor demand
Thy faving Aid with fruitlefs Pray'r,
But guard them by thy foft'ring Care.

14.

Why fhould the fouls, who Thee defy,
With impious Tongue reproachful cry,
" 'Tis not within th' Almighty's plan
" To fcrutinize the acts of Man ?"

15.

What eyes, like thine, eternal Sire,
Through fin's obfcureft depths inquire ?
What Judge, like Thee, on Virtue's foes
The needful vengance can impofe ?

16.

The meek obferver of thy Laws
To Thee commits his injur'd caufe ;
In Thee, each anxious fear refign'd,
The fatherlefs a Father find.

17.

O, break the arm of impious might ;
So fhall their threats no more excite
Our dread, nor thy offended eye
The triumphs of their guilt defcry.

18.

Thine is the throne : Beneath thy reign,
Immortal King ! the tribes profane
Behold their dreams of conqueft o'er,
And vanifh to be feen no more.

19. Thou,

19.

Thou, Lord, thy People's wish canst read,
Ere from their lips the pray'r proceed;
'Tis thine their drooping hearts to rear,
And when they call incline thine ear;

20.

'Tis Thine the Orphan's cheek to dry,
The guiltless Suff'rer's cause to try,
To rein each earthborn Tyrant's will,
And bid the Sons of Pride be still.

PSALM XI.

1.

ON God my stedfast hopes rely:
  Why urge ye then my soul to fly,
And swift on trembling wings convey'd
To seek the mountain's cov'ring shade?
See, prompt to ill, th' insidious foe
Now couch'd in secret bend the bow,
Now to the string adjust the dart,
That thirsts to wound the guiltless heart:
While Justice mourns her Base o'erthrown,
Say who the injur'd cause shall own?

2.

Thou, Lord, that cause wilt still sustain;
Thou, thron'd amid thy heav'nly fane,
Shalt cast, regardful, from on high
On suff'ring innocence thine eye,

Each

Each human heart intent to prove,
And bid the souls that seek thy Love,
Bleſt objects of thy conſtant care,
The fulneſs of thy bounty ſhare;
While lawleſs hands and hearts impure
Thy wrath and ſtedfaſt hate endure.

3.

Behold the lightnings wing their way,
Behold the fires vindictive ſtray;
While from thy hand the baleful draught,
With ſtorm and mingled ſulphur fraught,
In wild amaze the impious Train
Low to its utmoſt dregs ſhall drain:
For (juſt himſelf,) where'er it ſhines
To Juſtice God his Love inclines,
Delighted in the upright mind
His own reflected beams to find.

P S A L M XII.

1.

O Help me, Lord: For none I ſee,
   Whoſe acts conform to thy Decree;
Nor truth nor faith my ſearch can trace
Amid the ſons of human race:

2.

New Plans of fraud each Mind has known,
And ſpeaks a language not its own;
Their Lips have learn'd with ſpecious Art
To veil the Purpoſe of the Heart:

3. But

3.

But God with vengeance arm'd fhall rife,
The tongue of Flatt'ry to chaftife,
And Juftice to the lip of Pride
Its ftroke with aim unerring guide.

4.

What force, exclaims the impious Band,
Shall eloquence like ours withftand?
And fay, to whom the tafk belongs
To fix the bridle on our tongues.

5.

" Enough (th' eternal Sire has cried)
" Enough my fuff'ring Saints have figh'd,
" To Me difclos'd their ceafelefs fear,
" And pour'd their forrows in mine ear :

6.

" My hand fhall fee their wrongs redreft,
" And footh to peace their troubled breaft,
" Its faving Aid around them throw,
" And guard them from th' infulting Foe."

7.

Pure are thy words, almighty Lord,
As Silver, that, by art explor'd,
Has feen the fev'nth tormenting fire
Around th' inclofing vafe afpire.

8.

Thy Love thy Servants, Lord, fhall fhare,
And, fafe in thy protecting care,
Behold, unmov'd, an impious Age
Aim at their life its fruitlefs rage.

9. When

9.

When Men, by ev'ry Crime debas'd,
In Seats of fov'reign Rule are plac'd,
Then wrong and fraud the Earth o'erfpread,
And Vice triumphant lifts the head.

P S A L M   XIII.

1.

HOW long fhall I, my God, in vain,
     Preft by a weight of griefs, complain?
Say, fhall I fink in deep defpair,
For ever banifh'd from thy care ?

2.

Condemn'd thy abfent beams to mourn
Still to divided counfels turn
My lab'ring thought, and hear the foe
Exulting triumph in my woe ?

3.

Thy Suppliant's voice attentive weigh,
And bid, O bid, thy heav'nly ray
With healing influence o'er me rife,
Ere death's dark flumber clofe my eyes.

4.

What Tranfport would my Fall impart,
To each incens'd Oppofer's Heart,
Who would his utmoft Art addrefs
The Friend of Peace and Truth t' opprefs !

5.

" Behold," the hoftile tongue would cry,
" Beneath my feet behold him lie,
" The wretch that, hafting to his end,
" With pow'r fuperior durft contend."

8   6. But,

6.

But, while their ceaselefs threats I hear,
Thy mercy, Lord, difpels my fear;
My hopes on thy Salvation reft,
And fill with confcious joy my breaft.

7.

Well pleas'd that mercy to proclaim,
To Thee, Inftinct with holy flame,
To Thee my tongue from day to day
Shall meditate the grateful lay.

P S A L M XIV.

1.

BEHOLD the Fool, whofe heart denies
The God who form'd the Earth and Skies:
While, fearlefs, fin's worft paths he treads,
Mark how the dire example fpreads.

2.

Of Man's whole race not one we find
To Virtue's Heav'n-taught rules inclin'd,
Who 'midft infectious times has ftood
Unftain'd, and obftinately good.

3.

Th' eternal Monarch from on high
Caft on the fons of Earth his eye,
If haply fome he yet might fee
True to their God, from Error free.

4.

He look'd: but ah! not one could find
To Virtue's Heav'n-taught rules inclin'd:
Each, led from Wifdom's path aftray,
Purfues the tenour of his way.

D   5. O

5.

O fay, what frenzy thus could blind
Their fouls, that with remorfelefs mind
As bread my People they devour,
Nor fuppliant own their Maker's pow'r.

6.

Yet fee their thoughts tumultuous roll,
See various terrors fhake their foul:
For God amidft the Righteous dwells,
And each invading foe repels.

7.

And what are Ye, who thus deride
The fouls that in their God confide,
With wife fimplicity of mind
To his all-juft Decrees refign'd?

8.

Who, mightieft Lord, to *Ifrael*'s eyes
Shall bid the wifh'd Salvation rife,
From *Sion*'s hill its healing ray
Extend, and round us pour the day?

9.

When Thou thy captives fhalt reftore
Thy praife fhall found through *Judah*'s fhore,
And ceafelefs fhouts, thro' heav'n's wide frame
Loud-echoing, *Jacob*'s joy proclaim.

P S A L M XV.

1.

WHO fhall tow'rd thy chofen feat
Turn in glad approach his feet?
Who fhall at thine Altars bend?
Who to *Sion*'s Hill afcend?

Who,

Who, great God, a welcome Gueft,
On that hallow'd Mountain reft ?—
He whofe heart thy Love has warm'd,
He whofe Will, to thine conform'd,
Bids his Life unfullied run ;
He whofe word and thought are one.

2.

He who ne'er with cruel aim
Seeks to wound an honeft fame,
Nor with gloomy joy poffefs'd
Can a Brother's peace moleft,
Or to Slander's tongue fevere
Stoops with eafy faith his ear :
Who from fervile terror free
Spurns at thofe who fpurn at Thee,
And to each who Thee obeys
Love and lowlieft rev'rence pays.

3.

What he fwears, with ftedfaft will
To his lofs he fhall fulfil,
Nor by avaricious loan
Make the poor man's bread his own ;
Nor can bribes his fentence guide
'Gainft the guiltlefs to decide.
He who thus, with heart unftain'd,
Treads the path by Thee ordain'd,
He, great God, fhall own thy care,
And thy conftant bleffing fhare.

1.

FATHER of All! my foul defend;
On Thee my ftedfaft hopes depend.
" Thou, mightieft Lord, and none befide,
" Thou art my God," my heart has cried:

2.

In vain, with grateful zeal, I burn
Thy boundlefs goodnefs to return;
In vain would gifts by Me beftow'd
Augment the treafures of my God.

3.

Yet fhall my love on All defcend,
Whofe Souls to thy Decrees attend,
My heart's defire to each incline,
Whofe faintlike Virtue marks him Thine.

4.

The Wretch, who madly ftrays from Thee,
And bows to Gods mifcall'd the knee,
Shall find new forrows round him roll
And whelm in dread his confcious foul.

5.

Be witnefs to my guilt, if e'er
Their draughts of offer'd blood I fhare,
If, while thy breath my life fuftains,
Their name my hallow'd lip profanes.

6.

Thee, Lord, my patrimony, Thee
The portion of my cup I fee:
Thy care my envied lot fecures,
And life's beft gifts around me pours.

7. Thee

7.

Thee let me blefs, the faithful Guide,
Whofe counfels o'er my life prefide,
And wifdom to my wakeful breaft
At midnight's filent hour fuggeft.

8.

In all my acts, in each intent,
Thee to my foul my thoughts prefent,
Whofe fure defence my gate has barr'd,
And planted on my right a guard.

9.

For this my heart, for this my tongue,
Shall meditate the joyful fong;
Hope ev'n in death fhall be my gueft
And fmooth the pillow of my reft.

10.

Thou from the grave my foul fhalt free,
Nor leave thy Holy One to fee
Corruption's pow'r :—before my eyes
The op'ning paths of life fhall rife;

11.

Thofe paths that to thy prefence bear;
For plenitude of Blifs is there:
And pleafures, Lord, unmix'd with woe,
At thy right hand for ever flow.

P S A L M XVII.

I.

TO Thee, the Judge inthron'd on high,
Shall injur'd Innocence apply:
O let my pray'r by Thee be heard,
From undiffembling lips prefer'd;

O let

O let my Doom from Thee proceed,
And gracious mark the upright deed.

2.

When night's dark ſhades were round me
         pour'd,
Thy thoughts my ſpirit have explor'd;
Say, to thy all-diſcerning eyes
If aught of guilt within me riſe,
If offer'd violence and wrong
Have urg'd to Sin my thoughtleſs tongue.

3.

Taught by thy Word my ſtedfaſt mind
Has each nefarious path declin'd;
O ſtill my Guardian, ſtill my Guide,
Forbid my wav'ring feet to ſlide;
To Thee (for Thou the pray'r canſt hear,)
To Thee my ſuppliant voice I rear;

4.

O treat me not with cold diſdain,
Nor let my vows return in vain:
O Thou, whoſe hand th' oppreſſor quells,
And each invading pow'r repels
From him whoſe hopes on Thee repoſe,
To Me thy wondrous grace diſcloſe.

5.

What care the pupil of the eye
Demands, that care to Me apply;
Let thy prevailing beams diſpel
The clouds of grief that o'er me dwell,
" And keep, O keep me, King of Kings,
" Beneath thy own almighty wings."

6.

Rich in my fpoils, with murth'rous hate
A pamper'd croud around me wait ;
Their heart, with impious fury ftung,
To mad prefumption prompts their tongue,
Pride on their neck its chain has bound,
And Violence invefts them round.

7.

With watchful look they mark my way,
As lurks, expectant of the prey,
The Lion, or his tawny Brood
To rapine born, and nurs'd in blood ;
Rife, Lord, and let me, by thy aid
Preferv'd, their threatning jaws evade :

8.

With fword unfheath'd, and lifted hand,
Preventive crufh the lawlefs Band,
Whofe Days, with Life's full bleffings fraught,
To Earth's low fcene confine their thought;
Whofe eyes a num'rous race behold,
To heir their heaps of treafur'd gold.

9.

Far other blifs my foul fhall own,
A blifs to guilty minds unknown
O ! when, awaken'd by thy care,
Thy face I view, thy image bear,
How fhall my breaft with tranfport glow,
What full delight my heart o'erflow !

PSALM XVIII.

1.

BLEST Object of my foul's defire,
   To Thee my grateful thoughts afpire;
On Thee my ftedfaft hope I build ;
My God, my Reft, my Rock, my Shield :

2.

The Strength of my Salvation Thee,
And Tow'r of fure defence, I fee ;
Protected by thy pow'rful arm,
No danger can my foul alarm :

3.

What foe fhall e'er my terror raife,
While thus I pay my debt of praife,
And, as the doubtful field I tread,
To God my fuppliant hands outfpread ?

4.

Woes heap'd on woes my heart deplor'd,
While Sin's tumultuous torrents roar'd,
And, fpreading wide before my view,
Their gloomy horrors round me threw.

5.

The Sepulchre's extended hands
Had wrapt me in its ftrongeft bands,
And Death, infulting, o'er my head
Th' inextricable toils had fpread.

6.

My words, as griev'd to God I pray,
Wing to his heav'nly fane their way,
Through adverfe clouds their paffage clear,
Nor unaccepted reach his ear :

7. With

7.

With ftrong convulfions groan'd the ground,
The hills, with waving forefts crown'd,
Loos'd from their bafe, their fummits nod,
And own the prefence of their God :

8.

Collected clouds of wreathing fmoke
Forth from his angry noftrils broke,
And orbs of fire, with dreadful glare,
Rufh'd onward through the glowing air.

9.

Incumbent on the bending fky
The Lord defcended from on high,
And bade the darknefs of the pole
Beneath his feet tremendous roll.

10.

The Cherub to his car he join'd,
And on the wings of mightieft wind,
As down to Earth his journey lay,
Refiftlefs urg'd his rapid way.

11.

Thick-woven clouds, around him clos'd,
His fecret refidence compos'd,
And waters high-fufpended fpread
Their dark pavilion o'er his head.

12.

In vain reluctant to the Blaze
That previous pour'd its ftreaming rays,
As on he moves, the clouds retire,
Diffolv'd in hail and rufhing fire :

13. His

13.

His voice th' almighty Monarch rear'd,
Thro' heav'n's high vault in thunders heard,
And down in fiercer conflict came
The hailstones dire and mingled flame.

14.

With aim direct his shafts were sped,
In vain his foes before them fled;
Now here, now there, his lightnings stray,
And sure destruction marks their way:

15.

Earth's basis open to the eye,
And Ocean's springs, were seen to lie,
As, chiding loud, his fury past,
And o'er them breath'd the dreadful blast.

16.

God in my rescue from the skies
His arm extends, and bids me rise
Emergent from the flood profound,
Whose waves my struggling soul surround.

17.

His hand my strongest foes repell'd,
Their force by force superior quell'd,
And I, unequal to the fight,
Ev'n I have triumph'd in his might.

18.

Oppress'd with languor, grief, and pain,
Ere yet my nerves their strength regain,
His fierce assault th' Invader gave;
But Thou wert present, Lord, to save:

19. **My**

19.

My fpacious path by Thee outfpread,
With courfe fecure behold me tread;
From Thee, when terrors clos'd me round,
My foul its fulleft fuccour found.

20.

Bleft in the favour of my God,
I fpeak the grace on all beftow'd,
Who guiltlefs hands to him can raife,
And offer unpolluted praife.

21.

His precepts, fix'd before my view,
My thoughts with ftedfaft aim purfue,
Nor error's cloud nor arts of fin
My foul from his obedience win.

22.

Thou feeft, eternal Judge, my breaft
Each taint of inward guilt deteft;
Thine eye my innocence furveys,
Thy pow'r with fulleft blifs repays.

23.

Thy ways to ours conform: in Thee
The Holy fhall the Holy fee,
The Pure theP ure; the Perfect Mind
In Thee Perfection's felf fhall find:

24.

Their arts the men of froward turn
Surpafs'd by deeper art fhall mourn,
Wh 1: They their pow'rs with effort vain
Unite againft thepious Train.

25. By

25.

By Thee their Guardian, ever nigh,
The poor are fav'd; the haughty eye,
Chaftis'd by thy afflicting ftroke,
Bends to the earth its humbled look.

26.

While night's thick fhades around me ftand,
My lamp, illumin'd by thy hand,
Pours through the gloom its fteady ray,
And turns my darknefs into day.

27.

My arm, if Thou thine aid fupply,
Shall bid whole hofts before me fly;
My feet, if Thou my finews ftring,
High o'er the wall exulting fpring.

28.

Author of Good ! nor fin, nor guile
The purenefs of thy path defile;
On thy tried Word who build their truft,
Shall find their confidence was juft.

29.

What God but Thee fhall *Ifrael* know,
Or Who, O Who can fave but Thou?
'Tis God that arms me for the fight,
'Tis God that girds my foul with might;

30.

Upheld by Him, in air fublime,
Swift as the hind, the rock I climb,
Girded with ftrength, there fix my ftand,
Safe from each proud Invader's hand.

31. By

31.

By Him inform'd, with fureſt art
My hands direct the pointed dart,
And forceful break the ſteely bow,
New wreſted from the ſtruggling foe.

32.

Thou, mightieſt Lord, haſt o'er my head
The ſhield of thy Salvation ſpread;
Thee its defence my Soul has found,
And gratefully thy ſuccour own'd.

33.

By Thy right hand I walk'd upheld,
Great in thy mercy trod the field
With ſtep enlarg'd, and, Thou my Guide,
Nor fear'd to fall, nor knew to ſlide.

34.

With fierce purſuit my foes I preſs'd,
Beheld my ſpear their flight arreſt,
Nor bade my ſword its fury ſtay,
'Till proſtrate on the earth they lay.

35.

They bow'd, they fell, diſtain'd with gore;
They bow'd, they fell, and roſe no more:
My foes, beneath my feet o'erthrown,
The terrors of my hand have known.

36.

Bleſt Lord ! 'Twas Thy reſiſtleſs pow'r
That arm'd me for the dreadful hour,
Their backs expos'd to many a wound,
And ſtretch'd them breathleſs on the ground.

E   37. Aloud,

37.

Aloud, oppreſs'd with horror, cried
The rebel Throng ; but None replied :
To God they call ; but God their pray'r,
Abhorrent, ſcatters to the air.

38.

Behold their troops before me chas'd,
As duſt before the driving blaſt,
And trampled, as the yielding clay
Extended o'er the beaten way.

39.

When factious Crouds againſt me roſe,
How prompt thy hand to interpoſe !
O'er realms, that have but heard my name,
Through Thee the juſt command I claim ;

40.

The Tribes, that from their God eſtrang'd
Through climes to Me unknown had rang'd,
With flatt'ring lip their homage pay,
And trembling own a foreign ſway.

41.

In vain they ſeek themſelves to hide
In walls and forts their ſtrength and pride,
Each dreads my vengeance to ſuſtain,
Nor walls nor forts their fears reſtrain.

42.

Bleſt be the living God, whoſe aid,
When impious foes my peace invade,
Their rage inſtructs me to decline,
And makes his wiſh'd Salvation mine ;

43. His

43.

His pow'r inflicts th' avenging ftroke,
And bends the Nations to my yoke,
Eaeh force, that durft my reign conteft,
By His refiftlefs ftrength fupprefs'd.

44.

For this, thy pow'r my fong fhall claim,
And diftant regions hear thy fame,
Whofe hands thy *David* to the throne
Have rais'd ; whofe oil his temples own.

45.

Profperity and fair fuccefs
His counfels and his arms fhall blefs,
Thy Love on him and on his Line
With unextinguifh'd luftre fhine.

P S A L M   XIX.

1.

GOD the Heav'ns aloud proclaim
Through their wide-extended frame,
And the Firmament each hour
Speaks the wonders of his pow'r :

2.

Day to the fucceeding day
Joys the notice to convey,
And the Nights, in ceafelefs round,
Each to each repeat the found :

3.

Prompt, without or fpeech or tongue,
In his praife to form the fong,
To the Lord they raife the theme,
Who of Gods is God Supreme.

4.

Pleas'd to hear their voice extend
Far as to her utmoſt end,
Earth the Heav'n-taught knowledge boaſts
Through her many languag'd coaſts;

5.

While the Sun above her head
Sees his tabernacle ſpread,
And from out his chamber bright
Like a Bridegroom ſprings to ſight:

6.

See him with gigantic pace
Joyous run his deſtin'd race,
See him, ev'ry breaſt to chear,
Paſs through Heav'n in ſwift career;

7.

Now to fartheſt regions borne
Onward ſpeed, and now return,
And to All, with welcome ray,
Life and genial warmth convey.

8.

Warmth and life each thankful heart
Feels thy Law, great God, impart;
Clear from ev'ry ſpot it ſhines,
And the guilt-ſtain'd Thought refines;

9.

Truth's firm baſe its frame upholds,
While it Myſteries unfolds,
Which the childlike mind explores,
And to heav'nly ſcience ſoars.

10. Preſſ

10.

Preſt with ſorrows, doubts, and fears,
What like this the ſpirit chears,
Big with acts that ſhall ſuggeſt
Laſting joy to ev'ry breaſt ?

11.

What ſo perfect, what ſo pure ?
What to Reaſon's eye obſcure
Can ſuch wondrous light afford
As the dictates of thy Word ?

12.

Where thy Fear its fruit matures,
(Fruit, that endleſs years endures)
There the mind, with ſtedfaſt truſt,
Owns thy ſtatutes wiſe, and juſt.

13.

Nor can Gold ſuch worth acquire
From the ſev'nth exploring fire,
Nor the labour of the bees
E'er in ſweetneſs vie with Theſe :

14.

Taught by Them, thy Servant's breaſt
Joys the Bleſſings to atteſt
Heap'd on thoſe whoſe hearts ſincere
Learn thy Precepts to revere.

15.

Beſt Inſtructor, from thy ways
Who can tell how oft he ſtrays ?
Save from Error's growth my mind,
Leave not, Lord, one root behind :

E 3   16. Purge

Purge me from the guilt that lies
Wrapt within my heart's difguife ;
Let me thence, by Thee renew'd,
Each prefumptuous fin exclude :

17.

So my lot fhall ne'er be join'd
With the Men whofe impious mind,
Fearlefs of thy juft command,
Braves the vengeance of thy hand.

18.

Let my tongue, from error free,
Speak the words approv'd by Thee ;
To thy all-obferving eyes
Let my thoughts accepted rife :

19.

While I thus thy name adore,
And thy healing grace implore,
Bleft Redeemer, bow thine ear,
God my Strength, propitious hear.

PSALM XX.

1.

MAY He whom Heav'n and Earth obey
Regard thee in the dreadful day,
May *Jacob*'s Lord above thy head
His own victorious banner fpread.

2.

May He from out his hallow'd fhrine
Reach to thy aid the hand divine,
And ftrength into thy foul inftill
From beauteous *Sion*'s favour'd hill.

3. There

3.

There may thy incenſe to the ſkies
In ſweet memorial ever riſe ;
Thy victims there in ſmoke aſpire,
Touch'd by his own celeſtial fire.

4.

May He thy ev'ry wiſh approve,
May He indulgent from above
His wonted benefits impart,
And grant the wiſhes of thine heart ;

5.

May He in dangers intervene,
While We, his great Salvation ſeen,
Aſſiſt thy joy, thy triumphs ſhare,
And bleſs the God who hears thy pray'r.

6.

I ſee, I ſee th' Almighty ſhed
His bleſſings on th' anointed head,
Attentive from his holy Heav'n
Protect the crown Himſelf has giv'n.

7.

I ſee th' Almighty to thy foes
His all ſubduing ſtrength oppoſe,
And, cloth'd with mercy, reach his hand,
To ſave Thee from the impious band.

8.

Theſe urge to Fight the rattling Car,
And Thoſe the fiery Steed prepare,
Unenvied Both by Us, who ſee
Our ſure defence, great God, in Thee.

9, Driv'n

Driv'n by superior force they fly,
Or, faln, in heaps promiscuous lie,
While We our heads exulting raise,
And sing our great Deliv'rer's praise.

10.

O, when we praise, and when we pray,
Do Thou, whom Heav'n and Earth obey,
Accept the praise, confirm the pray'r,
And make our safety still thy care.

PSALM XXI.

1.

BY Thy unwearied strength upheld
To Thee the King his thanks shall yield,
And, taught by blest experience, know
What joys from Thy salvation flow.

2.

Thy cares his heart's desire complete;
His pray'r from Thy eternal seat,
As low to Thee his knees he bends,
In full acceptance back descends.

3.

Thou, Lord, preventive of his want,
The blessings of thy Love wilt grant,
And bid the golden circlet spread
Its purest splendors round his head.

4.

He ask'd thee Life, and finds it giv'n,
Life, lasting as the days of heav'n;
The conquests, which thy hands bestow,
With grace and glory bind his brow.

5. He,

5.

He, crown'd with bliſs perpetual, He
Thy face in full diſplay ſhall ſee,
And (for on Thee his hopes rely,)
Unmov'd each adverſe ſhock defy.

6.

Thy hand ſhall find each latent foe,
And vengeful ſtrike th' unerring blow,
Mark as their crimes for juſtice call,
And teach thy Terrors where to fall.

7.

Fierce as the kindled furnace glows,
Whoſe ſides the crackling thorns incloſe,
Thy wrath its flames ſhall round them pour,
And quick their boaſted ſtrength devour.

8.

Their fruit, a luckleſs progeny,
Uprooted from the ground ſhall die,
And Earth their tribe no more behold
Amidſt her families inroll'd.

9.

In vain each hoſtile art they try;
Behold, as trembling back they fly,
Thy ſhafts, adjuſted to the ſtring,
Impatient wait upon the wing.

10.

Maker of All, through Earth and Skies
O let thy pow'r conſpicuous riſe,
And furniſh to our grateful lays
A theme of everlaſting praiſe.

P S A L M

PSALM XXII.

1.

MY God, my God, O tell me, why
 Unheeded ſtill aſcends my cry,
Why thus from my afflicted heart
Thy preſence and thy health depart.

2.

Eternal Lord, throughout the day
With fruitleſs plaint to Thee I pray ;
Nor ſleeps the anguiſh of my ſoul,
When night's dark ſhades involve the pole.

3.

Yet unimpeach'd thy Faith appears,
Thy Sanctity my heart reveres,
O Thou, to whom in homage join
The Sons of *Jacob*'s choſen line.

4.

Thee, Lord, our Sires their ſtrength confeſt,
And found thee, as their ſtedfaſt breaſt
To Thee its full affiance gave,
Nor ſlow to hear, nor weak to ſave.

5.

Lord, what am I ? A Man in form,
Yet brother to the trampled worm ;
An outcaſt from the human kind,
To fierce deriſion's rage conſign'd :

6.

They ſhake the head, they ſhout, they gaze ;
Each eye, each lip, contempt betrays :
" On God, they cry, thy hope was ſtaid ;
" Be God, if His thou art, thy aid."

7. Thine,

7.

Thine, mightieft Father, thine I am;
By Thee from out the womb I came,
From Thee my ev'ry comfort fprung,
While yet upon the breaft I hung.

8.

Hail, from my birth and to my end
My God, my Guardian, and my Friend;
O hafte, thy needful help beftow,
And fave me from th' invading foe.

9.

O view me not with diftant eye,
While various griefs await me nigh:
Thy aid withheld, what friendly pow'r
Shall fhield me in the dang'rous hour?

10.

See *Bafan*'s bulls around me roar,
Nor rage the famifh'd Lions more,
When nightly through the ftarlefs gloom
Along the howling Wild they roam.

11.

My frame, disjoin'd, in fwift decay
Waftes like the running ftream away;
My heart in groans its grief proclaims,
And melts, as wax before the flames.

12.

Faft to my jaws my tongue is chain'd,
My flefh its vital moifture drain'd,
While, Lord, thy chaftifement it bears
Dry as the clayform'd vafe appears;

13. O how

13.

Yet, patient ftill of ev'ry pain
Unerring Wifdom can ordain,
I wait till Thou refume my breath,
And lodge me in the duft of death.

14.

A hoftile throng who Thee defpife,
Dogs fierce of kind, againft me rife ;
And, while faft-iffuing ftreams the gore,
My hands and feet relentlefs bore.

15.

My ftarting bones to ev'ry eye
Expos'd, O Ye that, paffing by,
In wonder (not in pity) join,
O fay, was ever grief like mine?

16.

My raiment each with each divides,
My vefture, as the lot decides,
Becomes fome new poffeffor's fpoil,
The prize that crowns his impious toil.

17.

My God, my Strength, recede not far,
But hafte, and make my foul thy care,
My foul, purfu'd by hoftile hate,
Afflicted, helplefs, defolate?

18.

My God, (for Thou their rage haft feen)
With timelieft fuccour intervene,
And turn th' impending fwords away,
Nor yield me to the Dog a prey.

19. The

The foaming Lion's wrath affuage,
. Nor let the Oryx, in his rage,
With headlong force againſt me borne,
Aim at my life the pointed horn.

20.

So will I joy thy honour'd name
Amidſt my brethren to proclaim,
And gath'ring Crouds ſhall hear my tongue
Thus to my God awake the ſong.

21.

" Exalt, ye Saints, the Pow'r divine,
" Exalt him, All of *Jacob*'s line,
" And let each tribe with duteous fear
" His boundleſs Majeſty revere.

22.

" 'Tis not in Him, with cold diſdain
" To hear the helpleſs Poor complain ;
" He kindly ſees their wrongs redreſt,
" And ſoothes to peace their troubled breaſt:

23.

" He (nor with unrelenting eye)
" Each falling tear, each heaving ſigh,
" Regards, attentive to perceive
" Their wants, and faithful to relieve."

24.

Such Strains thy Mercy ſhall inſpire,
While in the full-aſſembled Choir
To Thee the votive Song I raiſe,
And thankful pay my debt of praiſe.

F

25. To

25.

To You, ye humble, meek, and good,
Who afk from *Ifrael*'s Lord your food,
His hand indulgent from on high
Shall yield at full the wifh'd fupply:

26.

Who feek like You their God, like You
To Him their praifes fhall renew,
Whofe Love immortal life imparts,
And fwells with joy their confcious hearts.

27.

Maker of All! through ev'ry Land
Thy Deeds in full record fhall ftand,
And fartheft Realms converted join
In homage to the Name divine;

28.

Kings fhall in Thee their Mightier greet,
And lay their fcepters at thy feet:
(Thy grace by facrifice implor'd,)
Earth's tribes fhall fpread the feftal board:

29.

And All Mankind, whofe mortal frame
Th' infatiate Grave prepares to claim,
Thy Pow'r, immortal Judge, fhall own,
And proftrate kneel before thy Throne.

30.

See, while by Thee redeem'd I live,
A Race from Me their birth derive,
A Race by juft poffeffion thine,
Whofe hearts infpir'd, to truth incline:

31. Whofe

31.

Whofe tongue thy glory fhall difplay,
Inftruct the world thy will t' obey,
And bid thy righteous Acts engage
The wonder of the future Age.

P S A L M XXIII.

I.

LO, my Shepherd's hand divine!
Want fhall never more be mine.
In a pafture fair and large
He fhall feed his happy Charge,
And my couch with tend'reft care
'Midft the fpringing grafs prepare:
When I faint with fummer's heat,
He fhall lead my weary feet
To the ftreams that ftill and flow
Through the verdant meadow flow.

2.

He my foul anew fhall frame,
And, his mercy to proclaim,
When through devious paths I ftray,
Teach my fteps the better way:
Though the dreary vale I tread
By the fhades of death o'erfpread,
There I walk from terror free,
While my ev'ry wifh I fee
By thy rod and ftaff fupplied,
This my guard, and that my guide.

3.

While my foes are gazing on,
Thou thy fav'ring care haft fhown;

Thou my plenteous board haſt ſpread,
Thou with oil refreſh'd my head :
Fill'd by Thee my cup o'erflows,
For thy Love no limit knows ;
Conſtant, to my lateſt end
This my footſteps ſhall attend,
And ſhall bid thy hallow'd Dome
Yield me an eternal home.

P S A L M   XXIV.

I.

EARTH, big with Empires, to thy Reign
Submits, great God, its wide domain ;
Whate'er this Orb's vaſt bounds confine,
By juſt poſſeſſion, Lord, is thine :

2.

That Orb amid the watry waſte
Thy hands, beſt Architect, have plac'd,
And bid th' unfathomable Deep
Beneath its firm foundations ſleep.

3.

Lord, who ſhall to thy Hill aſcend ?
Who ſuppliant at thine altars bend,
Then joyful find a ſure abode,
And own the preſence of his God ?

4.

Whoſe hands and heart from guilt are free,
Who ne'er to idols bow'd the knee,
Nor, ſtudious of deceit, would try
By oaths to conſecrate a lye.

5.

On fuch th' Almighty from above
Shall heap the bleffings of his Love,
And, purg'd from fin's tranfmiffive ftain,
Admit them to his facred Fane.

6.

Such only form the chofen Choir,
Whofe feet, with licens'd ftep, afpire
To vifit *Sion*'s bleft Abode ;
Who feek the face of *Jacob*'s God.   -

7.

Lift, lift your heads, each hallow'd Gate,
Aloft, with fudden fpring, your weight,
Ye everlafting Portals, rear ;
Behold the King of glory near !

8.

And who this King of glory ? fay.
That Lord who bears th' eternal fway ;
Who, cloth'd with ftrength, to war defcends
And conqueft on his fword attends.

9.

Lift, lift your heads, each hallow'd Gate,
Aloft, with fudden fpring, your weight,
Ye everlafting Portals, rear ;
Behold the King of glory near !

10.

And who this King of glory ? fay.
The God, whom Heav'n's high Hofts obey :
In him that King of glory view,
And yield to Him the homage due.

PSALM XXV.

1.

TO Thee, great God, my foul fhall rife;
   On Thee my ftedfaft mind relies;
O fave me, Lord, from fhame and woe,
And blaft the triumphs of my foe.

2.

Nor fhame nor woe the heart attends,
Whofe truft on *Jacob*'s God depends : .
But grief, confufion, doubt, and fear
The fouls that rafhly fin fhall tear.

3.

Thy paths, bleft Source of light, difplay,
And teach my doubting fteps thy way.
God of my health, from morn to eve
In Thee my hopes have learn'd to live :

4.

O lead me in thy truth, and ftore
My heart with thy celeftial lore ;
Thy mercy, Lord, recall to mind,
Whofe beams from earlieft age have fhin'd.

5.

O let oblivion's thickeft veil
'Th' offences of my youth conceal,
That I with Them my lot may bear,
Whofe fouls thy kind remembrance fhare.

6.

Good, Lord, and juft art Thou ; thy Love
Returning Sinners joy to prove,
And led by thy aufpicious ray
Correct the error of their way.

7. In

7.

In Thee ſhall each of humble mind
The Friend and ſure Inſtructor find,
And each, whoſe truſt on Thee is plac'd,
Shall happineſs perpetual taſte ;

8.

Thus, while the dictates of thy Law,
His thoughts to full obedience awe,
With joy thy paths the Juſt ſhall tread,
By Mercy and by Truth outſpread.

9.

Thy wonted pity, Lord, impart,
While in the anguiſh of my heart
The burthen of my guilt I own,
And humbled bow before thy Throne.

10.

Ye Souls that to his fear incline,
Secure to God your ſteps reſign,
And learn from his directing hand
What path may beſt your choice demand.

11.

How bleſt, thy precepts, Lord, who knows!
As o'er Life's pilgrimage he goes,
See Peace and Safety nightly ſpread
Their tent around his favour'd head :

12.

See, rang'd in fair deſcent, his line
The lot which thy Decrees aſſign
Divide, and, long as time ſhall laſt,
The bleſſings of thy Bounty taſte.

13. Who

13.

Who bow to Thee th' attentive ear,
The fecrets of thy will fhall hear ;
Thy Compact, Lord, to fuch reveal'd,
Shall light and heav'nly tranfport yield.

14.

Wrapt in the hoftile fnare I lie,
Yet lift to Thee th' expecting eye,
Till thou my full relief decree,
And bid my captive foul go free.

15.

O turn thee, Lord, in pity turn,
Behold me helplefs and forlorn ;
See various griefs my heart opprefs ;
My wants fupply, my wrongs redrefs ;

16.

O let me thy attention win,
And feal the pardon of my fin ;
For who like Thee with quick'ning ray
Can chafe each cloud of grief away.

17.

While factious Crouds around me wait,
Inflam'd with rage, and impious hate,
Stretch to my aid the arm of pow'r,
And guard me in the dang'rous hour.

18.

Let not my foul, on Thee reclin'd,
Its forrows utter to the wind ;
Let Truth and fpotlefs Innocence
Their fuccours to my heart difpenfe.

19. Indulgent

19.

Indulgent to my pray'r, with Mine
My Country's wiſh'd deliv'rance join;
God of my hope, thy Love diſcloſe,
And heal, O heal, thy People's woes.

P S A L M   XXVI.

1.

BE Thou my Judge : thy ſearching eyes
My guiltleſs life have known :
On Thee my ſtedfaſt ſoul relies,
    Nor fear of lapſe ſhall own.

2.

O ſearch me ſtill ; my heart, my reins,
    With ſtricteſt view ſurvey:
Thy Love, great God, my hope ſuſtains,
    Thy Truth directs my way.

3.

The houſe of guile, and ſeat of lies,
    With ſtudious care I ſhun :
From Crouds that impious deeds deviſe
    My ſteps abhorrent run.

4.

In innocence I waſh my hands,
    Thy altar compaſs round,
And grateful lead the ſacred Bands,
    Whoſe hymns thy acts reſound.

5.

How oft, inſtinct with warmth divine,
    Thy threſhold have I trod !
How lov'd the Courts whoſe walls inſhrine
    The Glory of my God !

6. O let

6.

O let me not the vengeance fhare,
  That waits the guilty Tribe,
Whofe murth'rous hands each mifchief dare,
  And grafp the offer'd bribe :

7.

But pour, O pour, while thus I tread
  The path by Thee prepar'd,
Thy beams of mercy on my head,
  And round me plant a guard.

8.

Thou, Lord, my fteps haft fix'd aright,
  And pleas'd fhalt hear my tongue
With *Ifrael*'s thankful Sons unite
  To form the feftal Song.

P S A L M   XXVII.

I.

THOU, Lord, my fafety, Thou my light,
  What danger fhall my foul affright ?
Strength of my life ! What arm fhall dare
To hurt whom Thou haft own'd thy care ?

2.

When erft, impatient to devour,
Againft me rofe each hoftile pow'r,
Their fierce attempts fuccefslefs found,
They ftumbled, fell, and bit the ground.

3.

Though adverfe hofts the ftandard rear,
Thy fervant fhall without a fear
The gath'ring War around him fee,
And fix, fecure, his truft on Thee.

4. One

4.

One wish, with holy transport warm,
My heart has form'd and yet shall form ;
That in thy Presence I may stand,
And share the blessings of thy hand.

5.

One gift I ask ; that to my end
Fair *Sion*'s Dome I may attend,
There joyful find a sure abode,
And view the beauty of my God.

6.

For He within his hallow'd shrine
My secret refuge shall assign,
And, while the storms around me beat,
Fix on the rock my stedfast feet.

7.

My heart secure to God resign'd
In him its safety boasts to find,
For he, his arm beneath me spread,
High o'er my foes exalts my head.

8.

For this, with grateful joy bestow'd,
My off'ring shall his altar load,
My tongue its note exulting raise,
And dictate to the harp his praise.

9.

O hear me, Lord ; on Thee I call,
And prostrate at thy footstool fall :
Propitious in my cause appear,
And bow to my request thine ear.

10. " Seek

10.

" Seek Ye my face with duteous care,
" And frequent to my Throne repair,"
Thus to my heart I hear thee speak ;
Thy face, my heart replies, I seek :

11.

Look down, my only Hope ! look down,
Behold me, but without a frown,
And ne'er to my desiring eye
Thy presence, heav'nly Lord, deny :

12.

O let me, on thy aid reclin'd,
Thee still my great Salvation find,
Nor leave me, helpless and forlorn,
The absence of thy grace to mourn.

13.

When, doom'd the Orphan's lot to bear,
No Father's kind concern I share,
Nor o'er me wakes a Mother's eye,
My wants attentive to supply.

14.

Adopted by thy care, in Thee
The Parent and the Friend I see,
And nourish'd by thy soft'ring hand,
Within thy courts secure I stand.

15.

Instruct me, Lord, thy path to know,
And, while with secret art the foe
My doubting steps would turn aside,
Be Thou my Guardian and my Guide.

16. O

16.

O fave me from the hand of wrong;
My foul by each malignant tongue
With caufelefs infult loaded view,
And charg'd with guilt it never knew.

17.

O how had grief confum'd my frame,
But that I hop'd, while yet my name
Amidft the living ftands inroll'd,
Thy boundlefs Mercy to behold.

18.

With patient hope, with mind fedate,
On *Ifrael*'s God expectant wait;
Be ftrong, be ftedfaft: So thy heart
Shall feel his grace its aid impart.

PSALM XXVIII.

1.

GOD my Strength, to Thee I pray;
Turn not Thou thine ear away;
Left, while to thy Suppliant's cry
Thou thy anfwer fhalt deny,
Sudden I my place affume
'Midft the tenants of the tomb:
Gracious to my vows attend,
While the humble knee I bend,
And, infpir'd with holy fear,
Tow'rd thy fhrine my hands uprear.

2.

Give me not thy wrath to know,
Nor to feel the vengeful blow

G   By

By thy juſt decrees aſſign'd
To the Men of impious mind,
Who, their hearts intent on wrong,
Smooth with lies their venom'd tongue.
Let whate'er their thoughts deviſe,
Thus aloud thy Juſtice cries,
What their ruthleſs arm has dar'd,
Meet from Thee its full reward :

3.

While thy wrath with ſteady pace
Step by ſtep their feet ſhall trace,
And, though now their ſtubborn ear
Shun thy wondrous acts to hear,
Teach them to confeſs thy pow'r,
Shatter'd like ſome Heav'n-ſtruck Tow'r,
That before th' aſtoniſh'd ſight,
Stooping from its airy height,
'Midſt the thunder's awful roar,
Falls, to be rebuilt no more.

4.

Let me (for with pitying ear
God my pray'r has deign'd to hear,)
Let me thanks perpetual yield;
He my Strength, and He my Shield,
On his long-experienc'd aid
See my hope for ever ſtay'd,
While my heart, with joy poſſeſs'd,
Dances in my throbbing breaſt,
And my tongue in grateful lays
Conſecrates to Him its praiſe.

5. Thou

. 5.

Thou whofe arm is o'er us fpread,
Prompt to guard th' anointed head,
And from each invader's hand
Vindicate thy chofen Land,
Save thy People from diftrefs,
And thy Patrimony blefs !
Give them, Lord, thy Love to fhare,
Feed them with a Shepherd's care,
And their pow'r to lateft days
O'er their foes triumphant raife.

P S A L M   XXIX.

.1. .

SING, ye Sons of Might, O fing
  Praife to Heav'n's eternal King ;
Raife to Him fome new-taught fong,
To his praife the note prolong.

2.

Pow'r and ftrength to Him affign,
And before his hallow'd fhrine
Yield the homage that his Name
From a Creature's lips may claim.

3.

Hark ! his voice in thunder breaks ;
Hufh'd to filence, while he fpeaks,
Ocean's waves from pole to pole
Hear the awful accents roll :

G 2   4. See

4.

See, as louder yet they rife,
Echoing through the vaulted Skies,
Loftieft Cedars lie o'erthrown,
Cedars of fteep *Lebanon*.

5.

See, uprooted from its feat,
Lebanon itfelf retreat ;
Trembling at the threat divine,
Sirion haftes its flight to join :

6.

See them like the heifer borne,
Like the beaft whofe pointed horn
Strikes with dread the fylvan train,
Bound impetuous on the plain.

7.

Now the burfting clouds give way,
And the vivid lightnings play,
And the wilds by Man untrod
Hear, difmay'd, th' approaching God.

8.

Cades, o'er thy lonely wafte
Oft the dreaded founds have paft :
Oft his ftroke the Wood invades,
Widow'd of its leafy fhades.

9.

Mightieft oaks its fury know ;
While the pregnant Hind her throe
Inftant feels, and on the earth
Trembling drops th' unfinifh'd birth.

10. Proftrate

10.

Proftrate on the facred floor
Ifrael's Sons his name adore,
While his acts to ev'ry tongue
Yield its argument of fong.

11.

He the fwelling furge commands;
Fix'd his Throne for ever ftands;
He his People fhall increafe,
Arm with ftrength, and blefs with peace.

PSALM XXX.

1.

TO Thee, great Ruler of the fkies,
Whofe arm its conftant aid fupplies,
While vanquifh'd foes confefs my fway,
My heart its ready vows fhall pay;
My grateful tongue, immortal King,
Thy mercy fhall for ever fing.

2.

As, prefs'd with woe, to Thee I cried,
Thy hand its healing pow'r applied,
And, while increafing languors gave
The fignal to th' expecting grave
This mortal fabrick to receive,
Revers'd the doom, and bade me live.

3.

Ye faithful Sons of *Ifrael*'s name,
Your Maker's fanctity proclaim,
And, while his mercies on your breaft
In fweet memorial ftand imprefs'd,

To him in joyful accents raife
The fong of gratitude and praife.

4.

How well our great Preferver knows
To weigh and to relieve our woes !
Behold his Wrath's avenging blaft,
How flow to rife, how foon o'erpaft,
How prompt his Favour to difpenfe
Its life-imparting influence.

5.

How fpeedy his paternal love
Our deep afflictions to remove !
Grief for a night, obtrufive Gueft,
Beneath our roof perchance may reft,
But Joy, with the returning day,
Shall wipe each tranfient tear away.

6.

As pleas'd I caft my eyes around,
And view'd my life with bleffings crown'd,
(While, fafe in thy protecting hand,
High on the rock I took my ftand,)
In confidence of foul I faid,
" What ills fhall e'er my peace invade ?"

7.

But, inftant, Thou thy face hadft turn'd,
And proftrate on the earth I mourn'd:
I mourn'd, and, O my Guard, my Guide,
(With humbler fpirit thus I cried,)
Shall aught of profit, if the ground
My blood abforb, to Thee redound ?

8. Shall,

8.

Shall, vocal in thy praife, the Duft
Proclaim thy Counfels wife and juft,
And wake thy wondrous Acts to tell
Amid Corruption's dreary cell?
Thy aid, my God, in pity lend,
And gracious to my plaints attend.

9.

Again the face of joy I wear;
Thy hand, indulgent to my pray'r,
The fackcloth from my loins unbound,
With mirth's fair cincture wraps me round:
Thy ftrength my fainting fpirit chears, –
And checks my griefs and calms my fears.

10.

For this, with facred tranfport fill'd,
To Thee my foul its praife fhall yield,
My thankful heart with zeal fhall burn,
My tongue the bands of filence fpurn,
And pleas'd, through life, in grateful verfe
Thy Love, eternal Lord, rehearfe.

PSALM XXXI.

1.

LORD (for on Thee fupported ftand
My hopes,) O let thy aiding hand
The juftice of my caufe proclaim,
And fave me from impending fhame.

2. Thy

2.

Thy ear, thou Majefty divine,
Propitious to my pray'r incline :
Hafte to my help, and let thy pow'r
My rock prefent and brazen tow'r :

3.

That rock, that tow'r, my God, in Thee,
Snatch'd from furrounding ills, I fee ;
Shew me thy path, and fo thy Name
Shall praife and thanks perpetual claim.

4.

O let me, by thy counfel led,
That path with ftep unerring tread,
And, fav'd by thy preventive care,
Shake from my feet the broken fnare.

5.

God of my ftrength, the Wife, the Juft,
To Thee my fpirit I intruft ;
From Thee, when terrors clos'd me round,
My foul its full redemption found.

6.

My thoughts the felf-deceiving train,
Enflav'd to fuperftitions vain,
Abhor, and 'midft increafing woes
Their confidence on Thee repofe.

7.

Thy Mercy fhall my thanks employ;
My conftant theme, my higheft joy ;
For Thou, my foul by griefs purfu'd,
My ftate with pitying eye haft view'd.

8. Thy

8.

Thy hand, while rang'd in cloſe array
Inſulting hoſts around me lay,
Gave to the wind their vain deſign,
And made the paths of freedom mine.

9.

Once more, my ſight with inward grief
Conſum'd, vouchſafe me thy relief,
Confeſs me thine, diſpel the ſighs
That in my heaving boſom riſe;

10.

For while my ſoul its ceaſeleſs pains
Deep through its inmoſt frame ſuſtains,
Life's noon for eve exchang'd I bear,
And Age invited on by Care.

11.

The guilt that in my thought revolves
My ſtrength impairs, my joints diſſolves;
The ſcorn of Foes, and, keener yet,
The ſcorns of Friends, my ſoul beſet:

12.

My former gueſts, if in their way
My waſted form they now ſurvey,
With horror ſtruck the ſight forego,
And ſhun th' infection of my woe.

13.

With lonely ſtep the earth I tread,
Forgotten as the ſilent Dead,
Or as the vaſe of meaneſt clay,
In uſeleſs fragments caſt away.

14. My

14.

My fame opprobrious tongues invade,
While terrors wrap me in their shade,
And crouds with meditated rage
Against my life their pow'rs engage.

15.

Yet see me, Lord, in Thee confide ;
Thou art my God, my heart has cried ;
From Thee my time its limit knows ;
O save me from devouring foes.

16.

O let thy presence on me beam,
Thy clemency my life redeem,
Nor let me, Lord, the shame sustain
Thy aid to ask, and ask in vain.

17.

Theirs be the shame, thy pow'r who brave,
Nor cease their insults, till the grave,
Absorbing quick the guilty throng,
In endless silence seal their tongue :

18.

Such silence on their lips impose,
Whose words their pride-swoln heart disclose,
At Wisdom's Sons their malice aim,
And blast with lies the guiltless name.

19.

O, how shall All who seek thy Love
The fulness of thy bounty prove !
And teach th' admiring World to see
How blest the souls that trust in Thee !

20. Thy

20.

Thy Saints, while breath their life prolongs,
Sav'd by thy care from strife of tongues,
Shall fee thy tabernacle fpread
Its awful fplendors o'er their head.

21.

Bleft be the name of *Jacob*'s God,
Whofe Love, in happieft hour beftow'd,
Has giv'n within my lot to fall
The ftrong-built City's guarding wall.

22.

Awhile, with uncollected mind,
As banifh'd from thy fight, I pin'd;
But Thou thy Servant's pray'r haft heard,
In anguifh of my heart prefer'd.

23.

Ye Souls devoted to his fear,
With thankful love your God revere,
Who wakes your chofen Train to guard,
And deals to Pride its juft reward.

24.

Be ftrong, be ftedfaft : So your mind
From Him its full fupport fhall find,
(Ye Saints that in his care confide,)
Nor own nor afk a help befide.

PSALM XXXII.

I.

HOW bleft the Man, whofe confcious grief
From Thee, great God, has found relief;
Whofe guilt thy boundlefs Love has veil'd,
His fears compos'd, his weaknefs heal'd;

2. To

2.

To whom th' offences of his hand
No longer now imputed stand,
Who learns thy precepts to revere,
Whose heart is pure, whose tongue sincere.

3.

While deep within my lab'ring breast
My mind its dire disease suppress'd,
Incessant groans, that shun'd controul,
Betray'd the anguish of my soul.

4.

See Age-anticipating Care
My joints dissolve, my strength impair,
Relentless from my cheek each trace
Of youth and blooming health erase.

5.

When Night extends its dusky cone,
Beneath thy terrors, Lord, I groan;
The shades anon retreating see;
And Day to All restor'd, but Me.

6.

Behold my frame with drought consum'd,
That late with youthful vigour bloom'd;
Such drought the blasted fields betray,
Beneath the dog-star's burning ray.

7.

My humbled Soul its crimes shall own :—
Behold me bow before thy Throne,
To Thee my inmost guilt disclose,
And in thy bosom pour my woes.

8. But

8.

But lo! while yet my hands I rear,
The voice of Mercy to my ear
Defcends, and whifp'ring peace within
Confirms the pardon of my fin.

9.

For this fhall All who Thee adore,
Ere yet the day of grace be o'er,
To Thee with ftedfaft hope repair,
To Thee prefer th' unwearied pray'r:

10.

So, when affliction's tempefts rife,
And heave the billows to the fkies,
They, fafe in Thee, the ftorm fhall brave,
And diftant view the madding wave.

11.

When various griefs my fôul furround,
In Thee my fure retreat is found;
Thy wifh'd Salvation meets my eyes,
And fongs of triumph round me rife.

12.

Come, from thy God inftruction learn;
While, prompt from error's path to turn
Thy feet, thy ev'ry ftep I fcan,
Let Reafon's ufe befpeak thee Man;

13.

Nor imitate the Steed and Mule,
Whofe brutal mouth, averfe to rule,
To guard thee from their rage, muft feel
The forceful rein, and curbing fteel.

H   14. What

14.

What pangs the impious Tribe await,
While hope and joy his heart dilate,
Who trufts in Thee, O King of Kings,
And Mercy round him fpreads her wings!

15.

Ye Saints, exulting lift your voice,
Ye pure of mind, in Him rejoice,
Whofe prefence on the foul imprefs'd
With heav'nly tranfport fills the breaft.

PSALM XXXIII.

1.

YE Saints (to you the tafk belongs,
And Praife fits comely on your tongues;)
Blefs, blefs *Jehovah!* fweet the joy
When tafks like thefe the voice employ;
Wake to *Jehovah*'s name the lute,
Nor let the ten-ftring'd lyre be mute.

2.

O fing, in accents loud and ftrong,
O fing fome new-invented fong;
And let the finger's artful ftroke
The pfalt'ry's various pow'r provoke,
And teach the praife of *Ifrael*'s Lord
To vibrate on the founding chord.

3.

His words eternal Truth has feal'd;
His promifes in act fulfill'd
Shall Equity and Judgement prove
The changlefs objects of his love,

And

§

And bid the Earth's wide confines know
The gifts that from his bounty flow.

4.

His Word yon azure vault outspread,
Ere Time the Seasons onward led;
Form'd by his breath the starry host
Their unextinguish'd lustre boast;
While in their cavern'd storehouse sleep
The treasures of the watry deep.

5.

Thy Maker's name, O Earth, revere;
And let thy Sons with holy fear
To Him in low prostration bend,
And duteous his decrees attend.
He spake: And Heav'n, and Seas, and Land,
Appear'd.   He bade: And lo, they stand.

6.

Their counsels vain the Heathen Tribes
Unite; but God th' event prescribes,
And blasts at will each hope that springs
Within the breast of haughtiest Kings;
His counsel, from controul secure,
His counsel only shall endure.

7.

His thoughts to Time's remotest bound
With sure effect shall e'er be crown'd:
How blest the People that have known
Him for their God, and Him alone;
The Flock His heritage declar'd,
And objects of His fix'd regard!

H 2   8. Wide

8.

Wide o'er the Sons of Earth his eye
The Pow'r eternal from on high
Extends, (that Pow'r, whose hand, with art
Mysterious, forms the human heart,)
Through life's wild maze their steps pursues,
Each act, each thought, attentive views.

9.

Think not, ye Kings, (His aid resign'd,)
In well arm'd Hosts your help to find :
In vain the Warrior bold and young
Exults, his arm with vigour strung :
In vain, his Lord to save, the steed
Vaunts in the fight his strength and speed.

10.

Hail, sure Protector of the Just !
From Him who builds on Thee his trust
Thy arm averts with studious care
Each death that viewless wings the air ;
Thy hand with food his life sustains,
When drought infests the blasted plains.

11.

Our Souls by Thee, their Help and Shield,
With patient hope have stood upheld ;
Thy sacred Name our trust, each mind
From Thee shall joy perpetual find :
In mercy give us, Lord, to see
How just the hope that rests on Thee.

PSALM

PSALM XXXIV.

1.

THEE will I thank, and day by day
 Form to thy praife the joyful lay ;
From morn to eve the fong extend,
Thee boaft my Father, Thee my Friend :

2.

While pleas'd each heart of humble frame
Shall wake, great God, to hear thy fame ;
His voice let each triumphant raife,
And fing with Me your Maker's praife.

3.

To Him my Soul difclos'd its care ;
He heard, and prefent to my pray'r
(His faithful buckler o'er me held,)
Each terror from my breaft difpell'd.

4.

The fouls, that his decree regard,
Like Me his chearing light have fhar'd,
And fearlefs of repulfe or fhame
The promife of his mercy claim.

5.

Behold a heart with woes opprefs'd ;
Behold, its vows to God addrefs'd,
His hand its healing pow'r difplay,
And chafe each cloud of grief away.

6.

His Angel, nigh the juft man's tent
Encamp'd, each danger to prevent,
His fure protection round him throws,
Though harnefs'd Hofts his peace oppofe.

H 3

7. Hail,

7.

Hail, Saviour of the human race!
Hail, Fountain of exhauſtleſs grace!
Thrice happy, who on Thee recline,
Nor own nor aſk a help but thine.

8.

O taſte with me; O taſte and prove
The bleſſings of his boundleſs love;
His fear preſerve, ye juſt and pure,
And live from dread of want ſecure.

9.

The ſtrengthful Lion's tawny brood
With thirſt and penury of food
Are ſtung; but who in God confide
Shall find their ev'ry wiſh ſupplied.

10.

Ye Children, come; my precepts hear,
And learn the dictates of his fear:
O come; if long extent of days,
With bleſſings crown'd, thy hope can raiſe:

11.

Averſe from each injurious art,
Let falſehood from thy lips depart;
Be Good thy choice; from Evil ceaſe;
And plight the ready hand to peace.

12.

Him ſerve, whoſe fav'ring eyes ſurvey
The hearts that his commands obey;
Him ſerve, whoſe ever open ear
With juſt regard their pray'r ſhall hear.

13. But

13.

But terrors planted on his brow
Inftruct the ftubborn foul to bow,
And vengeance, kindled to a flame,
Blots from the earth the impious name.

14.

With fuppliant voice, in each diftrefs,
His fole fupport, his fole redrefs,
From God the Man of faithful mind
Shall feek, and what he feeks fhall find.

15.

A fpirit griev'd is facrifice
Delightful to th' all-feeing eyes;
God, ever watchful, ever near,
The meek and contrite foul fhall chear;

16.

What though the Juft, by his decree,
Awhile a Man of griefs we fee,
His Love fhall foon its aid beftow,
Relieve his cares, and foothe his woe.

17.

To violence expos'd, his frame
Thy fix'd attention, Lord, fhall claim;
Nor Hell's worft rage one bone fhall dare
To break, when Thou haft bid to fpare.

18.

But ill on All who ill intend
In full proportion fhall defcend:
Who tow'rd the Juft in hatred join,
Shall feel, great God, the weight of thine.

19. 'Tis

19.

'Tis thine thy Saints from woes to free;
Nor Time throughout its courſe ſhall ſee
The ſoul, whoſe hope on Thee is ſtaid,
Neglected mourn thy abſent aid.

PSALM XXXV.

1.

DO Thou, juſt God, my cauſe defend,
O let thy pow'r its aid extend,
And make my quarrel thine; my foes
Let thy reſiſtleſs arm oppoſe;
Ariſe thy ſpeedieſt help to yield,
And reach the corſlet, reach the ſhield,
Graſp in thy hand the glitt'ring lance,
And obvious in the breach advance;
Say to my troubled Soul; " In Me
" Thy ſtrength and ſure ſalvation ſee."

2.

Let ſhame their glowing cheeks o'erſpread,
Whoſe ceaſeleſs threats excite my dread;
And let them, ſtruck with wild affright,
Inglorious backward urge their flight,
Diſpers'd, as chaff before the wind,
Thy Angel preſſing cloſe behind,
Along the dark and ſlipp'ry way,
Whoſe paths their ſtagg'ring ſteps betray;
And from the arm ethereal find
The vengeance to their guilt aſſign'd.

3.

Thou ſeeſt them, Lord, with cauſeleſs hate,
Beſide my path inſidious wait,

With

With caufelefs hate the pit prepare,
And plant before my fteps their fnare.
O let deftruction's fudden ftroke,
While thus thy juftice they provoke,
Defcend, vindictive, on their head;
Faft in the net for Me outfpread
Involv'd, let each repentant groan,
And reap the mifchiefs he has fown.

4.

But Thou, my Soul, with awful joy
On God thy ftedfaft thought employ,
And, his Salvation taught to prove,
Record the wonders of his Love:
Each bone whofe ftrength fupports my frame
With grateful tranfport fhall exclaim,
Lord! whom like Thee fhall Mortals find,
For ever juft, for ever kind,
Like Thee prepar'd th' afflicted poor
From ftern Oppreffion to fecure.

5.

Thus poor and thus opprefs'd with wrong
Awhile was I: a hoftile Throng
(Whofe Tongue to fraud has loos'd the reins
And lie with lie connected feigns)
Againft me urg'd, to fcandal prone,
The guilt my breaft had never known,
And left me helplefs and forlorn
The friendfhip ill repay'd to mourn,
That, when Affliction's weight they bare,
Had taught my heart their woes to fhare:

6. While

6.

While ſickneſs wrapt them in its chain,
And fix'd them on the bed of pain,
My heart, that no affection ow'd,
With ſympathizing pity glow'd,
I knew their ſuff'rings to bewail,
And ſunk with grief, with faſting pale,
To God, in ſorrow's garb array'd,
With humbleſt interceſſion pray'd,
And found the pray'r their pride has ſpurn'd
With bleſſings on my head return'd :

7.

Diſſolv'd in tears, with languor worn,
What miſery my ſoul has borne !
Nor Friend for Friend ſincerer woes,
Nor Brother for a Brother, knows ;
Nor feels the Son his melting breaſt
With deeper ſenſe of grief impreſs'd,
That graſps a dying Mother's hand,
And waits to take her laſt command,
Or o'er her loſs in ſecret pines,
And wraps the ſackcloth round his loins.

8.

Not ſuch the pity ſhown to Me :
Ev'n abjects my abjection ſee
With ſcornful gaze, as round me ſtand, –
In adverſe league, a lawleſs Band,
Theſe taught with well-diſſembled art
To veil the purpoſe of their heart,
While Thoſe in open hate engage,
And ceaſeleſs vent their murth'rous rage,

                    Now

Now furious grind their teeth, and now
Infulting aim the deathful blow.

9.

How long wilt Thou, my God, how long
With patient eye behold my wrong ?
How long fhall I, with anguifh torn,
Thy face, my God, averted mourn ?
With vain and fruitlefs hope attend
Till Thou, my Guardian and my Friend,
The Lion's dreaded rage controul,
And refcue my deferted foul,
That, 'mid th' affembled Tribes, my tongue
May raife to Thee the thankful fong ?

10.

O let not my uninjur'd foes,
With fpeaking eye, amidft my woes,
As round they ftand in clofe array,
The triumphs of their heart betray :
Behold them, Lord, their arts addrefs,
The friends of peace and truth t' opprefs,
But chief my name with infults load :
" Thou wretch abandon'd of thy God,
" In vain," they clamour, " what our eyes
" Atteft, thy confcious tongue denies."

11.

My God, (for Thou their rage haft feen,)
With timelieft fuccour intervene,
Nor filent long, Almighty Sire,
Remain, nor diftant far retire;
Arife, thy faving pow'r difclofe,
And heal with pitying Hand my woes;
Awake,

Awake, thy aiding ſtrength excite,
Awake, and vindicate my right ;
Let Juſtice teach them, by thy ſtroke,
Their frantic triumphs to revoke.

12.

Let not their heart, its wiſh complete,
With ſecret joy tranſported beat,
Or boaſting hail th' expected hour,
That gives me to the Murth'rer's pow'r;
But back my threaten'd life demand
From ſtern Oppreſſion's iron hand : ˙
Let All who make my grief their ſcorn
Their blaſted hopes aſtoniſh'd mourn ;
Let ſtern rebuke and foul diſgrace
With ſhame perpetual clothe their face.

13.

Lo, nigh me rang'd, with thankful voice,
The friends of innocence rejoice,
And " Bleſt," they cry, " be *Jacob*'s Lord,
" The God by Heav'n and Earth ador'd,
" Who joys his Servant's cauſe to plead,
" And crowns with peace his favour'd head."
While, loudeſt in the choir, my tongue
To notes of praiſe ſhall tune its ſong,
And pleas'd through each revolving day
Thy Juſtice, mightieſt Lord, diſplay.

PSALM XXXVI.

I.

BEHOLD the wretch, in error loſt,
Whoſe ſtubborn heart with impious boaſt
His Law rejects, his fear denies,
Who form'd the earth, and ſeas, and ſkies;

2.

He ne'er repentant looks within,
To view the meaſure of his ſin;
His tongue to falſehood train'd, his mind
No more to acts of good inclin'd;

3.

Concerted miſchiefs croud his breaſt,
And rob his midnight hours of reſt;
Nor Wiſdom to her paths his will
Can turn, or wean his ſoul from ill.

4.

Thy Mercy, Lord, to Heav'n extends,
Thy Truth the lofty clouds tranſcends;
Fix'd as the Mountain's ſolid baſe
Thy righteouſneſs maintains her place.

5.

Who ſeeks to trace the Will divine
By Reaſon's aid, with ſcanty line
(Prepoſt'rous,) would the Deep explore,
And meaſure with his ſpan its ſhore.

6.

Nor reſt thy cares alone confin'd
To Us, the Sons of human kind;
Thy hand th' unconſcious Brute ſuſtains,
And ſpreads his paſture on the plains:

.I   7. But

7.

But We, with pious truſt, who know
What gifts we to thy Mercy owe,
(O, what that Mercy can excel?)
Beneath thy foſt'ring wings ſhall dwell.

8.

To each who ſeeks thy name behold
Thy Houſe its richeſt ſtores unfold,
And bliſs unintermix'd with woe
In fulleſt ſtreams their breaſt o'erflow.

9.

From out thy Seat, immortal King,
Forth iſſues Life's perennial ſpring;
Thy light with unextinguiſh'd rays
Shall o'er our heads auſpicious blaze.

10.

Still may the ſouls who Thee have known
The Bleſſings of thy Mercy own,
And each who bears a ſpotleſs mind
His refuge in thy Juſtice find.

11.

Me let thy care, Almighty Friend,
From Pride's injurious foot defend;
Each impious hand that ſeeks my hurt
Let thy ſuperior ſtrength avert.

12.

O bid before my ſight each foe
The terrors of thy vengeance know;
Lo, there they fall, their triumphs o'er,
And proſtrate lie, to riſe no more.

P S A L M

PSALM XXXVII.

1.

LET not the Sinner's wealth or might
    The envy of thy foul excite:
Anon thine eye fhall fee him fade
Quick as the flow'r or vernal blade,
That now rejoicing lifts the head,
Now with'ring on the earth is fpread.

2.

But Thou thy will to Heav'n's high Lord
(His Faith thy truft, thy rule his Word,)
Submit, and nourifh'd by his hand
Inherit from his gift the Land:
In Him delight, on Him depend;
Him chufe thy Guide, thy Way, thy End.

3.

So fhall his Love thy wifhes grant,
His Care anticipate thy want,
And bid thy acts in light ferene
Fair as the rifing morn be feen,
Thy Juftice as the noon of day
Diffufive pour its cloudlefs ray.

4.

With patient hope await his will,
Nor let the fight of profp'rous ill
Impel thee with difquiet vain
His wife difpofals to arraign,
Left wrath and doubt thy confcience blind,
And urge to acts of guilt thy mind.

5.

See, from their dwelling torn, th' unjuft
To thofe who fix on God their truft

(So wills the Majesty divine,)
Their forfeit heritage resign :
Wait but awhile, then look around ;
No more the impious race are found.

6.

But see the meek and pious Band
(Advanc'd by God's almighty hand
The pow'r among them to divide,
To fierce Ambition's sword denied,)
Earth's bounds possess, and, Peace their care,
The fulness of its blessings share.

7.

Gnashing his teeth the fool prepares
To catch the upright in his snares ;
But God his frantic rage derides,
And sees the Day, as on it glides,
Whose beams, with wrath uncommon red,
Shall stream in vengeance o'er his head.

8.

On You, ye Poor, with vain intent,
The sword is drawn, the bow is bent ;
The sword, with better aim impress'd,
Descends into its Owner's breast ;
Reluctant to the Archer's will
Bursts the tough bow, and mocks his skill.

9.

Exchange not Ye your scanty store
For heaps of guilt-polluted ore :
That God, ye Saints, whose Love ye seek,
The arm of lawless pow'r shall break,
And bid the Just protected stand
Beneath the shadow of his hand.

10. By

10.

By Him your years determin'd flow ;
The Lot, which his Decrees beſtow,
From Sire to Son, till time ſhall end,
In ſure ſucceſſion ſhall deſcend ;
No diſtant time ſhall ſee his love
Its bleſſings from his Saints remove.

11.

When War's dire flames around you burn,
From You the darts their points ſhall turn ;
Each blaſt that taints the red'ning ſky
From Your exempted fields ſhall fly ;
Nor ſhame nor want the heart attends
Whoſe truſt on *Jacob*'s God depends.

12.

Who know not Thee, great God, to dread,
As Victims for the ſlaughter fed,
Conſum'd by Heav'n's avenging fire
Shall periſh and in ſmoke aſpire :
How ſwift how ſudden is their fate,
What horrors, Lord, their death await!

13.

While faithleſs Theſe th' intruſted loan
With baſe ingratitude diſown,
His plenteous alms the Juſt can give,
And pleas'd a Brother's wants relieve ;
Earth's goods thy Bleſſing to the Pure
Shall grant, and what it grants inſure :

14.

While guilty ſouls the Curſe divine
To full exciſion ſhall conſign ;

The Juſt, bleſt objeſt of thy Love,
Thou, Lord, wilt lead, his path approve,
Thy faithful hands his ſteps ſuſtain ;
Nor falls he, but to riſe again.

15.

Once was I young, and now am old,
Yet ne'er the Righteous could behold
By God deſerted, nor his ſeed
Requeſting at my gate their bread :
Secure he lives, and for his heirs
Proſperity and peace prepares.

16.

From Ill recede ; to Good incline
Thy thought; and endleſs life be thine.
Delighted whom his Laws delight
Th' Almighty views ; nor Day nor Night
The ſoul that bows to his Decree
Abandon'd from his Love ſhall ſee.

17.

Behold, ye Juſt, th' eternal Doom
The Sinner's ſhort-liv'd days conſume :
His fruit a luckleſs progeny
Uprooted from the ground ſhall die;
While happier Ye to Yours aſſign'd
A heritage perpetual find.

18.

How bleſt whom Thou, great God, haſt taught!
His lips, with ſacred ſcience fraught,
The leſſons of thy truth impart ;
And, grav'd within his inmoſt heart,
Thy Law, the ever faithful Guide,
Forbids his ſtedfaſt feet to ſlide.

x   19. Each

19.

Each art the murth'rous tribe effay,
And mark the guiltlefs for their prey;
But God his refcue has decreed;
Himfelf will rife his caufe to plead,
Refute th' Accufer's perjur'd tongue,
And fave him from the hand of wrong.

20.

Wait on thy God; obferve his ways:
His pow'r aloft thy head fhall raife;
Exerted in thy right his hand
Shall vindicate to Thee the Land,
And bid, before thy fight, his foe
The terrors of his vengeance know.

21.

The profp'ring Sinner once I view'd;
Strong as the healthful Tree he ftood,
That, fhadowing wide its native foil,
Nor knows, nor afks, the planter's toil:
I went, I came, and look'd again;
I look'd, but fought his place in vain.

22.

Behold the Juft, and mark his end;
See Peace his eve of life attend:
But fee, ah! fee a diff'rent fate
The Sinner's wretched courfe await;
For lo, upon his lateft hour
The ftorms of heavieft vengeance low'r.

23.

To God the Juft his fafety owes,
Him owns his Strength amidft his woes,

Affur'd

Affur'd that He fhall each defend
Whofe conftant hopes on Him depend,
And, while his foes their peace invade,
Reach, in their caufe, his promis'd aid.

P S A L M   XXXVIII.

I.

O Spare me, Lord, nor o'er my head
    The fulnefs of thy vengeance fhed :
Pierc'd by thy fhafts, great God, I ftand,
And feel the preffure of thy hand.

2.

Thou feeft, from health eftrang'd, my frame
The terrors of thy wrath proclaim,
While confcious guilt alarms my breaft,
And robs my tortur'd joints of reft.

3.

Whelm'd with a weight of fins I mourn,
A weight too heavy to be borne ;
My wounds, whofe fmart thofe fins repays,
The wide-infected air betrays.

4.

See ! bow'd, from morn to eve, with woe,
And wrapt in fackcloth drear, I go ;
My reins with hidden torments wrung,
Each limb difeas'd, each nerve unftrung.

5.

Aloud my fuff'rings I bemoan,
And fainting pour the frequent groan ;
But Thou, ere yet my groans proceed,
My griefs and inmoft wifh canft read.

6. Behold

6.

Behold my heart with anguifh torn,
My ftrength with long affliction worn,
And ftretch'd before my wafted fight
The fhadows of approaching night.

7.

Each kind confoler of my care,
Who wont my plenteous board to fhare,
With pitying eye, with filent gaze
My alter'd lineaments furveys.

8.

My Friends, and next Allies by birth,
(Once dear Companions of my mirth,
When wing'd with health the moments flew)
My griefs with diftant horror view.

9.

With fnares my foes befet my way,
Intent on death throughout the day
With fierceft rage my name revile,
And difcipline their thoughts to guile:

10.

Invented crimes, and taunts fevere,
With fteadieft patience, Lord, I hear,
Unmov'd, as One who deaf and mute
Nor cenfure feels, nor can refute:

11.

For Thou, beft Advocate, art nigh;
On Thee, great God, my hopes rely;
O vindicate my fame from wrong,
And filence the reproachful tongue.

12. Thou

12.

Thou know'ft the tenour of my pray'r ;
O let me not their infults bear :
But hear, and to my foul difplay
Thy Mercy's all-enliv'ning ray.

13.

Mark, when my fteps have chanc'd to flide,
The fhouts that rife on ev'ry fide,
And, echoing through the wounded air,
The triumphs of their heart declare.

14.

'Thou feeft how prone to lapfe my feet,
What woes my eyes inceffant meet ;
Nor fhuns my foul its guilt to own,
But forrowing bows before thy throne.

15.

How ftrong, how num'rous, are the foes
That unprovok'd my peace oppofe,
Their veins with health's full current warm,
And ftrung with active might their arm !

16.

Ill for my Good return'd I find,
Nor know from aught (but that, inclin'd
To Good, their deeds I fhun,) to date
The ground of their prepoft'rous hate.

17.

O let me, rais'd by Thee, no more
The abfence of thine aid deplore ;
God of my life, recede not far,
But hafte, and make that life thy care.

P S A L M

PSALM XXXIX.

1.

MY steps Difcretion's rules fhall guide;
Nor error from my lips fhall flide,
(Thus to myfelf refolv'd I faid;)
Nor word, in Wifdom's fcale unweigh'd;

2.

While lawlefs crouds attend me nigh,
And mark me with infidious eye,
Behold me with the fteady rein
Each effort of my tongue reftrain.

3.

Awhile my foul its purpofe keeps;
A ftubborn filence feals my lips:
But O! from themes of good withheld,
How oft my full-fwoln heart rebell'd!

4.

My thoughts in various tumult roll;
At length, impatient of controul,
Forth from my ftruggling bofom brake
The kindled flame; and thus I fpake:

5.

Taught by thy Wifdom, let me learn
How foon my fabric fhall return
To Earth, and in the filent tomb
Its feat of lafting reft affume.

6.

O let me, heav'nly Lord, extend
My view to life's approaching end;
What are my days? (a fpan their line;)
And what my age compar'd with thine?

7. Our

7.

Our life advancing to its clofe,
While fcarce its earlieft dawn it knows,
Swift through an empty fhade we run,
And Vanity and Man are one:

8.

With anxious pain this Son of care
Toils to inrich an unknown heir,
And, eying oft his heapy ftore,
With vain difquiet thirfts for more.

9.

Where, Lord, fhall I my refuge fee?
On whom repofe my hope but Thee?
O purge my guilt, nor let my foe
Exulting mock my heighten'd woe.

10.

Convinc'd that thy paternal hand
Inflicts but what my fins demand,
I fpeechlefs fate; nor plaintive word,
Nor murmur, from my lips was heard.

11.

But O, in thy appointed hour
Withdraw thy rod; left Nature's pow'r,
While griefs on griefs my heart affail,
Unequal to the conflict, fail.

12.

O, how thy chaftifements impair
The human form, however fair!
How frail the ftrongeft frame we fee,
If Thou the Sinner's fate decree!

13. As

13.

As when the fretting moths confume
The labour of the curious loom,
The texture fails, the dyes decay,
And all its luftre fades away.

14.

Such, Man, thy ftate! then, humbled, own
That Vanity and Thou are one;
Thyfelf when in the balance weigh'd
A Nothing, and thy life a fhade.

15.

To Thee, great God, my knees I bend;
To Thee my ceafelefs pray'rs afcend;
O let my forrows reach thine ears,
And mark my fighs, my groans, my tears.

16.

God of my Fathers! Here, as They,
I walk the Pilgrim of a day;
A tranfient Gueft, thy works admire,
And inftant to my home retire.

17.

O fpare me, Lord, awhile, O fpare,
And Nature's ruin'd ftrength repair,
Ere, life's fhort circuit wander'd o'er,
I perifh, and am feen no more.

PSALM XL.

1.

WITH patient hope my God I fought;
He to his Suppliant's want his thought
In happieft hour applied:

K   He

He from the dark and miry pit
High on the rock has rais'd my feet ;
 Nor fear my steps to slide.

2.

His praise inspires my grateful tongue,
And dictates to my lips a song
 In strains unheard before.
Admiring crouds his work shall see,
Their strength on Him repose with Me,
 With Me his name adore.

3.

Blest, who in Thee, great God, confide,
Nor madly trust the arm of pride,
 And helps that but betray.
Thy Mercies, Lord, all praise surmount,
Nor numbers can their sum recount,
 Nor words their worth display.

4.

Nor Sacrifice thy Love can win,
Nor Off'rings from the stain of sin
 Obnoxious Man shall clear :
Thy hand my mortal frame prepares,
(Thy hand, whose signature it bears,)
 And opes my willing ear.

5.

And, since the Blood of Victims slain,
And hallow'd Gifts, attempt in vain
 T' avert th' Offender's doom,
Myself th' atonement will provide ;
Lo ! (touch'd with pity thus I cried,)
 I come, my God, I come.

§   6. Thy

6.

Thy Book, by facred Bards unroll'd,
My full obedience has foretold
 To Thy myfterious Will.
His juft affent thy Servant gives,
Thy words my Breaft with joy receives,
 My Hands with zeal fulfil.

7.

The faithful Witnefs to thy fame,
Aloud thy Juftice I proclaim
 To *Abraham*'s chofen Race :
My lips, Thou know'ft, have ne'er declin'd
To preach the Theme by Thee injoin'd,
 The Wonders of thy Grace.

8.

With ftrong defire my bofom glows
Thy Truth and Mercy to difclofe,
 In Man's relief difplay'd :
O let that Truth difpel my woe,
That Mercy, Lord, around me throw
 Its all-protecting fhade.

9.

While griefs on griefs my cup have mix'd,
On earth my downward looks are fix'd ;
 The Sins whofe weight I bear,
(Thofe Sins, that number'd by the eye
The hairs that fhade my head outvie,)
 My heart with anguifh tear.

10.

Hafte to thy Servant's refcue, hafte ;
My Soul, by hoftile numbers chas'd,
 To Thee directs its pray'r.

In wild confusion backward borne
Their wish defeated let them mourn,
   And lost in empty air.

11.

Be shame their just reward assign'd,
While round me with relentless mind
   Derision's shout they raise:
Thy Bliss let All who seek thee share,
And, taught thy Love, that Love declare
   In songs of ceaseless praise.

12.

While These in thy Salvation joy,
Increasing griefs my thought employ,
   And speediest aid demand:
My Helper and Redeemer, hear;
O, instant in my cause appear,
   And reach thy saving hand.

P S A L M XLI.

1.

BLEST, who with gen'rous pity glows,
  Who learns to feel another's woes,
Bows to the poor man's want his ear,
And wipes the helpless Orphan's tear:

2.

Who to th' afflicted gives relief,
And kindly soothes each anxious grief;
In ev'ry want, in ev'ry woe,
Himself thy pity, Lord, shall know;

            3. Thy

3.

Thy Love his life ſhall guard, thy hand
Give to his lot the choſen land,
Nor leave him in the dreadful day
To unrelenting foes a prey.

4.

When languid with diſeaſe and pain,
Thou, Lord, his ſpirit wilt ſuſtain,
Prop with thine arm his ſinking head,
And turn with tend'reſt care his bed.

5.

O let me, Lord, thy mercy ſhare,
(Thus to my God I form'd the pray'r,)
Health to my fainting ſoul diſpenſe,
That humbled owns its dire offence.

6.

" When ſhall he periſh ?" Thus my foes
With ruthleſs tongue their wiſh diſcloſe ;
" Why lingers Death's appointed hour
" Oblivion on his name to pour ?"

7.

The hoſtile viſitants appear
Beſide my couch, and drop the tear,
Though, feigning, o'er my griefs they mourn
Their hearts with ſecret malice burn.

8.

See them, ſcarce parted from my gate,
Aloud proclaim their ſettled hate ;
Now pleas'd they form ſome dark deſign,
Now whiſp'ring thus in curſes join :

9.

" Still may the guilt unpurg'd remain,
" That binds him on the bed of pain ;
" Nor let him from that bed arife,
" But clofe in endlefs fleep his eyes."

10.

Yea Thou, the friend to whom my heart
Its inmoft counfels wont t' impart,
Ev'n Thou, in fubtlety difguis'd,
The Man whom chief of friends I priz'd ;

11.

For whom the focial board I fpread,
And broke with lib'ral hand my bread,
With lifted heel, (fevere return !)
The partner of thy breaft couldft fpurn.

12.

Maker of All ! be Thou my guard :
Give me, (my ftrength by Thee repair'd,)
Give me to teach the faithlefs band
To own the juftice of thy hand.

13.

So, while my pray'rs indulg'd approve
My Soul the object of thy Love,
My foes, with inward anguifh torn,
Shall each his blafted triumphs mourn ;

14.

And I (for Thou thy aid fhalt yield,)
In innocence of heart upheld
Thy Courts fhall ever tread, and there
The fulnefs of thy prefence fhare.

15. O

15.

O thankful blefs th' Almighty Lord,
The God by *Jacob*'s Sons ador'd ;
With joyful hearts his Love proclaim,
And praife, O praife, his holy name.

16.

His fame, ere Time its courfe began,
O'er Heav'n's wide region echoing ran ;
To Him through endlefs ages raife
One fong of oft-repeated praife.

PSALM XLII.

1.

AS pants the Hart for cooling fprings,
So longs my Soul, O King of Kings,
Thy face in near approach to fee,
So thirfts, great Source of Life, for Thee.

2.

With ardent zeal, with ftrong defires
To Thee, to Thee my Soul afpires ;
When fhall I reach thy bleft abode ?
When meet the prefence of my God ?

3.

Tears, Lord, Thou know'ft, have been my
        bread,
By day, by night, profufely fhed,
While thus they urge me to defpair :
" Where's now thy God, thou Outcaft,
        where ?"

4. While

4.

While griefs like thefe befet my Soul,
While thus my thoughts tumultuous roll,
To Thee my heart afcends in pray'r,
And in thy bofom pours its care.

5.

Oft, Lord, in luxury of woe
Back to thofe happier hours I go,
When up fair *Sion's* high afcent
The Tribes in long proceffion went;

6.

There, while thy praife in grateful fongs
Refounded from a thoufand tongues,
I, rank'd amid the feftive Train,
Exulting trod thy hallow'd Fane.

7.

Why thus, my Soul, with care opprefs'd ?
And whence the woes that fill my breaft ?
In all thy cares, in all thy woes,
On God thy ftedfaft hope repofe ;

8.

To Him my thanks fhall ftill be paid,
My fure Defence, my conftant Aid;
His Name my zeal fhall ever raife,
And dictate to my lips his praife.

9.

When griefs like thefe befet my foul,
My thoughts with vain impatience roll,
Thy mercies, Lord, before my eyes
Shall yet in fweet remembrance rife ;

10. Though

10.

Though now with mournful ftep and flow
O'er *Jordan*'s lonely banks I go,
And, exil'd from thy much-lov'd Dome,
On diftant *Hermon* penfive roam.

11.

Deeps to confed'rate Deeps aloud
Have call'd, and from the burfting cloud
Their licens'd rage the ftorms have fhed,
And heap'd the billows o'er my head.

12.

Yet 'midft the ftorm, and 'midft the wave,
Thy Love the beams of comfort gave ;
Thy name by day employs my tongue,
By night infpires my pray'r, and fong.

13.

God of my ftrength, attend my cry,
Say why, my great Preferver, why,
Excluded from thy fight I go,
And bend beneath a weight of woe ?

14.

Why fharper than the biting fteel
Th' infulting Foe's reproach I feel,
While thus they urge me to defpair :
" Where's now thy God, thou Outcaft,
    where ?"

15.

Why thus, my Soul, with care opprefs'd ?
And whence the woes that fill my breaft ?
In all thy cares, in all thy woes,
On God thy ftedfaft hope repofe ;

16. To

16.

To Him my thanks ſhall ſtill be paid,
My ſure Defence, my conſtant Aid ;
His Name my zeal ſhall ever raiſe,
And dictate to my lips his praiſe.

P S A L M   XLIII.

1.

O Weigh me, Lord, in equal ſcale,
    And let my injur'd cauſe prevail :
O ſave me from an impious Throng,
The Sons of Violence and Wrong.

2.

God of my ſtrength, to Thee I cry ;
Say why, by Thee rejected, why,
I bend beneath a weight of woe,
And bear the inſults of the Foe.

3.

O let thy Light attend my way,
Thy Truth afford its ſteady ray,
To *Sion*'s Hill direct my feet,
And bring me to thy hallow'd Seat :

4.

Admitted to thy Altars there,
My hands to Thee the gift ſhall bear,
Whoſe Mercies, to my heart reveal'd,
A theme of endleſs tranſport yield.

5.

Thy praiſe, O God, my God, the lyre
Shall wake, thy Love its ſong inſpire,
And thankful teach the rapt'rous lay
Thy bounteous goodneſs to diſplay.

6. Why

6.

Why thus, my Soul, with care opprefs'd?
And whence the woes that fill my breaft?
In all thy cares, in all thy woes,
On God thy ftedfaft hope repofe;

7.

To Him my thanks fhall ftill be paid,
My fure Defence, my conftant Aid;
His Name my zeal fhall ever raife,
And dictate to my lips his praife.

PSALM XLIV.

1.

TAught by our Sires, great God, our ear
Thy wondrous Acts has wak'd to hear,
The Mercies to their Tribes reveal'd,
When Ages long o'erpaft beheld
By Thee diflodg'd an impious race
Yield to their chofen Seed a place;

2.

When *Ifrael's* Sons, thy foes o'erthrown,
Obtain'd poffeffions not their own;
Where, planted by the hand divine,
With large increafe their profp'ring Line
Are blefs'd, and nourifh'd by thy care
The fulnefs of thy bounty fhare.

3.

For not the arm of human might,
Nor fword of fteel, upheld their right;
Thy pow'r exerted in their aid,
Thy prefence o'er their heads difplay'd,

Proclaim'd

Proclaim'd them favour'd from on high,
And bade each force before them fly.

4.

Thee, Lord, our King, and Thee alone,
Attentive to thy Laws we own;
Indulgent ftill, Almighty Friend,
Thy Arm in *Ifrael*'s caufe extend,
And let us, on thy aid reclin'd,
Thee ftill our great Salvation find.

5.

Through Thee our Hofts unmov'd fhall ftand,
Strike with the horn each adverfe band,
Thy name invok'd, their fury meet,
And tread them breathlefs at their feet:
Not from our fword or from our bow
Our fouls fuch confidence fhall know;

6.

Thou, Lord, each adverfe pow'r fhalt quell,
Thy ftrength their gath'ring troops difpel:
That ftrength our boaft, thy hallow'd name,
Our hymns of loudeft praife fhall claim,
While Time fhall roll its rapid tide,
And Day and Night thy works divide.

7.

But now, thy wonted aid withheld,
Repuls'd, afham'd, we quit the field;
No more we fee, to battle led,
Th' Almighty Conqu'ror at our head,
But quick retreat in wild difmay,
Abandon'd to our foes a prey.

8. Beneath

8.

Beneath thy anger, Lord, we groan,
The flock whom thou hadſt ſeal'd thine own,
As Beaſts for food decreed we die,
Or, ſpar'd, as worthleſs in thine eye
See ! ſold for nought our Lords we change,
And loſt through diſtant climates range.

9.

Each neighb'ring Realm with ſcornful gaze
Thy People's ruin'd ſtate ſurveys ;
Our name, amid the Nations round,
A proverb in each mouth is found;
Aſſembled Crouds inſulting ſtand,
And fierce Deriſion claps the hand.

10.

How feels my heart the dire diſgrace !
How glows with ceaſeleſs ſhame my face,
While thus, diveſted of thy fear,
With keen reproach they wound my ear,
And with revengeful hand fulfil
The dictates of their lawleſs will !

11.

Yet, torn with grief, with dread oppreſs'd,
Thy eyes can witneſs that our breaſt
Its truſt from Thee has ne'er remov'd,
Nor faithleſs to thy Compact prov'd,
For lo ! the dictates of thy Law
Our thoughts to full obedience awe :

12.

No Lord but Thee thy Servants greet,
Nor wander from thy paths our feet,

L   Though,

Though, fir'd with ceaseless rage, a croud
Advance, and round us roar aloud,
Though 'midst the dragon's haunts we tread,
And death's dark shades are o'er us spread.

13.

If ever, of the name divine
Forgetful, we our faith resign,
Or if, averse to thy command,
To Stranger-Gods we lift the hand,
Say, shall our crime thy search elude,
Whose eyes our inmost thoughts have view'd?

14.

Thy Cause we still avow ; thy Cause
The hostile sword against us draws,
And numbers to the death our train,
As Sheep, whose blood the hallow'd fane,
Before the altar's kindled flames,
By regular allotment claims.

15.

Arise, eternal God, arise;
Why sits this slumber on thine eyes ?
Awake, nor from thy care expel
Thy once regarded *Israel:*
Say why from our afflicted race,
Why veils th' impervious cloud thy face?

16.

O tell us why thine ear denies
To hear thy captive People's cries,
As sunk with sorrow's weight we bend,
And prostrate in the dust descend :
Arise, thy saving pow'r disclose,
And heal with pitying hand our woes.

P S A L M

PSALM XLV.

1.

MY heart its noblest Theme has found:
O Thou, with regal splendor crown'd,
Thy pow'r, thy greatness taught to know,
How shall my lips with praise o'erflow !

2.

To Thee the grateful strains belong ;
Thy Worth shall bid my willing tongue,
Quick as the pen of readiest art,
The dictates of my soul impart.

3.

Hail, fairer than the Sons of Men !
Grace on thy lips and Beauty reign,
That speak thee honour'd from above,
And blest with God's eternal Love.

4.

Hail, Thou whom Nations own their Lord !
Gird on thy thigh the glitt'ring sword ;
By Mercy, Truth, and Justice led,
Ride glorious on, thy conquests spread :

5.

Thy stubborn foes, a guilty race,
Thy hand with faithful search shall trace,
Mark, as their crimes for vengeance call,
And teach thy terrors where to fall :

6.

While, edg'd with wrath, thy ev'ry dart
Shall pierce some proud Oppoſer's heart,
Assert the cause of *Judah*'s King,
And dip in impious blood its wing:

7.

O God, through ages lasts thy Throne,
Thy Scepter Justice calls her own,
Thy heart th' all perfect Law pursues,
And guilt with fix'd abhorrence views :

8.

For this thy God, who rules the skies,
Has o'er thine Equals bid thee rise,
And, pleas'd, the oil of gladness shed
In large profusion on thy head.

9.

Myrrh, Aloes, Caffia, to the sense
Their all-reviving sweets dispense,
While, recent from the iv'ry cell,
Their mingled odours round thee dwell.

10.

Their Daughters mightiest Kings behold
Amid thy Virgin Train inroll'd ;
And, seated on thy right, the Queen
Array'd in robes of gold is seen.

11.

Hear, Daughter, and attentive weigh
The precepts of the Heav'n-taught Lay ;
Within thy thought retain no more
Thy Father's house and native shore :

12.

So shall the King delighted see
Thy spotless Form ; and O, be He,
That Lord whom Heav'n's high hosts revere,
Thy only Love, thy only Fear.

13. Im-

13.

Imperial *Tyre*, that, thron'd on high,
O'er fubject feas extends her eye,
Her Gifts, O Prince, fhall bring to Thee,
And fuppliant Nobles ftoop the knee.

14.

The Virgin (Offspring of a King,)
Whom now thy happy Choice we fing,
(Herfelf with each perfection bleft)
Ere Thee fhe greets, affumes the veft;

15.

That veft, where 'mid th' inwoven gold
A thoufand colours we behold,
That, kindled by the beams of day,
The needle's utmoft art difplay.

16.

By eminence of beauty known
Amidft her fair Affociates, on
She moves, and joys with them to tread
The paths that to thy prefence lead.

17.

No more the Patriarchs of thy line
In Time's long records chief fhall fhine;
Thy greater Sons, to Empire born,
Its future annals fhall adorn.

18.

Thy Pow'r to Them deriv'd difplay,
And ftretch thro' Earth their boundlefs fway;
O'er fubject realms their wide command
Through diftant times confirm'd fhall ftand.

L 3   19. Thofe

19.

Thofe realms, while thus to Thee I raife
A lafting Monument of praife,
With thankful voice fhall join the ftrain,
And own the Bleffings of thy Reign.

P S A L M   XLVI.

1.

ON Thee, great Ruler of the Skies,
On Thee our ftedfaft hope relies :
When hoftile pow'rs againft us join,
What Aid fo prefent, Lord, as thine ?

2.

By Thee fecur'd, no fears we own,
Though Earth, convuls'd, beneath us groan,
Though tempefts o'er her furface fweep,
And whirl her hills into the Deep :

3.

Though, arm'd with rage, before our eyes
That Deep in all its horrors rife,
While, as the tumult fpreads around,
The mountains tremble at the found.

4.

Behold fair *Sion*'s bleft retreat,
Where God has fix'd his awful Seat ;
Whofe walls to heav'n's Almighty Lord
His chofen refidence afford :

5.

No Tempefts there licentious ftray,
But foft along their level way
The facred Streams their courfe maintain,
And crown with health her happy plain.

6.

God, ever watchful, ever nigh,
Bids ftorms around her harmlefs fly ;
His early care each foe withftands,
And backward turns the yielding Bands.

7.

See, rous'd by Difcord's fierce alarms,
The headlong Nations rufh to arms ;
But God aloud afferts his fway,
And Earth's whole fabrick melts away.

8.

On Heav'n's high Lord our truft we build ;
The God of *Jacob* is our Shield ;
His arm, exerted in our right,
Shall turn each adverfe pow'r to flight.

9.

O come, behold a fcene of dread,
Behold a World with flaughter fpread ;
And know, 'tis God who bids each Land
Thus feel the terrors of his hand.

10.

'Tis His, again the Earth to chear,
To break the bow, to fnap the fpear,
To wrap in flames the glitt'ring car,
And hufh the tumult of the war.

11.

Be ftill, ye Sons of Pride, and own
That I am God, and I alone :
Exalted o'er each heathen Land,
Exalted o'er the Earth I ftand ;

12. On

12.

On Heav'n's high Lord our truſt we build;
The God of *Jacob* is our Shield,
His arm, exerted in our right,
Shall turn each adverſe pow'r to flight.

P S A L M   XLVII.

1.

ARISE, ye People, clap the hand;
.Exulting ſtrike the chord :
Let ev'ry Iſle, and ev'ry Land,
    Confeſs th' Almighty Lord.

2.

How awful his myſterious Name !
    How high advanc'd his Seat !
Who bids the Nations own our claim,
    And caſts them at our feet.

3.

He to our lot a Land aſſign'd,
    His favour'd *Jacob*'s boaſt,
And bleſt with gifts of various kind
    Her health-incircled coaſt.

4.

Hear, while the ſhouts wide-echoing round
    Th' aſcending God proclaim,
The anſw'ring trump through Heav'n reſound,
    And ſhake its vaulted frame.

5.

Sing to our God; in loudeſt ſtrain
    Perpetual praiſes ſing :
O'er Earth's wide bounds extends his reign ;
    O praiſe our God and King.

6. Prepare,

6.

Prepare, prepare, with tuneful art,
    In one affembled throng,
Your fhares of harmony to part,
    And raife the Heav'n-taught Song.

7.

His fway the Sons of human kind
    With humbleft homage own ;
And Sanctity with pow'r combin'd
    Supports his lafting throne.

8.

Kings from afar conven'd behold,
    Whofe breafts with zeal have glow'd
Among the tribes to ftand inroll'd,
    That bow to *Abraham*'s God.

9.

For He, whofe hands amid the fkies
    Th' eternal fcepter wield,
To Earth's whole race his care applies,
    And o'er them fpreads the fhield.

PSALM XLVIII.

1.

GREAT is our God : With warmeft zeal
    O let his name be bleft,
Within the precincts of his Hill,
    And City of his reft.

2.

Fair is that Hill ; how wondrous fair !
    Imperial *Sion*'s Seat :
There centers, Earth, thy Joy, and there
    Its meafure owns complete.

3.

Her Walls, while there his lov'd receſs
 The Northern Heav'n ſurveys,
With ſafety God vouchſafes to bleſs,
 And pleas'd her ſcepter ſways.

4.

Earth's haughty Monarchs thither came;
 They came, they ſaw, they fled,
Amazement ſhook their inmoſt frame,
 And undiſſembled dread.

5.

Such fears they ſhare as Matrons find
 That feel th' increaſing throe,
Struck by that God, whoſe ſhatt'ring wind
 Thy Ships, O *Tharſis*, know.

6.

Lord! what our ears long ſince have known,
 Our eyes delighted trace,
Thy Love in long ſucceſſion ſhown
 To *Salem*'s choſen race.

7.

Thrice bleſt Abode! whoſe ev'ry tow'r
 By Thee ſupported ſtands,
That God whoſe wide-extended pow'r
 Th' ethereal Hoſt commands.

8.

When, proſtrate at thy hallow'd Shrine,
 Thy mercies each ſurveys,
Tranſported with the view, we join
 In wonder, love, and praiſe.

9. Thy

9.

Thy Name, through Earth's wide confines
    ſpread,
  Eternal honours crown;
Each ſentence by thy hand decreed
    Fair Juſtice ſtamps her own.

10.

Let *Sion*'s Heav'n-devoted Mount
    With ſhouts of triumph ring,
And *Judah*'s Daughters pleas'd recount
    The Judgments of her King.

11.

Go, walk her ſacred ſtreets along,
    And let her tow'rs be told;
With curious eye her bulwarks ſtrong
    And beauteous domes behold.

12.

So ſhall the fair deſcription laſt,
    Preſerv'd in full record,
And tell what glories once have grac'd
    The Seat of *Jacob*'s Lord.

13.

To Him our thankful hearts ſhall bow,
    Nor own a God beſide;
To life's laſt period Him avow
    The ever faithful Guide.

P S A L M

PSALM XLIX.

1.

YE Nations, hear : Ye Sons of Earth,
   Of higheſt or obſcureſt birth,
Ye who from wealth's full board are fed,
And Ye who eat with toil your bread.

2.

My words with juſt attention weigh,
And liſten to the hallow'd Lay;
While, touch'd with holy fire, my tongue
Forms to the harp the myſtic ſong.

3.

My lips ſhall Wiſdom's leſſons yield,
My heart, with nobleſt ſcience fill'd,
Shall prompt me with obedient ear
The Heav'n-deſcending truths to hear.

4.

   Why ſhould my ſoul with anxious dread
Behold the foes around me ſpread,
Who build on wealth their truſt, and ſtore
In boaſted heaps the glit'ring ore ?

5.

Ceaſe, Mortals, ceaſe your pride ; nor dream
That riches ſhall from death redeem,
Or from the all-diſpoſing hand
A Brother's forfeit life demand.

6.

In vain would Friendſhip's zeal eſſay
The full equivalent to pay,
In vain the flitting breath to ſave,
And plead exemption from the grave;

7. In

7.

In vain, though *Ophir's* wealthieft mine
Its treafures to the purchafe join;
Then, taught the Soul's beft price to know,
At once the frantic thought forego.

8.

Thou feeft the Man in Wifdom's fchool
Long tutor'd, like the untaught fool
To death fubmit, and leave his heir
His heaps of gather'd wealth to fhare.

9.

What though they build the Dome fublime,
Proof to the rage of eating Time,
While Lands fubjected to their claim
Take from their haughty Lord a name,

10.

Yet Man, with erring pride elate,
And high in pow'r, in honour great,
Shares with the Brute an equal doom,
And fleeps forgotten in the tomb.

11.

Their hope, thus fond thus faithlefs found,
Their Sons affume; in endlefs round
Another and another race
Their Fathers' wayward fteps fhall trace.

12.

Together now behold them laid,
As Sheep, when Night extends her fhade,
While Death within the vaulted rock,
Stern Shepherd, guards the flumb'ring flock:

M   13. Corruption

13.

Corruption there its work fhall ply,
And, wrapt in darknefs as they lie,
Each feature fair, each boafted grace,
With unrelenting hand efface.

14.

Ye Juft, exulting lift your eyes ;
Behold the promis'd Morn arife,
That bids you, o'er each haughty foe
Exalted, endlefs triumphs know :

15.

My Soul, amidft your happy train,
The wifh'd redemption fhall obtain,
By God adopted, Death fhall brave,
And mock the difappointed Grave.

16.

Let not the Sight thy heart difmay,
If Man's proud Offspring thou furvey
With growing wealth incircled round,
Or mark his houfe with honours crown'd :

17.

Think not his treafures, at his end,
Shall with him to the grave defcend,
Or the vain pomp, that ftrikes thy view,
Through Death's dark fhade its Lord purfue.

18.

His life with each delight was fraught,
How blefs'd his pamper'd Soul its lot !
Thee too, while pleafure crowns thy days,
Admiring Crouds perchance may praife;

5   19. Yet

Yet Thou, like Him, the way ſhalt tread,
Which, one by one, thy Sires have led,
And 'midſt th' impenetrable gloom
Shalt find with Them thy laſting home.

20.

For Man, with erring pride elate,
And high in pow'r, in honour great,
Shares with the Brute an equal doom,
And ſleeps forgotten in the tomb.

PSALM L.

1.

THE Lord, th' Almighty Monarch, ſpake,
And bade the Earth the ſummons take,
Far as his eyes the realms ſurvey
Of riſing and declining day.

2.

Reveal'd from *Sion*'s ſacred bound,
The Seat with matchleſs beauty crown'd,
Our God his courſe ſhall downward bend,
Nor ſilent to his Work deſcend.

3.

At his approach the fire ſhall blaze,
And kindled pour its ſtreaming rays;
Devouring flames ſhall march before,
And mightieſt tempeſts round him roar.

4.

Heav'n from above ſhall hear his call,
And Thou, the vaſt terreſtrial Ball! [meet,
While Man's whole race their Judge ſhall
In countleſs throngs before his Seat.

M 2   5. " My

5.

" My Saints collect from diftant Poles,
" Collect the juft and faithful Souls,
" With whom my compact firm has ftood,
" Seal'd with the fpotlefs Victim's blood."

6.

Th' applauding Heav'ns the changelefs Doom,
While God the balance fhall affume,
In full memorial fhall record,
And own the Juftice of their Lord.

7.

With humbleft awe, my People, hear ;
For God, thy God, his voice fhall rear :
Myfelf, O *Ifrael*, will atteft
The guilt that ftains thy erring breaft.

8.

Though at the Altar's kindled fire
No bleeding Victim fhould expire,
Not ritual Sacrifice withheld
My theme of juft complaint fhall yield :

9.

Still let thy Stall the Steer detain,
Still let thy Goat untouch'd remain
Amidft his herd-mates : from thy hands
Nor Goat nor Steer thy Lord demands :

10.

Mine are the Beafts that range the wood,
Mine all the tame or favage Brood
Whofe train the Earth's wide pafture fills,
And wanders o'er her thoufand hills.

11. Each

11.

Each fowl, that from its airy flight
Defcends upon the mountain's height,
Each brute, that o'er the champaign ftrays,
My all-obferving eye furveys.

12.

Admit, I hunger; fhall thy God
Defcend from Thee to afk his food,
Lord of the World and all its Store
Thy aid, thou Child of Earth, implore?

13.

Shall Bulls to eafe my want be flain,
Or blood of Goats my thirft reftrain?
Go, fuppliant at my altar bow,
And pay thy thanks, and pay thy vow:

14.

(Be this thy Off'ring:) In thy woes
On Me with ftedfaft hope repofe;
So fhall my ear receive thy pray'r,
And, grateful, Thou my mercy fhare.

15.

Thou Wretch by difcipline unaw'd,
(Thus to the Impious fpeaks my God,)
Thy fecret crimes to Me are known;
I fee my Laws behind thee thrown:

16.

And Thou, doft Thou with lips profane
The precepts of my will explain,
And, rank'd thyfelf amid my foes,
My terms of offer'd grace propofe?

M 3   17. Say,

17.

Say, has the Thief to Thee applied,
And Thou thy wanted aid denied ?
Or fail'd th' Adult'rer e'er to fee
A partner of his guilt in Thee ?

18.

Train'd in each well-diffembled art
To veil the purpofe of thine heart,
Thy tongue to fraud has loos'd the reins,
And lye with lye connected feigns.

19.

Haft thou not fat, with cruel aim
Reflecting on a Brother's fame,
And with invented fcandal ftain'd
Whom erft one womb with Thee contain'd ?

20.

While yet my anger I fupprefs'd
Within the fecrets of my breaft,
And filent deign'd thy crimes to fee,
Thy folly pictur'd Me like Thee :

21.

But foon my op'ning lips fhall yield
The juft rebuke fo long withheld,
And bid, before thy confcious eyes,
Thy guilt in all its horror rife.

22.

Ye Souls forgetful of my fear,
With full regard my dictates hear ;
Left, at my word, your life the Grave
Demand, and none be nigh to fave.

23. Who

23.

Who yields the Sacrifice of praise,
His beft-accepted homage pays:
Who forms his fteps aright, fhall know
What Joys from my Salvation flow.

PSALM LI.

1.

O Lord, whofe Mercies vaft amount,
  Nor words nor numbers can recount,
Let now thy clemency divine
Confpicuous in my pardon fhine:

2.

O let the fulnefs of thy grace
Each error of my life efface,
Its influence to my foul convey,
And wafh my ev'ry ftain away.

3.

My confcious heart its guilt fhall own;
My Deed to Thee, and Thee alone,
Obnoxious, nor the day nor night
Conceals from my abhorring fight.

4.

Right is thy fentence, holieft Lord,
(God of my hope) thy ev'ry word
In truth's unvarying balance weigh'd
Thy ev'ry act by Juftice fway'd.

5.

Thou from the birth my foul couldft view,
As fhap'd in fin my breath I drew,
And feeft me guilt's tranfmiffive ftain
Through life's revolving courfe retain.

6. But

6.

But thy decrees, Almighty Sire,
Integrity of heart require;
Thy hand, corrective of my will,
Shall wisdom in my breast instill:

7.

With hallow'd hyssop sprinkled o'er,
My soul its spots shall mourn no more,
But, cleans'd by Thee, the whiteness know
That clothes the new-descended snow.

8.

How shall my ear thy pard'ning voice
Transported welcome! How rejoice
My bones, with vital moisture fill'd,
That, crush'd by Thee, by Thee are heal'd!

9.

O turn, great Ruler of the Skies,
Turn from my Sin thy searching eyes,
Nor let th' offences of my hand
Within thy book recorded stand.

10.

Give me a will to thine subdu'd,
A conscience pure, a soul renew'd,
Nor let me, wrapt in endless gloom,
An outcast from thy presence roam.

11.

O let thy Spirit to my heart
Once more his quick'ning aid impart,
My mind from ev'ry fear release,
And sooth my troubled thoughts to peace.

12. So

12.

So fhall the Souls, whom Error's fway
Has urg'd from Thee, bleft Lord, to ftray,
From Me thy heav'nly precepts learn,
And humbled to their God return.

13.

O would thy healing grace beftow'd
Abfolve me from my debt of blood,
How fhould my breaft with tranfport glow,
What Gratitude my heart o'erflow !

14.

How fhould my tongue thy Juftice fing,
Invifible, Immortal King,
And, long as breath extends my days,
The God of my Salvation praife !

15.

Not Victims, Lord, in folemn rite
Prefented, thy defire excite ;
Elfe fhould my hand with zealous care
Th' exacted holocauft prepare.

16.

Prompt is thy pow'r, when ills invade,
The meek and contrite foul to aid ;
A Spirit griev'd is facrifice
Delightful to th' all-feeing eyes ;

17.

The heart, that, taught its guilt to know,
Repentant heaves with inward woe,
Shall find its pray'r, its groans, its fighs,
To Thee in full acceptance rife.

18. Thy

18.

Thy grace to *Sion*, Lord, extend,
And bid fair *Salem*'s walls afcend :
So fhall the Sons of *Jacob*'s line
With pureft off'rings load thy Shrine ;

19.

And, while in many a lengthen'd wreath
Their incenfe fhall its odours breathe,
Before thy altar doom'd to bleed
The flaughter'd fteer the flames fhall feed.

P S A L M LII.

1.

WHY, Tyrant, boafts thy heart the
pow'r
To work a Brother's woe ;
While God his mercy bids each hour
In ftreams unmeafur'd flow ?

2.

With joy thy tongue, to falfehood prone,
Its venom deals around ;
Nor razor fharpen'd on the ftone
Inflicts fo deep a wound.

3.

Thy lips far readier Ill than Good
And Lies than Truth have fought ;
Nor e'er has word that aim'd at blood
Unwelcom'd met thy thought.

4. But

4.

But God, whofe wrath thy crimes inflame,
    Shall pluck thee from thy home,
Root from the land of life thy name,
    And feal thy changelefs doom.

5.

The Juft, with thankful awe poffefs'd,
    Shall view thy blafted pride,
And, from their fierceft foe releas'd,
    Thy impious boafts deride.

6.

" Lo there the wretch in trefpafs bold,
    " Who God's fupport difdain'd,
" And on his heaps of treafur'd gold
    " His frantic hope fuftain'd."

7.

Frefh as the verdant olive, I
    Within thy Courts fhall ftand,
And, fix'd, indulgent Lord, rely
    On thy protecting hand.

8.

Thy Acts my praife fhall ever claim,
    Thy Name, amidft my woes,
(How grateful to thy Saints that Name!)
    My ev'ry fear compofe.

PSALM LIII.

1.

BEHOLD the Fool, whose heart denies
The God who form'd the Earth and
Skies :
While, fearless, sin's worst paths he treads,
Mark how the dire example spreads.

2.

Of Man's whole race not one we find
To Virtue's Heav'n-taught rules inclin'd,
Who 'midst infectious times has stood
Unstain'd, and obstinately good.

3.

Th' eternal Monarch from on high
Cast on the Sons of Earth his eye,
If haply some he yet might see
True to their God, from error free.

4.

He look'd : But ah ! not one could find
To Virtue's Heav'n-taught rules inclin'd :
Each, led from Wisdom's path astray,
Pursues the tenour of his way.

5.

O say, what frenzy thus could blind
Their Souls, that with remorseless mind
As bread my People they devour,
Nor suppliant own their Maker's pow'r.

6.

Yet see their thoughts tumultuous roll,
See causeless terrors shake their soul;
By just alarms of conscience driv'n
To tremble at the wrath of Heav'n !

7. Wide

7.

Wide o'er the field the bones are ſpread
Of Chiefs who by thy ſword have bled,
And ſpeak the doom that All muſt ſhare,
Whom God abandons from his care.

8.

Who, mightieſt Lord, to *Iſrael*'s eyes
Shall bid the wiſh'd Salvation riſe,
From *Sion*'s. hill its healing ray
Extend, and round us pour the day ?

9.

When Thou thy captives ſhaſt reſtore,
Thy praiſe ſhall ſound through *Judah*'s ſhore,
And ceaſeleſs ſhouts, through heav'n's wide
     frame
Loud echoing, *Jacob*'s joy proclaim.

P S A L M LIV.

1.

THY Name my ſtedfaſt heart avows;
  Do Thou my injur'd cauſe eſpouſe,
    And be thy Strength my aid:
My plaints, eternal Monarch, hear,
And let them by thy pitying ear
    With full regard be weigh'd.

2.

For Nations from thy fear eſtrang'd,
With Tyrants fierce, againſt me rang'd,
    My guiltleſs ſoul purſue:
But 'midſt my helpers Heav'n's high Lord
Shall ſtand, and faithful to his word
    Each adverſe pow'r ſubdue.

N   3. O

3.

O let my heart, their rage repell'd,
Itself a willing off'ring yield;
    To Thee its praise shall flow,
While to my thought thy Mercies rise,
That gave me with exulting eyes
    To see my prostrate foe.

P S A L M   LV.

1.

O Hear my voice, All-potent Sire,
    Nor distant from the pray'r retire,
Whose accents to thine ear impart
The anguish of my heaving heart.

2.

A Croud, whose thoughts from Thee have
     stray'd,
With falsehood arm'd, my peace invade,
And, leagu'd in sin, reproaching foes
With settled hate my steps inclose.

3.

Oppression's shouts around me roar,
Death's blackest horrors whelm me o'er,
And griefs and fears, that shun controul,
Shake to its inmost depth my soul.

4.

O who shall give me (thus my breast
Its vain inquietude exprefs'd,)
The Dove's light wing, that through the air
My soul to peaceful rest may bear?

                       5. How

5.

How would I mount the wafting wind,
How leave the wrathful ftorms behind,
And in the Defert's lone retreat
Contented fix my lafting Seat!

6.

Thy vengeance, Lord, inflict; their tongue
Divide; for Tumult, Strife, and Wrong,
Where'er I turn, before my eyes
In giant forms amid them rife;

7.

Within their wall's unhallow'd bound
By day, by night, they take their round;
Nor ceafe their guilty ftreets to hear
The voice of falfehood, grief, and fear.

8.

If foes profeft had aim'd the wound,
My foul fome fafe recefs had found,
Or, difciplin'd by previous care,
Had learn'd th' expected ill to bear;

9.

But Thou, 'twas Thou, the Friend difguis'd,
The Man, whom chief of Friends I priz'd,
To whom, its Counfellor and Guide,
My foul in ev'ry doubt applied:

10.

In bands of fweeteft union join'd,
Each wifh, each fecret of the mind,
We fhar'd, and 'midft th' affembled Train
Familiar trod the hallow'd Fane.

11. Let

11.

Let Earth its op'ning jaws extend,
While living to the grave defcend
The lawlefs Throng ; whofe Land profane
Hell's worft-invented mifchiefs ftain.

12.

God, as with fervent lips I pray,
At dawn, at noon, at clofe of day,
Shall ftoop to my complaint his ear,
And inftant in my caufe appear.

13.

He, when the battle round me bled,
From hoftile myriads fcreen'd my head,
Gave to my pray'r the wifh'd-for peace,
And bade the dreadful tumult ceafe.

14.

That Pow'r who reign'd thro' ages paft,
Whofe counfels fhall for ever laft,
That Pow'r my conteft fhall decide,
And humble to the duft their pride.

15.

See, unprovok'd, the reftlefs foe
Aim at thy Saints the deathful blow,
(Thy fear, great God, behind him thrown,)
And compacts oft confirm'd difown.

16.

While War's fierce flames within him burn,
As milk new foaming from the churn
Smooth are his lips ; as oil his words ;
Yet wound they deep as keeneft fwords.

17. O

17.

O caſt thee fearleſs on thy God ;
He, prompt to ſave, the grateful load
Within his foſt'ring arms ſhall bear,
And feed thee with a parent's care.

18.

Author of good ! beneath thy hand
Secure from lapſe the Juſt ſhall ſtand,
While (ſuch thy Mandate !) on his foes
Deſtruction's pit its mouth ſhall cloſe.

19.

Who thirſt for blood, who falſehoods raiſe,
To death ſhall yield, ere half their days
Be number'd, while, exulting, I
On Thee with ſtedfaſt hope rely.

PSALM LVI.

1.

O Reach me, Lord, thy aiding pow'r,
   While hoſtile troops my ſtrength devour;
My ſtrength devour, and day by day
With fierceſt threats my heart diſmay:
Yet Truſt in Thee my ſpirit chears,
And checks my ſighs, and wipes my tears.

2.

Thy promiſe, Lord, to notes of praiſe
In each diſtreſs my ſong ſhall raiſe ;
Thy word my breaſt with joy ſhall ſwell,
And all my anxious cares diſpel:
God in my cauſe his arm will rear ;
And Man, ſhall Man excite my fear ?

N 3   3. My

3.

My words they torture ; and, their thought
Each hour with deepeſt malice fraught,
In impious council nightly meet,
To watch, with murth'rous aim, my feet,
And guileful, onward as I tread,
Beſide my path their nets outſpread.

4.

On wrong, and ſuperſtition vain,
Their hope the frantic tribe ſuſtain ;
But teach them, Lord, thy wrath to know,
And quell the inſults of my foe ;
O let thine arm their crimes repay,
Who ſeek my footſteps to betray.

5.

My grief to thine obſerving eye,
As chas'd from realm to realm I fly,
In full diſplay, great God, appears ;
O treaſure in thy vaſe my tears :
But ſee ! already by thy hand
Recorded in thy book they ſtand.

6.

Whene'er to Thee, my God, I cry,
Secure of help the fight I try,
For thou thine aid, when aſk'd, wilt give,
And teach my fainting hope to live ;
While hoſts beneath my falchion bleed,
And back with headlong flight recede.

7.

Thy promiſe, Lord, to notes of praiſe
In each diſtreſs my ſong ſhall raiſe ;

4

Thy

Thy word my breaſt with joy ſhall ſwell,
Thy promiſe, Lord, my woes diſpel:
God in my cauſe his arm will rear;
And Man, ſhall Man excite my fear?

8.

Their thanks, their vows, (thy juſt demand,)
My lips ſhall yield: Thy fav'ring hand
My feet from error, from the grave
My fainting ſoul, has deign'd to ſave,
And bids me ſtill, to Thee allied,
Within the land of life reſide.

P S A L M   LVII.

I.

THY Mercy, Lord, amidſt my woes,
To my deſiring eyes diſcloſe;
Propitious to thy ſervant's heart
Thy wonted clemency impart:

2.

Let me, my hope on Thee reclin'd,
Beneath thy wings a refuge find,
Till thy prevailing beams diſpel
The clouds of grief that o'er me dwell.

3.

To Thee, the God who reigns on high,
To Thee with ſuppliant voice I cry,
Aſſur'd that Thou, indulgent ſtill,
My plaint ſhalt hear, my pray'r fulfil,

4. Thy

4.

Thy timeliest aid from heav'n extend,
My fame from obloquy defend,
And bid thy 'Truth and Mercy shed
Their kindest influence on my head.

5.

The Lions round me roar aloud;
And, fir'd with causeless rage, a Croud
Advance, (thy foes, eternal Lord,)
Whose teeth are spears, whose tongue a sword.

6.

Inthron'd thyself above the skies,
O bid thy fullest glory rise,
And to the earth with cloudless ray
The wonders of thy pow'r display.

7.

Oft, as amid the snares I tread,
Each hour by hostile fraud outspread,
What clouds of grief around me roll,
What dreadful storms invade my soul !

8

What fears, what woes, my bosom prove !
Yet, sav'd by thy preventing Love,
Th' artificers of death I see
Fall'n in the pit prepar'd for me.

9.

My heart is fix'd, Almighty Sire,
My heart is fix'd : to Thee aspire
My thoughts, and dictate to my lays
An argument of endless praise.

10. Awake

10.

Awake, thou glory of my frame,
Awake, my tongue, to loud acclaim;
Pſalt'ry awake, and joyful pay
To God the tribute of the day;

11.

Awake my lute, and new-ſtrung lyre;
Inſtinct, myſelf, with holy fire
I wake; and lo, the dawning ſun
Already hears the ſtrain begun.

12.

From Me aſſembling crouds ſhall burn
The triumphs of thy Love to learn,
And, rapt with zeal, the Nations round
Catchf rom my lips the ſacred ſound.

13.

Lo! to the clouds thy Truth extends,
And Heav'n's ſtupendous height tranſcends;
Far as to earth's extremeſt bound
In all thy works is mercy found:

14.

Inthron'd thyſelf above the ſkies,
O bid thy fulleſt glory riſe,
And to the earth with cloudleſs ray
The wonders of thy pow'r diſplay.

P S A L M   LVIII.

1.

YE whoſe lips the cauſe decide,
  Say, does Truth your ſentence guide?
Are your thoughts by Juſtice ſway'd,
And in Reaſon's balance weigh'd?

Let

Let your confcious tongues atteft
What ye harbour in your breaft.

2.

Hearts ye bear, that deep within
Cherifh each fuggefted fin,
While on fierce contention bent
Arts of mifchief ye invent,
And the dictates of your will
With remorfelefs hands fulfil.

3.

From the womb, in error's way
See the infant finner ftray:
Nurtur'd in deceit and wrong
See him with advent'rous tongue
(Prompt his earlieft fkill to try,)
Lifp the meditated lye.

4.

See their veins with venom fwell;
Arm'd with fuch, the Adder fell
Stops her ear, in many a fold
'Mid the fhelt'ring brake uproll'd,
While each note the Charmer tries,
And his utmoft art defies.

5.

Smite, great God, the Lions' cheek,
And their fangs indignant break.
While they arm them for the war,
And their quiver'd ftores prepare,
Let th' Oppreffors feel thy pow'r,
Let thy fword their ftrength devour;

6. Let

6.

Let them waſte in ſwift decay,
As the Torrents paſs away,
As the earth-bred Snails conſume,
As th' Abortions of the womb
(Life's ſhort circuit ſcarce begun,)
Periſh ere they ſee the ſun.

7.

Ere the Caldron learn to glow
From the kindling thorns below,
Let thy hotter wrath be ſhed
Quick on each rebellious head :
Let thy whirlwinds, through the ſky,
Miniſters' of vengeance, fly.

8.

Let them, Lord, at thy beheſt,
Sweep from earth the living Peſt :
While the Souls that truſt in Thee
Pleas'd their cauſe aveng'd ſhall ſee,
And, the dreadful conflict o'er,
Waſh their ſteps in hoſtile gore.

9.

" Doubtleſs," each convinc'd ſhall cry,
" Doubtleſs, there's a God on high,
" Who in awful Pomp array'd,
" Comes to judge the world he made,
" All who His commands regard,
" Reap at length their full reward."

PSALM

PSALM LIX.

1.

TH' impending storm, my God, assuage ;
High o'er the foes, that round me rage,
Exalt me, (foes, whose stubborn mind,
To wrong and violence resign'd,
Thy sacred Laws has long withstood,)
And save me from the Man of blood.

2.

Assembling crouds the deadly snare,
Without my crime, great God, prepare ;
Without my crime, in sin allied,
To diff'rent paths their course divide :
O, obvious to my pray'r, arise,
Nor let their guilt escape thine eyes.

3.

Leader of Hosts, and *Israel*'s God !
Stretch o'er the Heathen tribes thy rod,
Nor let them vauntingly each hour
With mad presumption brave thy pow'r,
But instant from thy seat arise
The proud transgressors to chastise.

4.

When eve's dark shades o'er heav'n are hung,
See ! as the Dog with fury stung,
While hideous yells their wrath betray,
From street to street they urge their way;
Swords in their lips, without a fear
Their threats they vent: for who shall hear ?

5. Thou

5.

Thou, Lord, their menace fhalt deride,
And check with juft reproach their pride.
Rock of my ftrength ! to Thee on high
My Soul fhall lift the ftedfaft eye,
Whofe aid, e'er yet invok'd, each foe
Beneath my conqu'ring feet fhall throw.

6.

Let not thy wrath, O God our fhield,
Their name to full excifion yield,
Left, vanifh'd from th' obferving eye,
Th' example of thy vengeance die ;
But, arm'd with pow'r, through foreign lands
Diftribute wide their vanquifh'd Bands.

7.

Such vengeance from thine arm, great Sire,
Their tongues repeated crimes require,
Their thoughts, inflam'd with impious pride,
Their oaths to guile's worft ends applied,
And urge thee with impartial doom
Each bold tranfgreffor to confume:

8.

Strike, Lord, O ftrike the needful blow,
And teach an erring World to know,
How vain its efforts to withftand
The force of thy refiftlefs hand ;
While *Jacob*'s Sons thy pow'r obey,
And Earth's wide confines own thy fway.

9.

When eve's dark fhades o'er heav'n are hung,
Still, as the Dog with fury ftung,

O   Still

Still let them clam'ring for their prey,
From ſtreet to ſtreet purſue their way,
Inſatiate; while their deſtin'd ſpoil
Eluſive mocks their fruitleſs toil.

10.

I, Lord, ſecure in Thee, thy might
Will praiſe, and with the riſing light
Thy Love, that in the dreadful day
Redeem'd me, on my harp diſplay,
Thee own my refuge, (heav'nly King!)
And Mercy's unexhauſted Spring.

P S A L M LX.

1.

REPULS'D, diſpers'd, chaſtis'd by Thee,
O grant us, Lord, thy face to ſee,
And let the People, once thy care,
Again thy fav'ring preſence ſhare.

2.

How trembles this divided Land
Beneath the terrors of thy hand!
O Thou, the God whom we adore,
Its breaches heal, its peace reſtore.

3.

Thy juſt Decrees to *Iſrael's* eyes
Have bid a ſcene of ſorrow riſe,
And to his pallid lips the wine
Of dire Aſtoniſhment conſign.

4.

Yet ſee, thy hands a ſtandard rear;
Beneath it Each, who owns thy fear,

Engag'd

Engag'd in Truth's neglected caufe,
His fword, fecure of conqueft, draws.

5.

Such, objects of thy tend'reft Love,
Defend propitious from above;
Let Me with Them thy Mercy fhare,
And hear, O hear, my ceafelefs pray'r.

6.

God's truth fhall ne'er forget to guard
The promife by his lips declar'd;
And what th' Almighty Monarch wills,
My ready hand with Joy fulfills.

7.

Behold me *Sichem*'s plain divide;
My line, to *Succoth*'s vale applied,
Its bound defcribes; Thee mine I fee,
O *Gilead*, and, *Manaffes*, Thee.

8.

Thou, *Ephraim*, art my ftrong defence,
Thou, *Judah*, fhalt my Law difpenfe;
A diff'rent lot fhall *Moab* find,
A Vafe to vileft ufe affign'd;

9.

A doom like his fhall *Edom* meet,
And wipe the duft from off my feet.
Philiftia fhall her tribute bring,
And own in Me her future King.

10.

Who, as our troops in clofe array
To *Edom*'s forts direct their way,
Arm'd with refiftlefs ftrength fhall bid
Her gates unfold, her bolts recede?

11.

Behold us, Lord, oppress'd with woe,
As exil'd from thy care we go:
Shall *Israel's* hosts, thy aid withheld,
Still unsuccessful take the field?

12.

Our hope, on Man repos'd in vain,
O let thy Strength, great God, sustain,
And let us on thy aid reclin'd,
In thee our firm Protector find:

13.

Thus arm'd, each adverse pow'r we dare,
And dauntless meet the rushing war,
While from thy sword our foes retire,
Or trampled in the dust expire.

P S A L M   LXI.

1.

OPPRESS'D with grief, in exile lost,
    To Thee from *Judah's* utmost coast
My voice, eternal God, I send:
O hear my plaint; my pray'r attend.

2.

High on the rock my footsteps rear;
There let me stand unmov'd, and hear
The storms, that now around me beat,
At distance roll beneath my feet.

3.

Thee, Lord, I seek, whene'er my foes
With dire intent my path inclose,
And own thee in the dang'rous hour
My firmest Hope, my strongest Tow'r.

4. Remote

Remote from fear, within thy ſhrine
Thou, Lord, my dwelling ſhalt aſſign;
And, while the ſtorms around me beat,
Fix on the rock my ſtedfaſt feet.

5.

Thy wings ſhall wrap me in their ſhade;
Thou, Thou haſt heard me when I pray'd,
And yielded to my wiſh the joys
Of Thoſe whoſe care thy Will employs.

6.

Long Life ſhall *Iſrael*'s King behold,
And ages count on ages roll'd;
With laſting joy thy ſervant's eyes
Shall ſee his children's children riſe:

7.

Safe in thy preſence let him ſtand,
And ſhare the bleſſings of thy hand;
His dwelling let thy Truth defend,
Thy Mercy on his ſteps attend.

8.

So ſhall thy Love awake my ſong,
Thy Name the willing note prolong,
While warm'd with zeal, my vows I pay,
And bleſs thee to my lateſt day.

P S A L M   LXII.

1.

MY Soul in God its reſt has found;
When various griefs befet me round,
His Love ſhall ſure deliv'rance yield;
By Him through life I walk upheld,

And

And safe from lapse my course maintain,
Or, falling, instant rise again.

2.

How long, Artificers of ill,
Shall schemes of death employ your skill?
Behold the mischiefs ye intend
Retorted on your heads descend:
Your semblance see yon loosen'd Wall,
Yon Bulwark, nodding to its fall.

3.

Vain are the wiles for Him prepar'd,
Whom Heav'n's high Lord vouchsafes to
        guard;
See, vers'd in fraud, the impious Throng
With blessings charge their guileful tongue,
While deep within the heart's disguise
The secret curse invelop'd lies.

4.

But Thou, my Soul, on God reclin'd,
In Him thy wish'd for rest shalt find;
His Love shall sure deliv'rance yield;
By Him through life I walk upheld,
Superior brave the hostile Train,
And safe from lapse my course maintain.

5.

Thee, Lord, my Glory, Thee alone
My Rock, my Health, my Strength, I own;
Ye Tribes, in God your help behold,
To Him, with me, your hearts unfold;
Each want confess, each grief reveal;
For who, O who like Him can heal?

6. O

6.

O Vanity, thy Name is MAN :
Intent the human mind to scan,
Come, try, if aught of weight there seem ;
Suspend the balance, fix the beam :
In vain.—With equal ease were weigh'd
The flitting air, or empty shade.

7.

Trust not in Wrong and Fraud ; no more
On Hope's light wing presumptuous soar ;
Let gather'd wealth before thee lie
Beheld with unretorted eye,
Nor let the glitt'ring heap impart
One wish to thy deluded heart.

8.

Once from his throne th' Almighty spake,
And forth again the accents brake :
" See Pow'r in Me with Mercy dwells,
" And where my fear the mind impels
" Each act I mark with kind regard,
" And pleas'd confer the just reward."

PSALM LXIII.

1.

THOU art my God ; to Thee my eyes
I lift, e'er yet the dawn arise :
With sacred thirst, O Lord, I burn,
My Heart, my Flesh, thy absence mourn,
As o'er th' unhospitable way
Amidst a barren waste I stray,

2. Yet

2.

Yet here, by heav'nly Wifdom led,
Expectant wait, till o'er my head
Thy beams in mild effulgence play,
And turn my darknefs into day ;
Thofe beams which oft my eyes beheld
From *Salem's* hallow'd Shrine reveal'd.

3.

Thy Love my lips fhall ever tell,
(Can Life itfelf that Love excell ?)
Nor ceafe, while breath prolongs my days,
In thankful notes the hymn to raife :
To Thee thy Servant, Lord, as now,
His hands fhall rear, his knees fhall bow.

4.

For nought like this my foul can chear ;
Nor marrow from the fatted fteer
Could e'er to the luxurious fenfe
Such full delight, my God, difpenfe,
As what my fatiate foul enjoys,
Whene'er thy praife my tongue employs.

5.

Thou Moon, be witnefs if my bed
Forgetful of my God I fpread ;
And Thou, revolving Sun, if e'er
I wake unconfcious of his care :
Each night and each returning day
To him my grateful vows I pay.

6.

Safe in the fhadow of thy wings,
In Thee I joy, O King of Kings ;

When

When dangers threaten to devour,
Superior to each adverfe pow'r
Thy Arm extends the help divine,
And long Experience calls it mine.

7.

Behold my foes in dread retire,
Or proftrate at my feet expire:
While to my conqu'ring fword they yield,
The Beafts that nightly range the field
Amid the flaughter'd heaps fhall ftray,
And rav'nous feize their licens'd prey.

8.

By Thee exalted to the throne
Shall *Judah*'s King thy mercies own;
And bleft be Each, my God, whofe tongue
With Him fhall raife the grateful fong,
Who fuppliant at thy fhrine fhall kneel,
While fhame the Lyar's lips fhall feal.

P S A L M LXIV.

I.

THINE ear, thou Majefty divine,
Propitious to my pray'r incline,
O hear, my voice in pity hear,
And fave my life from hoftile fear.

2.

Behold the men of impious mind,
Their pow'rs in fecret league combin'd,
With factious rage my foul purfue,
And hide, O hide me from their view.

3. Behold

3.

Behold the slaughter-breathing Throng
Whet as a sword their baleful tongue,
And words, as arrows keen, prepare,
That edg'd with death shall walk the air.

4.

Conceal'd they ev'ry fear disclaim,
And level at the Just their aim,
Nor rest, till in the blameless heart
Their hand has lodg'd the sudden dart.

5.

Their dire designs, in guilt allied,
They form ; secure, their snares provide ;
" And who our aim shall thwart ? What eye
" (They ask,) the hidden death descry ?"

6.

With future mischiefs teem their breasts,
(As each to each new wiles suggests,)
And seek in art's obscurest veil
Their guilty purpose to conceal.

7.

Ah ! Wretches, whither will ye fly ?
Behold the arrow from on high
Descend, that bears upon its wing
The wrath of Heav'n's offended King.

8.

Their tongue, that seeks another's hurt,
Itself their footsteps shall subvert,
And passers by with inward dread
Behold them on the earth outspread.

9. Each

9.

Each heart fhall own, with rev'rent thought,
That Thou the work, great God, haft wrought,
And, pleas'd, thy chaftifements fhall trace,
Inflicted on their guilty race ;

10.

While, refcu'd from their rage, the pure
In peaceful reft fhall live fecure,
And with triumphant joy the juft
Exulting fix on Thee their truft.

PSALM LXV.

1.

THEE *Sion's* praife, O Lord, attends,
To Thee the frequent vow afcends
From each whom *Salem's* walls behold
Among her faithful fons inroll'd :
To Thee, whofe ready ear the pray'r
Prevents, fhall Man's whole race repair :

2.

Behold, their Maker taught to own,
Behold them bow before thy throne,
Amidft them at thy footftool I,
Prefs'd with a weight of guilt, apply,
Affur'd from Thy free grace to win
The wifh'd atonement of my fin.

3.

Bleft, who by fweet experience knows,
What Joys thy Prefence, Lord, beftows,
The Man, who, privileg'd by Thee,
Thy face in near approach fhall fee,

Behold

Behold thy beams effulgent play,
And in thy Dwelling fix his ftay.

4.

Let *Ifrael*'s Tribes, their foes o'erthrown,
The terrors of thy Juftice own,
O Thou, the Hope of human race,
Of all whom Earth's wide arms embrace,
Of all who toft by tempefts fweep
The furface of the pathlefs Deep.

5.

In Thee they truft, who girt with pow'r
Haft bid the Mountains heav'nward tow'r,
And fix'd their Bafe ;—who know'ft to rein
The infults of the foaming Main,
Check the brute waves that roar aloud,
And ftill the madnefs of the Croud.

6.

Remoteft Realms with dire difmay
Thy wonders, mightieft Lord, furvey;
Struck with furprize thy pow'r they own,
And humbled bow before thy throne ;
While, as they walk th' ethereal Round,
The Morn and Eve thy praife refound.

7.

Thy vifits teach the grateful foil
To recompenfe the tiller's toil :
By unexhaufted fprings fupplied
Thy River pours its copious tide,
And bids the ftrength-infufing grain
Earth's countlefs Family fuftain.

x   8. The

8.

The Clouds, in frequent fhow'rs diftill'd,
Drop fatnefs on the pregnant field,
Break the tough glebe, the furrows chear,
And crown with good the gliding year;
Th' exulting Hills, th' extended Wafte,
Thy gifts in rich profufion tafte.

9.

Nurs'd by thy care the fleecy train
Invefts with white the rural plain,
While, as beneath the fav'ring fkies.
In crouded ranks the harvefts rife,
The laughing Vale affumes a tongue,
And burfts triumphant into fong.

PSALM LXVI.

I.

YE Sons of Men, in God rejoice;
Lift in one choir your thankful voice,
And fpread through Earth's extended frame
The honour of your Maker's name.

2.

Ye Nations round affembled meet!
Thus let your fong his praife repeat;
Eternal Ruler of the fkies,
How awful are thy works, how wife!

3.

Thy late obdurate foes behold,
By thy fuperior ftrength controul'd,
With flatt'ring lip their homage pay,
And Earth's whole empire own thy fway.

P   4. Each

4.

Each tribe of human race to Thee
Shall suppliant bend the humble knee,
Each tongue in hymns of praise shall join,
And joyful bless the name divine.

5.

O come, and view with rev'rent thought
The acts by Heav'n's high Monarch wrought,
His wonders shown since Time began,
And friendlike intercourse with Man.

6.

His word the Deep's vast channel dried,
And backward roll'd th' obedient Tide;
Aw'd by his voice the briny flood   .
In liquid heaps suspended stood:

7.

Now safe athwart its sandy bed
By Him our rescu'd troops are led,
Now lost in grateful transport stand,
And shouts of triumph shake the strand.

8.

Time's latest period long o'erpast,
His pow'r shall self-supported last;
His eyes the earth survey;—in vain
Its rebel sons oppose his reign.

9.

Ye Nations all of various tongue,
To *Jacob*'s God exalt the song;
Sing, sing aloud, that Nature's ear
His praise through all her bounds may hear,

10. Whose

10.

Whofe wakeful care within our breaft
(Though countlefs foes our peace infeft,)
Still gives the vital pulfe to beat,
And guards from dread of lapfe our feet.

11.

Oft has thy hand, All-potent Lord,
By various proof our faith explor'd,
And bid the flame each heart refine,
As filver recent from the mine :

12.

Now round us waves ihe net, and now
Beneath Oppreffion's weight we bow,
While o'er our heads the Sons of pride
With hoftile fcorn exulting ride.

13.

Through fires, through torrents, led by Thee,
At length th' expected Land we fee,
Where ftreams irriguous cleave the foil,
And crown with wealth the tiller's toil.

14.

Lo, to thy Dome, my God and King,
The facred Holocauft I bring,
That late, opprefs'd by forrow's cloud,
To Thee with fervent lip I vow'd :

15.

Before thy Altar's kindled fire
The promis'd victims fhall expire,
Here bleed the full-fed Goat, and here
The fleecy Ram, and ftubborn Steer.

P 2   16. O

16.

O come, Ye Souls that fear your God,.
And learn his grace on Me beftow'd,
As, fupplicating loud, my tongue
Wak'd to his praife the hallow'd fong.

17.

Had confcious guilt my bofom ftain'd,.
How had his ear my pray'r difdain'd,.
That upward now through tracts of day
In fure acceptance wings its way !

18.

Bleft be my God, who, thron'd on high,.
Rejects not from his care my cry,
Nor, while afflictions round me rife,.
His mercy to my foul denies.

P S A L M LXVII..

1.

MAY God his fav'ring ear incline,.
And bid his face on *Ifrael* fhine,.
That All thy counfels, Lord, may know,
Where Earth extends, or Oceans flow,
And, thankful, to their wondring eyes
Behold thy wifh'd Salvation rife..

To Thee, of life th' eternal Spring,.
Invifible, All-potent King,
One chorus let the Nations raife,
One fhout of univerfal praife.

2.

Ye diftant Realms your voice employ
In fongs of gratitude and joy;

Exult

Exult each Tribe, exult each Land ;
Heav'n's mighty Lord with equal hand
The balance holds, and Earth's domain
Shall own to lateſt age his reign.
    To Thee, of life th' eternal Spring,
    Inviſible, All-potent King,
    One chorus let the Nations raiſe,
    One ſhout of univerſal praiſe.

3.

So, warm'd by genial ſuns, the field
With full increaſe its fruits ſhall yield,
And God, thy God, O *Iſrael*, ſhed
His choiceſt bleſſings on thy head:
God ſhall on us his bleſſings ſhow'r,
And Man's whole race revere his pow'r.
    To Thee, of life th' eternal Spring,
    Inviſible, All-potent King,
    One chorus let the Nations raiſe,
    One ſhout of univerſal praiſe.

P S A L M LXVIII.

1.

LET God ariſe, and let his foes,
    His arm unable to oppoſe,
Back from the field, with wild affright
O'erwhelm'd, precipitate their flight.

2.

Behold, great God, the impious Hoſt
Like ſmoke in quick diſperſion loſt :
Behold them, at thy look, expire,
Diſſolv'd, as wax before the fire ;

P 3   3. While

3.

While all who own thy juſt command
Exulting in thy preſence ſtand,
And bid the ſhout of triumph riſe
Loud echoing to the diſtant ſkies.

4.

Your ſongs for *Iſrael*'s God prepare,
Who, ſeated on his regal Car,
Triumphant o'er the Deſert wide
In ſolemn ſtate is ſeen to ride:

5.

His name JEHOVAH; Theme of praiſe
Exhauſtleſs!—in His preſence raiſe
The grateful ſtrain, and joyous ſing
The Mercies of your heav'nly King.

6.

Their Parent Him the Orphans hail;
He bids the Widow's cauſe prevail,
And, ſhrin'd above th' empyreal ſky,
Extends to All his equal eye;

7.

A manſion to the Outcaſt gives,
The Captive from his chain relieves;
But bids the Sinner wear away
In barren wilds his ſhorten'd day.

8.

When o'er the long-extended Waſte
Thy Preſence before *Iſrael* paſt,
And, beaming o'er thy People's head,
Their Bands to certain conqueſt led,—

9. Earth,

9.

Earth, groaning to its centre, reel'd;
The Heav'ns, in clouds diſſolv'd, beheld
The footſteps of th' approaching God,
Ev'n *Sinai* bow'd with lowly nod.

10.

While yet the burning ſands they tread,
Thy kindlieſt rains, around them ſhed,
Beſpeak them fav'rites of thy care,
And Nature's wearied pow'rs repair.

11.

Thus joy the Tribes whom Thou haſt lov'd,
Thus boaſt their lot by. Thee improv'd,
Whoſe aid the humble and the poor
Shall ne'er with fruitleſs vows implore.

12.

Heav'n's mighty Monarch gave the word;
His mandate *Sion's* Daughters heard,
And thus in one aſſembled throng
With ſweet accordance form the Song:

13.

" Kings with their hoſts have fled; and We,
" Who fate from toils of battle free,
" (Content the houſhold's care to guide;)
" The Victor's richeſt ſpoils divide."

14.

Again (their form obſcur'd awhile
By taſks of ſervitude and toil,)
Again the Sons of *Abraham's* line
Array'd in ſpotleſs luſtre ſhine,—

15.

As Doves, while obvious to the Sun
From plume to plume the fplendors run,
Their wings in filver dipt unfold,
And necks that glow with living gold.

16.

While back thy foes, O *Ifrael*, turn,
Thy God amid thy gloom a morn
Prefents, unfullied as the fnow
Diffus'd o'er *Salmon*'s ample brow.

17.

No more, O *Bafan*, vaunt thy height,
That ftrikes with awe the diftant fight;
No more, ye fwelling Mountains, rife
In haughty triumph to the fkies:

18.

On humbler *Sion*'s favour'd head
His tent th' eternal King has fpread,
Her facred Hill his choice confeft,
And lafting manfion of his reft.

19.

Ten thoufand Cars, and yet again
Ten thoufand Cars, in lengthen'd train
Along her hallow'd way proceed,
While God the Pomp vouchfafes to lead,—

20.

Thus *Ifrael* views within her fhrine
(Bleft feat of Majefty divine,)
The fcene that erft his Tribes beheld
On *Sinai*'s myftic top reveal'd.

21. Admiring

21.

Admiring Crouds with upcaft eye
Have feen thee, Lord, afcend on high:
Behind Thee move a captive Train,
Faft fetter'd with the fervile chain,

22.

While gifts through Thee on All below
From Heav'n's high throne tranfmitted flow,
A Race, who fhun'd thy Laws to own,
Thy Prefence and thy Aid have known.

23.

To God, our ever-conftant Aid,
Be thanks and ceafelefs honour paid:
To whom belongs the pow'r to fave
His fervants from th' expecting grave,

24.

On Him thy wifh'd falvation refts;
Him, *Ifrael*, praife; whofe high behefts
Death's dreaded march thro' Earth's domain
To paths by Him prefcrib'd reftrain.

25.

To Each whofe heart rejects his fway,
His terrors fhall their guilt repay;
Deftruction, with unwearied pace,
Through Sin's dark maze their path fhall trace;

26.

Intent on plans of future ill,
His ftroke the hairy fcalp fhall feel,
And fhare the vengeance, thus aloud
Denounc'd on the rebellious Croud.

27. " Once

27.

" Once more from *Bafan*'s fertile plain,
" Once more from the divided Main
" Thee, *Jacob*, my refiftlefs hand
" Shall lead, and guard thy chofen Band.

28.

" When foes thy fword prefumptuous brave,
" Thy feet the fanguine ftream fhall lave,
" Thy dogs devour the flaughter'd throng,
" And tinge with impious gore their tongue."

29.

My God, my King, with joyful view
Thy fteps our wond'ring eyes purfue,
As on thou moveft to thy fhrine
Attended by thy chofen Line.

30.

Before the Singers walk; behind
The Minftrels tread, in concert join'd,
While, in the midft, the Virgin train
Awake the trimbrel's loudeft ftrain.

31.

" Your praifes" (thus begins the lay,)
" To Heav'n's eternal Sov'reign pay,
" Ye Tribes that boaft your hallow'd Race
" From *Ifrael*'s fruitful fource to trace."

32.

Leaft of that Race, Thou, *Benjamin*,
With mightier *Judah* there art feen,
While *Naphthali*'s glad Chiefs confpire
With *Zebulon* to form the choir.

33. Strong

33.

Strong in thy God, O *Ifrael*, rife;
And Thou, great Ruler of the Skies,
Thy Work perpetuate; and increafe
Thy People's ftrength by lafting peace.

34.

O let thy grace and boundlefs love,
Fair *Salem*'s fhrine incircling, move
Affembled Kings her Courts to greet,
And caft their gifts before thy feet.

35.

The Beaft, that from his reedy bed
On *Nile*'s proud bank uplifts the head,
Rebuke, and check the impious band
Who lift to idol Gods the hand;

36.

From whom the Heifer, and the Steer,
The offer'd Vow unconfcious hear,
While to the filver's tinkling found
Their feet in folemn dance rebound.

37.

Their thirft of war, great God, reftrain,
And backward drive their fcatter'd train:
So, fummon'd from her fartheft end,
Shall *Egypt*'s Lords to *Salem* bend;

38.

So fhall *Arabia*'s fertile land
Extend to Thee the fuppliant hand:
The various Realms that Earth divide,
Shall fing to *Ifrael* s God and Guide:

39. He

39.

He o'er the fkies, in awful ftate,
From earlieft age, exalted fate;
His voice, in frequent thunders giv'n,
Tremendous fhakes the vault of Heav'n.

40.

To Him the pow'r afcribe, whofe rays
To *Jacob's* view confpicuous blaze,
Who downward from th' ethereal height
O'er fubject Worlds extends his fight.

41.

What terrors from thy prefence flow!
O Thou, of *Ifrael's* foes the Foe,
Whofe ftrength his arm for toil prepares,
And crowns with fure fuccefs his wars.

42.

Bleft be the name of *Ifrael's* Lord,
The God by *Jacob's* fons ador'd,
To Him, till Time fhall reach its end,
Let fongs of higheft praife afcend.

P S A L M LXIX.

1.

TO Thee I call; O hafte thee near,
My voice, great God, indulgent hear;
Extend thy powerful arm, and fave
My foul from the voracious wave.

2.

In depths of mire behold me bound;
In vain my finking feet the ground
Explore; while high above my head
The whelming floods their billows fpread.

3. Faint

3.

Faint are my limbs, my palate dry,
While ceaſeleſs to my God I cry;
With waſting orbs my eyes attend
To ſee his promis'd grace deſcend.

4.

Behold my Foes around me ſpread,
The hairs that ſhade my hapleſs head
Outnumb'ring; Foes, that, arm'd with pow'r,
My ſoul have labour'd to devour;

5.

Yet pure of each offence I ſtand,
Plight to their terms my willing hand,
Nor ſhun (Extortion's eaſy prey,)
The wrong-imputed debt to pay.

6.

To Thee, my God, to Thee alone
The errors of my heart are known:
Thine eyes my inmoſt guilt have view'd,
Nor can my thought thy ſearch elude.

7.

O let not, heav'nly Lord, thine aid
Thus long to my requeſt delay'd
Their hope to hoſtile ſcorn conſign,
Whoſe hearts on *Iſrael*'s God recline.

8.

Thy Cauſe, by Me avow'd, my fame
To inſult gives, my cheek to ſhame:
The impious mockers on me gaze,
Each eye, each lip contempt betrays.

Q   9. Domeſtic

9.

Domeſtic Wrath and kindred Hate,
In thy defence, my ſoul await ;
The Brothers of my blood in Me
An Alien and an Outcaſt ſee.

10.

The zeal that to thy houſe I bear
My ſoul conſumes; each taunt ſevere ·
That loud-tongu'd Rage for Thee intends,
On Me with fulleſt weight deſcends.

11.

Diſſolv'd in tears, with faſting worn,
What obloquy my ſoul has borne !
My loins with ſorrow's garb o'erſpread
With jeſts their cruel fancy fed :

12.

I paſs the crouded gate, purſu'd
By laughter and reproaches rude,
The proverb of the Drunkard's tongue,
And theme familiar of his ſong.

13.

O let me in th' accepted hour
In pray'r to Thee my ſpirit pour ;
Thine ear in full accordance bend,
And pleas'd thy promis'd help extend.

14.

Snatch from the miry depths my feet;
Back let my furious foes retreat,
Safe from their hate thy Servant keep,
Nor leave him ſinking in the deep.

7   15. O then

15.

O then the fwelling ftorm affuage,
Ere yet the flood's remorfelefs rage
In dreadful whirlpools wrap me round,
And plunge me in the dark profound.

16.

Hear, Lord, and to my foul difplay
Thy Mercy's all-enliv'ning ray;
Look down, eternal God, look down,
Behold me, but without a frown:

17.

Ne'er to thy Servant's longing eye
Thy face, amidft my woes, deny,
Hafte to my aid, O hafte thee near,
Releafe my foul from hoftile fear.

18.

Thine ears have heard each infult keen,
Thine eyes, juft Lord, my fhame have feen,
And ftedfaft mark'd the adverfe Band,
That leagu'd in guilt around me ftand.

19.

My foul, by evil tongues affail'd,
Unequal to the conflict fail'd:
I wifh'd, in vain, fome friend to find,
Whofe voice might foothe my troubled mind.

20.

Thefe, 'mid the Croud that wait me nigh,
Gall to my loathing lips apply;
While Thefe my thirft's afflictive rage
With juice of fharpeft tafte affuage.

21.

While pleas'd the focial board they fhare,
Let Death around it plant a fnare,
And what fhould blifs and health beftow
With aim inverted work their woe.

22.

Let blindnefs check their fell defigns,
Bow with affliction's weight their loins,
And let thy Wrath, with loofen'd rein,
Defcending crufh the rebel Train.

23.

Let Horror and Deftruction drear
Amid their tents the ftandard rear,
Nor human habitant be found
Within their dome's capacious round:

24.

Since, unprovok'd, with murth'rous view,
Whom Thou haft fmitten they purfue,
And feek, inftinct with cruel joy,
The Man of forrows to deftroy.

25.

Let Each (for nought their hearts could bend)
From depth to depth in fin defcend,
Ne'er, touch'd by healing Mercy, fee
The path that leads to Blifs and Thee;

26.

Let vengeance, kindled to a flame,
Blot from the earth their hateful name,
Nor let them, 'mid thy chofen Band,
In life's fair page recorded ftand.

27. And

27.

And O ! while prefs'd with ills I lie,
Caſt on my ſtate a pitying eye,
And let thy Mercy to my grief
In full ſufficience yield relief.

28.

For this to Thee my voice I rear;
Nor ſhall the hoof'd and horned Steer,
New draughted from the fat'ning field,
A Sacrifice ſo grateful yield.

29.

Ye humble Souls, that ſeek his aid,
His Love, in my releaſe diſplay'd,
His Love your dying hearts ſhall chear,
Who ſtoops the captive poor to hear.

30.

O praiſe him, Heav'n, and Seas, and Earth,
And All whom Nature wakes to birth :
Him praiſe, who *Sion* deigns to ſhield,
Whoſe hand ſhall *Judah*'s Cities build :

31.

He bids her Sons the Land divide,
Where unmoleſted ſhall reſide,
Through rolling Time's extended Year,
A Race devoted to his fear.

PSALM LXX.

1.

HASTE to my aid, my Saviour, haſte ;
My Soul, by hoſtile numbers chas'd,
To Thee directs its pray'r:

In wild confusion backward borne
Their wish defeated let them mourn,
   And lost in empty air.

2.

Be shame their just reward affign'd,
While round me with relentless mind
   Derision's shout they raise:
Thy Bliss let All who seek thee share,
And, taught thy Love, that Love declare
   In songs of ceaseless praise.

3.

While These in thy Salvation joy,
Increasing griefs my thought employ,
   And speediest aid demand.
My Helper and Redeemer, hear;
O, instant in my cause appear,
   And reach thy saving hand.

P S A L M LXXI.

1.

ON Thee, O God, with steady frame,
  (O blast not Thou my hope with shame)
On Thee my Soul its trust has staid,
And asks thy Justice to its aid:

2.

Thy Servant, God of Gods supreme,
O hear, and hasten to redeem;
Be Thou my Rock, and safe Resort;—
My Rock thou art, my strongest Fort:

              3. Thy

3.

Thy lips my refcue have decreed,
And bid each threaten'd ill recede :
O let thy promis'd help o'erthrow
Each impious and revengeful Foe.

4.

On Thee my hopes fupported ftand ;
My Life from earlieft youth thy hand
(That Life which firft from Thee began,)
Preferv'd, and led me up to Man.

5.

When lodg'd within the womb I lay,
Thy Care produc'd me to the day,
And, while that Care my years prolongs,
Thy Name fhall animate my fongs.

6.

Though Crouds, with filent gaze, in Me
A fpectacle of wonder fee,
Amidft my grief, amidft my pain,
Thy Love fhall ftill my faith fuftain.

7.

Thy arm in my relief employ,
That foon, my hope abforb'd in joy,
From op'ning dawn to clofing eve
Thy praifes on my tongue may live.

8.

O let me not, Almighty Friend,
While with a weight of Age I bend,
And wearied Nature's fuccours fail,
The abfence of thine aid bewail.

9. " Behold"

9.

" Behold" (fuch words the ranc'rous héart
Suggefts, while, pleas'd, with fecret art
My foes the deathful fnare provide,)
" A Wretch whom God has caft afide :

10.

" Come" (thus, by lawlefs counfel led,
Aloud they cry) " deftruction fpread ;
" Purfue, and mark him for the grave ;
" Purfue ; for None is nigh to fave."

11.

My God, my God, depart not far,
But hafte, and make my life thy care ;
O obvious to my pray'r arife ;
Nor let their guilt efcape thine eyes.

12.

Let Shame, let Death their deeds repay,
Who wifh my guiltlefs foul their prey,
And black Difgrace their name o'erfpread,
Who aim their mifchiefs at my head.

13.

My heart fhall ftill on Thee depend ;
My thankful voice to Thee afcend,
And, through the day, my God and King,
Thy Juftice, thy Salvation, fing.

14.

Thy Mercies, Lord, all praife furmount,
No numbers can their fum recount,
For ne'er can words in equal ftrain
The meafure of thy love explain.

15. Lo!

15.

Lo! in thy ſtrength I take my way,
Thou art my God, and thou my ſtay;
Thy righteouſneſs alone, and love
My heart ſhall warm, my ſong improve.

16.

Thy Leſſons on my youthful breaſt
Fair Wiſdom's ſacred lines impreſs'd,
And taught me, each advancing hour,
To ſpeak the wonders of thy Pow'r.

17.

Recede not now, while grey with years
His hands to Thee thy Servant rears,
Nor e'er thy wonted help withhold,
Till, pleas'd, my tongue thy Acts has told:

18.

Such Acts as ſhall the ear invite
Of All who now th' ethereal light
Enjoy, and oft rehears'd engage
The wonder of each future age.

19.

How great thy pow'r, thy works how great!
Say, what in Earth, or Heav'n's high ſeat,
What ſhall the ſearching eye to Thee
Or equal, Lord, or ſecond, ſee?

20.

How haſt thou bid my ſoul to know
A long viciſſitude of woe,
Yet, back return'd, with quick'ning ray
Haſt chas'd each cloud of grief away!

21. Thy

21.

Thy hand, when Earth had clos'd me round,
Has snatch'd me from the dark profound,
My head with endless honours bless'd,
And sooth'd my anxious thoughts to rest.

22.

O Thou, whom, wrapt in holy fear,
The Sons of *Israel*'s Line revere;
Thy Pow'r, thy Mercy shall my lay
In sweet harmonious sounds display.

23.

Thy Truth my psalt'ry shall inspire,
And tune to loudest notes my lyre,
My willing lips with praise o'erflow,
My rescu'd soul with transport glow.

24.

From morn to night, indulgent Lord,
My tongue thy Justice shall record;
That gave the period to my woes,
And whelm'd in shame my vaunting foes.

P S A L M LXXII.

1.

INSTRUCT, great God, the kingly heart,
Nor cease thy guidance to impart,
T'ill, pleas'd, the Heir of *Judah*'s throne
Thy precept's full extent has known.

2.

So shall his hand dispense thy Laws,
Prompt to defend the poor man's cause,
In his protecting arm the meek
With sure success their aid shall seek.

3. Peace

3.

Peace from the fort-clad Mountain's brow
Shall blefs the happy plains below,
And Juftice from each rocky cell
Shall Violence and Fraud expel.

4.

In Him the Souls to fcorn confign'd
The Advocate and Friend fhall find ;
His arm their injur'd race fhall right,
And crufh the proud Oppreffor's might.

5.

Thy fear fucceeding Times fhall own,
Long as the Sun and waxing Moon,
With varied light, in fwift career,
Alternate guide the circling year.

6.

Behold his influence downward pour,
Delightful as the copious fhow'r,
Whofe drops refrefh the new-fhorn plain,
And fwell with life the foodful grain.

7.

His Care the Juft aloft fhall raife,
Nor fair Profperity his days
Defift to crown, till round the pole
The meafur'd Months fhall ceafe to roll.

8.

From Sea to Sea his wide Command
Shall reach, and from *Euphrates'* ftrand
Through Realms of various tongue extend
Far as to Earth's remoteft end.

9. To

9.

To Him the Defert's Tribes fhall kneel ;
His Foes, that on their conqu'ring fteel
Repos'd erewhile their frantic truft,
Shall proftrate fall, and lick the duft.

10.

Before his throne affembled meet
The Chiefs, at whofe imperial feet
Arabia's far-divided fhores
Prolific fpread their richeft ftores.

11.

See Kings from *Tharfis* and each ifle,
Their prefents bring with willing toil ;
Each Prince to Him fhall homage pay,
Each Nation own his equal Sway.

12.

He, when the helplefs Poor fhall cry,
Shall hear propitious from on high,
Health to their fainting fouls convey,
And challenge from the Grave its prey.

13.

Nor Fraud, nor Rapine's iron hand
Shall dare to touch the pious Band ;
For facred is their blood, and high
Its price in his paternal eye.

14.

Long fhall he live, and *Sheba*'s gold
In tributary heaps behold
Difplay'd, while Crouds fhall fuppliant bow,
And thankful pay their daily vow.

15. Lift

15.

Lift to the Mountain's height your eyes;
And fee the yellow harvefts rife,
Wide-waving, as the verdure fpread
On *Lebanon*'s exalted head.

16.

Behold his Cities o'er the plain
Pour from their gates a num'rous Train,
And healthful as the vernal Birth,
That fhades with green the joyous Earth.

17.

From age to age the Orb of day
His brighter glories fhall furvey,
While Man's whole Race his Love confefs,
And, bleft in Him, his Name fhall blefs.

18.

Exalt, exalt your heav'nly Lord,
In all his wond'rous acts ador'd:
To Him in loftieft praifes join,
And blefs the Majefty divine;

19.

That Majefty whofe cloudlefs rays
O'er Earth's capacious round fhall blaze:
To Him again in praifes join;
O, blefs the Majefty divine.

PSALM LXXIII.

1.

YES: mightieft Lord! My foul has known
Thy Love to *Ifrael*'s Offspring fhown,
And owns the Blifs by Thee ordain'd
To each who bears a heart unftain'd.

R

2. Yet

2.

Yet griev'd awhile thy paths, my God,
With hesitating step I trod,
And, but for Thee, the faithful Guide,
My erring feet had swerv'd aside.

3.

As fix'd in happiest state I see
The foes to Virtue, Truth, and Thee,
Their Blessings on my thoughts imprefs'd
With envy near had fill'd my breast :

4.

Health strings their nerves ; and Death, (their
hour
Approaching), with remitted pow'r.
And flow advance his easy doom
Inflicting, bows them to the tomb.

5.

Forbid the gen'ral lot to share
Of pain, affliction, want, and care,
The lawless Tribe with cruel skill
Augment the woes that others feel.

6.

Pride on their neck its chain has bound,
And Violence invests them round ;
Their swelling eyes and pamper'd frame
Their boundless appetite proclaim :

7.

Their wishes by success outrun,
Their headlong wills controulment shun ;
And words with fury wing'd impart
The genuine dictates of their heart.

8. Lo,

8.

Lo, train'd to infolence and wrong,
Againſt the Heav'ns their impious tongue
Defiance and reproach has hurl'd,
And unreſiſted walks the world.

9.

Untaught to ſcan thy wiſe Decree,
With wonder, Lord, thy People ſee
Life's choiceſt gifts their want ſupply,
Whoſe breaſts thy ev'ry threat defy:

10.

Who aſk, " Shall He our acts ſurvey,
" Whoſe hands th' ethereal ſcepter ſway ?
" Shall He, inthron'd above the ſtars,
" To Earth's low ſcene extend his cares ?"

11.

While daring Mortals thus each hour
Thee, Lord, inſult, and brave thy pow'r,
Yet, ſunk in eaſe, and bleſt with health,
Amaſs in heaps their growing wealth;

12.

In vain, (thy Servant cried,) in vain,
I purge my breaſt from ev'ry ſtain,
My acts conform to thy commands,
And waſh in innocence my hands.

13.

Each day oppreſt with fierceſt pains,
Thy ſcourge my chaſten'd Soul ſuſtains ;
Each Morn, that riſing ſtreaks the ſky,
Awakes me but to miſery.

14. My

14.

My heart, while thus by grief affail'd,
In filence long its thought has veil'd,
Left Doubts like mine thy Saints betray
From thy Decrees, great God, to ftray.

15.

Thy Conduct weigh'd, awhile my mind
Its hidden Caufe effay'd to find;
That Caufe, as deeper it inquires,
Still farther from its fearch retires.

16.

Thy Fane at length I feek; and there,
(My anxious foul effus'd in pray'r,)
Inftructed by thy Spirit, read
The period to their guilt decreed.

17.

I fee Thee on the flipp'ry feat
Of high Ambition plant their feet,
Then mark them as they downward bend,
And headlong to the earth defcend.

18.

Thy hand in unexpected hour
Deftroys the phantom of their pow'r,
How fwift, how fudden is their fate!
What horrors, Lord, their death await!

19.

Wrapt in Oblivion's fhade they lie,
Their image vanifh'd from the eye,
As the light fabric of a Dream,
Diffolv'd by day's intruding beam.

20. Such

20.

Such woes, in error's fetters chain'd,
Such heart-felt anguiſh, I ſuſtain'd,
Inſenſate, as the Brutes that rove
Th' extended Wild, or ſhady Grove:

21.

Yet ſtill thy Care confeſs'd me thine;
My hand within the hand divine
Was lock'd; Thou, Thou, Almighty friend,
Propitioys ſhalt my cauſe defend.

22.

By thy directive counſel led,
Life's maze I yet, ſecure, ſhall tread,
And wait till thy appointed hour
The promis'd Glory round me pour.

23.

O ſay, in Heav'n's capacious round
What Friend like Thee my Soul has found;
Or who, great God, on Earth reſides,
Whoſe love with thine my breaſt divides.

24.

My heart, my fleſh, have fail'd; but Thee
My laſting heritage I ſee;
Thy ſtrength my fainting ſpirit chears,
And checks my grief, and calms my fears.

25.

Who, taught to ſpurn his equal ſway,
From *Iſrael's* God adult'rous ſtray,
His Juſtice, with reverſeleſs doom,
In Life's full vigour ſhall conſume:

R 3   '26. While,

26.

While, warm with holy tranfport, I
To Him with fure fuccefs apply,
Him truft, and, guarded by his Care,.
To Man's whole race his acts declare.

P S A L M   LXXIV.

1.

OThou, whofe hand has *Ifrael* led,
His fold enlarg'd, his pafture fpread,
Why haft thou doom'd us thus to bear
A long exclufion from thy care ?

2.

Why thus beneath thy anger groan
The Flock whom Thou haft feal'd thine own
Call to thy thought the facred Band
Once own'd the purchafe of thy hand :

3.

The Heritage by Thee redeem'd,
Fair *Sion*'s Mount, where copious ftream'd
Th' eternal light, and fpoke her Shrine
'The Seat of Majefty divine :

4.

Lift to that Seat thy fteps again ;
See Defolation fpread her reign
Around it, and its wide extent
Each mark of hoftile rage prefent.

5.

With clamours fierce a lawlefs Train
The filence of thy Courts profane,
And bid their ftandard to the fkies
Aloft in haughty triumph rife.

6. As

6.

As when the Woodman's ſtroke invades
The lofty Grove's thick-woven ſhades,
So through thy Temple's awful bounds,
Now here, now there, the axe reſounds;

7.

Down, down in ſhapeleſs ruins fall
The ſculptures fair that grac'd its wall,
Rich with the foreſt's nobleſt ſpoil,
And wrought by Heav'n-directed toil.

8.

Along the violated Dome
Th' intruding flames licentious roam,
Swift, ſwift the fiery deluge ſtrays
And wraps thy Fabric in its blaze.

9.

Thy ſpacious Courts, and Tow'rs ſublime,
Whoſe roofs through long-revolving time
With holy wonder ſtruck each eye,
Now heap'd in dire confuſion lie.

10.

" Come," (thus th' inſulting foe has cried,)
" Come, deal the vengeance far and wide ;
" And let the flames with equal doom
" Each Houſe of _Iſrael's_ God conſume."

11.

They ſpeak : and, inſtant, all around
The blazing ruins ſtrew the ground.
No more thy wonders to our eyes,
Bleſt ſignals of thy preſence, riſe ;

4   12. No

12.

No more the Prophet's lips thy will
In myſtic Oracles reveal,
Or to thy People's view diſcloſe
The deſtin'd period of their woes.

13.

But ſay, O ſay, great God, how long
Thus unchaſtis'd the hoſtile tongue
Shall mock thy pow'r, thy fear diſclaim,
And load with loud reproach thy Name.

14.

While Crimes like theſe redreſs demand,
Why in thy boſom ſleeps thy hand?
O pluck it forth, and let the foe
Repentant feel th' inflicted blow.

15.

Thee from of old my King I ſee,
Nor knows my heart a Friend but Thee:
Thine arm alone, in *Jacob*'s right,
Has turn'd each adverſe pow'r to flight.

16.

At thy command, the watry Deeps
Suſpended ſtood, in liquid heaps;
And ſafe, as o'er the ſandy waſte,
Th' admiring troops betwixt them paſt;

17.

The proud Leviathan, his head
Low to thy ſtroke ſubmitted, bled,
And, 'midſt returning waves, his train
Around their mighty King are ſlain.

18. While

18.

While Rapine waits upon the ftrand,
And calls from far her hungry Band,
That fcatter'd range the Defert wide,
The promis'd banquet to divide.

19.

Thy ftroke the rock's dark entrails clave ;
Forth from its depth the foaming wave
Sprang inftant, and with lengthen'd train
Irriguous lav'd the thirfty plain.

20.

Thy Mandate *Jordan*'s channel dried,
And backward roll'd his wondring tide ;
While *Ifrael*'s Sons, by Thee, O God,
Conducted, fafe the channel trod.

21.

By Thee prepar'd, the Night and Day
Alternate walk th' ethereal way ;
Thy Art the Light's thin texture fpun,
And with it cloth'd the jocund Sun ;

22.

Thy hand the Earth's vaft fabric rounds,
Its balance fixes, marks its bounds,
With fummer's fhow'rs its glebe unbinds,
Or warps it with the wintry winds.

23.

Parent of Nature ! God fupreme !
While Folly's Sons thy acts blafpheme,
O vindicate thy Name from wrong,
And filence the reproachful tongue.

24. Let

24.

Let not the fangs of cruel pow'r
Thy trembling Turtle's life devour,
Nor dark Oblivion's shade our pain
For ever from thy thought detain.

25.

O give the Flock that bears thy Name,
Thy fed'ral mercy yet to claim:
Behold within each cavern'd cell
Fraud, Violence, and Rapine dwell.

26.

Behold; and let th' afflicted Poor,
From terror and from shame secure,
With grateful heart, and joyous tongue,
Wake to thy praise the hallow'd song.

27.

Rise, mightiest Lord, thy cause defend:
Wide o'er a guilty Race extend
Thy rod, and let the needful blow
Repress the licenfe of the Foe.

28.

O let thy hand correct their fin,
Whose hearts thy mercy fails to win,
Whose mad presumption ev'ry hour
With heighten'd rage insults thy pow'r.

P S A L M LXXV.

1.

THY Name, immortal God, thy name
Our love and highest praise shall claim,
Whose Acts attest thee ever near,
And plant within each heart thy fear.

2. To

2.

To Me, to Me the hour is known,
When, feated on th' appointed Throne,
My Juftice fhall affert its Laws,
And arbitrate each dubious caufe.

3.

Though all the Land before mine eye
Diffolv'd in wide confufion lie,
Secure from lapfe its pillars ftand,
And reft on my fupporting hand.

4.

Lift not the horn, ye Sons of pride,
(Aloud with fierce rebuke I cried,)
Lift not the horn; nor thus in vain,
With ftubborn neck oppofe my reign.

5.

Shall pow'r, to Eaft or Weft inclin'd,
Float cafual on the wafting wind,
Or iffue from the Climes, that blaze
Beneath the Sun's meridian rays:

6.

That God, who erft the Heav'ns outfpread,
The regal crown from head to head
Transfers: Wealth, Honour, Pow'r, his Doom
At will fhall grant, at will refume.

7.

His hand the full-charg'd cup prefents,
While red with wrath its wine ferments,
Whofe mixture Earth's rebellious Train
Low to its utmoft dregs fhall drain.

8. But

8.

But I, with facred tranfport fill'd,
To *Jacob*'s God my praife will yield;
Through Life's continu'd round, my tongue
Shall wake to Him the joyous fong.

9.

Behold me, conqu'ring in his right,
Now crufh the horn of impious Might,
Now bid the Juft, that proftrate lies,
With lifted head triumphant rife.

P S A L M   LXXVI.

1.

THY Confines, *Judah*, God have known,
His greatnefs *Ifrael*'s Offspring own,
His glories *Salem*'s temple fill,
And reft·on *Sion*'s facred hill.

2.

There broke his hand the fword and fhield,
And caft them ufelefs on the field;
There fnap'd the arrows wing'd with fire,
And bade the raging War expire.

3.

O cloth'd with Majefty divine,
O fay, what ftrength fhall equal thine;
Not fuch the Mountains boaft, whofe feat
To robbers yield a fafe retreat.

4.

When erft, impatient to devour,
Infulting rofe each hoftile pow'r,
Who wont with fpoils the earth to heap,
Now fpoil'd themfelves have flept their fleep:

5. Amaz'd

5.

Amaz'd the Chiefs were seen to stand ;
Nor knew the once resistless hand
Its task, but, summon'd to their aid,
Shrunk trembling back and disobey'd.

6.

The Steed, the Car that o'er the plain
Rush'd headlong on, nor heard the rein,
With horror struck confess thee nigh,
And wrapt in iron slumber lie.

7.

Thou, Thou alone our fear shalt claim ;
O who, when, kindled to a flame,
Thy Vengeance shall its debt demand,
Shall dare within thy sight to stand ?

8.

  Earth heard, when God the judgment gave,
And rose his injur'd Saints to save,
In silent dread beheld his look,
And instant to her centre shook.

9.

While impious Crouds oppose thy Reign,
Thou, Lord, their fury shalt restrain,
Thy stroke correct their stubborn will,
And teach them at thy shrine to kneel.

10.

Low to our God, ye Nations, bow,
Yield to his Name the faithful vow,
Him serve with fear, and duteous bring
Your presents to the heav'nly King ;

S   11. That

11.

That King, whofe fword, in wrath applied,
Lops in mid growth the Tyrant's pride,
And threatful bids each earthly throne
His mightier fway fubmiffive own.

P S A L M　LXXVII.

1.

TO God my fuppliant voice I rear,
　　With holy violence his ear
Solicit, and expectant kneel,
Till He my inward anguifh heal.

2.

To Him with fervent zeal I cried,
In whom alone my hopes refide;
With ftretch'd-out hand, and reftlefs thought,
Befet with woes, his aid I fought:

3.

When night's dark fhades the earth inveft,
And weary Nature finks to reft,
Still, deaf to comfort, I complain,
And give my ftruggling griefs the rein.

4.

Now fix'd on God, to Him in pray'r
My fainting fpirit pour'd its care,
And words, in artlefs form compos'd,
The tumult of my foul difclos'd:

5.

Now, dumb with forrow while I weep,
My eyes their ceafelefs vigils keep:
Anon my mind its fearch began;
And back to diftant years I ran,—

8　　　　　　　　　　　　6. The

6.

The years whofe wonders to my tongue
Yield fruitful themes of joyous fong,
And deep inquiry to my breaft
At midnight's thoughtful hour fuggeft.

7.

Will God a heart opprefs'd as mine
For ever to its griefs refign?
Has Mercy from his bofom fled?
My hope his promife vainly fed?

8.

Forgets th' Almighty to be kind?
And fhall his Love, in wrath confin'd,
No more its wonted aid beftow,
Or fix a meafure to my woe?

9.

Now Reafon's pow'rs collected rife,
And thus each anxious doubt chaftife;
Though preft with various ills I ftand,
And mourn the changes of his hand,—

10.

His Works, atchiev'd in ages paft,
Shall fix'd in my remembrance laft;
His Wonders on my thought fhall dwell,
My tongue his Acts unwearied tell.

11.

For Sanctity thy counfel guides,
And o'er thy paths, Bleft Sire, prefides:
Where finds, O where, the fearching eye
A God, with *Ifrael's* God to vie?

12. Maker

12.

Maker of All ! At thy command
Revers'd the Laws of Nature ftand;
Stupendous fcenes thy Acts afford,
And bid the Nations know their Lord.

13.

Let *Jacob* and let *Jofeph* fay,
How ftrong thy Arm to chafe away
Each woe that waits thy People near,
Each danger that excites their fear.

14.

The Deeps beheld thee, heav'nly King!
The Deeps beheld thee; and each Spring,
That rofe from out their fandy bed,
Tumultuous own'd its fudden dread.

15.

Inceffant from the burfting cloud
Down ftream'd the bidden rain; aloud
Peal'd the big thunder; through the fky
Thy flaming fhafts were feen to fly;

16.

And, as thy voice around the pole
In awful threats was heard to roll,
Earth trembling groan'd, while o'er her head
Its livid fheet the lightning fpread.

17.

Wide yawn'd the Flood from fhore to fhore,
And op'd a path unknown before,
While *Ifrael*'s Guardian and his God
With tracklefs ftep its channel trod.

18. As

18.

As sheep to diftant paftures led,
Secure thy people march'd, convey'd
By *Mofes'* and by *Aaron*'s hand
To promis'd *Canaan*'s happy Land.

P S A L M   LXXVIII.

1.

Y E Nations, to my Law give ear,
 The dictates of my lips revere,
While Heav'n-taught Parables they yield,
And Truths in myftic fong conceal'd:

2.

Truths, which, from earlieft ages heard,
To Us in facred truft transferr'd,
From Sire to Son fucceffive flow,
That lateft times our God may know;

3.

That lateft times in thankful verfe
His boundlefs Mercies may rehearfe,
And own the Wonders of his hand
Whofe pow'r prefides o'er *Judah*'s land.

4.

He, bounteous Parent of mankind,
His Law to *Jacob*'s race confign'd,
(Fit theme!—and worthy to engage
Th' attention of each future age!)

5.

That Children, yet unborn, might learn
That Law, and yield the juft return;
Truft in his aid, his works record,
And mark the precepts of his word:

S 3   6. Unlike

6.

Unlike the Fathers of their line,
Who, rebels to the Will divine,
Turn'd from that Word their stubborn ear,
Nor sought his Love, nor own'd his Fear.

7.

Such *Ephraim*'s sons; a heartless train,
That, arm'd for war, but arm'd in vain,
With bows unbended from the fight
In wild diforder urg'd their flight.

8.

His sacred League, and juft Decrees,
Th' Almighty Lord forgotten sees,
His wonders by their Sires beheld
On *Nile*'s wide banks, and *Zoan*'s field.

9.

What hand but His from side to side
Could bid the foaming Deep divide,
In liquid heaps suspended stand,
And safe transmit the chosen Band?

10.

That hand the cloud around them threw,
Day's kindled fervors to subdue;
And, lit by Him, with friendly ray
The fire nocturnal led their way.

11.

To quench their thirst the copious wave,
Call'd from the rock, its waters gave,
And onward pour'd with headlong haste
Luxuriant lav'd the burning Waste:

12. Strange

12.

Strange to relate ! Yet, stranger still,
Their Bands, rebellious to his Will,
In rash and heighten'd sin conspire,
And dare to wrath the heav'nly Sire,

13.

As o'er the Waste their course they held,
By lawless appetite impell'd,
Each, from th' Almighty's lib'ral hands,
Meat for his fancied want demands.

14.

" Will God, to give his People bread,
" A table in the Desert spread ?
" Our eyes have own'd the flinty Rock
" Obsequious to his mighty stroke,—

15.

" Have seen the streams, with lengthen'd train,
" Run copious o'er the thirsty plain ;
" But can his stores, exhaustless still,
" With flesh our hungring myriads fill ?"

16.

He hears, and now in kindling flames
His vengeance dire at *Israel* aims,
Whose impious speech a heart betray'd
Distrustful of his promis'd aid.

17.

For them He opes the doors of Heav'n,
Back to their wish the clouds are driv'n,
And, downward pour'd, th' ethereal grain
In wide profusion fills the plain.

18. Their

18.

Their wants attentive to fupply,
He gives them Manna from on high :
His fulleſt bounties they have known,
And angels food, and their's are one.

19.

The Winds, that o'er the Defert fly,
New paths, by Him directed, try,
And onward, through th' aerial way,
In flocks the vagrant fowls convey.

20.

Till o'er their tents the cloud impends,
And down the living ſhow'r deſcends,
Thick as the duſt, or as the ſand
That lies upon the fea-beat ſtrand.

21.

Fed to the full, th' infenfate throng
At will the joyous feaſt prolong,
No more their frenzy they reſtrain,
But give their wild defires the rein :

22.

While o'er their heads the vengeful fword
Hangs viewlefs, and but waits the word
To ſnatch their Princes to the tomb,
And *Iſrael*'s choiceſt ſtrength confume.

23.

Yet fuff'rings ſtill to fuff'rings join'd
Fail to correct their faithlefs mind,
Though ſhorten'd in duration ſlow
Their years, and meaſur'd out by woe.

24. When

24.

When struck by his resistless hand,
Their Tribes lie scatter'd o'er the land,
Thus scourg'd his pow'r they humbly own,
And early bow before his throne.

25.

With seeming gratitude possess'd,
His arm each tongue their shield confess'd;
And " who so strong to save," they cry,
" As Thou, great Ruler of the Sky?"

26.

Dissembling praise their lips prepare,
And solemn mockery of pray'r,
While, deep within, a mind they nurse
To Truth and to his Laws averse.

27.

Yet He their trespass can forgive,
And bid th' obdurate Sinners live;
Oft arts of mild persuasion tries,
Nor lets his whole displeasure rise.

28.

Indulgent He their frame survey'd,
Of flesh and frailty knew them made,
A Wind, that life's short passage o'er
Flits transient, and returns no more.

29.

The conscious Wilderness shall tell
How oft the thankless Race rebel;
How oft, by mercies unsubdu'd,
They grieve their Maker, just and good.

30. Yea,

30.

Yea, frantic, to their will they bind
The Counfels of th' eternal mind,
And boldly challenge to the teft
His Pow'r, fo late their Aid confeft,—

31.

When *Cham's* proud offspring felt his Hand
Diffuſing vengeance through their Land,
And fcenes, each hour, to Nature new,
In dreadful feries met their view.

32.

Their *Nile* corrupted now they mourn,
And, though with fierceft thirft they burn,
Start back, affrighted, from the flood;
For Ah! its channel foams with blood.

33.

Athirft for human gore, the Fly
In countlefs legions fills the fky,
And fwarming Frogs, where'er they tread,
With dire intruſion round them fpread.

34.

The Beetle, cluft'ring on their trees,
Now haftes the ripen'd fruit to feize,
While Locufts fell the tiller's toil
Confume, and riot in the fpoil.

35.

By furious Blafts deftroy'd, and torn,
Their fall'n ſhades the forefts mourn;
Their froft-burnt fig-trees fade and die,
Their vines by hailftones ruin'd lie:

36. The

36.

The sturdy tenants of the stall
Beneath the rattling tempests fall;
The flocks, by fire ethereal slain,
In heaps promiscuous strew the plain.

37.

Wrath, horror, trouble, at his word,
Quick on the guilty Race were pour'd,
And Angel-Forms with dreadful haste
From door to door vindictive past.

38.

With course direct his Vengeance flew,
Its path, by Him instructed, knew,
And Pestilence with noxious breath
Sow'd through the air the seeds of death:

39.

Now to the grave, with anguish torn,
Each Mother yields her eldest-born,
And *Egypt*, through her wasted shores,
The first-fruits of her strength deplores.

40.

Now, *Israel*, shines the Day to Thee,
That bids thy captive Sons go free,
Safe as beneath the shepherd's care
The flocks from waste to waste repair.

41.

Each hostile fear by Him dispell'd,
Their destin'd course his People held,
While deep beneath the whelming wave
Their proud Pursuers found a grave.

42. Behold

42.

Behold them, borne to feats of reft,
Seats by his hallow'd prefence bleft,
With joyful ftep the Mount afcend,
By his victorious arm obtain'd.

43.

Lo! there, refiftlefs, *Jacob's* Line
The Tribes whom *Canaan's* tents confine
By Heav'n's high Doom appointed quell,
And from their forfeit Lands expel.

44.

Yet, like their Sires, perverfe they prove,
Reject the offers of his Love,
And led from Wifdom's path aftray
Purfue the tenour of their way;

45.

As ftarts aflant the Bow of fteel,
And faithlefs mocks the archer's fkill,
They, rebels to his juft command,
Elude the guidancè of his hand.

46.

On interdicted Hills uprais'd,
With impious flame their altars blaz'd,
While figures by the Artift made
Thy honours, mightieft Lord, invade.

47.

See, urg'd to wrath, th' eternal Sire
From *Silo's* hallow'd Tent retire,
And quit the feat fo lov'd before,
Refolv'd with Man to dwell no more.

48. His

48.

His Ark, inviolated fhrine
Of Strength and Majefty divine,
Now wanders captive o'er the plains,
Where Guilt in all its horror reigns.

49.

Prevailing foes, conven'd from far,
On *Ifrael* pour the tide of war,
While God his Houfhold from on high
Beholds with alienated eye.

50.

No Virgins to the nuptial band
Affenting give the plighted hand,
While, fnatch'd by the devouring fire,
Their Sons in early youth expire.

51.

The fword deftruction round them fpread,
Nor fpar'd the Prieft's anointed head;
Nor lives the Widow to bemoan
Her Hufband's fate, but meets her own.

52.

His People's cry th' Eternal hears;
As wak'd from fleep, his ftrength he rears,
Shouts like a Giant chear'd with wine,
And wrathful lifts the Arm divine:

53.

Th' averted Foe that Arm confeft,
With fhame and dire difeafe opprefs'd,
Struck with furprize and wild affright
Inglorious backward urg'd their flight.

T   54. But

54.

But where, O *Israel*, shall thy God
Returning chuse his blest Abode ?
Nor *Ephraim*'s Dwellings to his eyes,
Nor Thine, *Manasseh*, grateful rise :

55.

On *Judah*'s Tribe he plac'd his care ;
Thy Temple, *Sion*, founded there,
From age to age his Love demands,
Fix'd as the ground whereon it stands.

56.

That Tribe his *David*'s birth has known,
Rais'd from a sheep-fold to a Throne,
O'er *Jacob*'s realms to stretch the rod
And feed the heritage of God.

57.

As o'er the waste the teeming ewes
His eye with wakeful care pursues,
A Voice arrests the youthful Swain,
And calls him from the humble plain.

58.

He hears, and, while each kingly art
Thy succours to his breast impart,
(All-potent Lord !) with faithful mind
Absolves the charge by Thee assign'd.

P S A L M LXXIX.

I.

O *Israel*'s Father, King, and God !
The Heathen Pow'rs thy lov'd abode
Rapacious seize ; the Heathen Pow'rs
Thy shrine profane ; and *Salem*'s Tow'rs

That

That ftruck with facred awe the eye,
Now whelm'd in wide confufion lie.

2.

Beafts, and each Bird that wings the air,
Thy flaughter'd Saints infatiate tear,
Whofe blood beneath the Victor's fword
In ftreams round *Salem's* walls was pour'd;
None wept their fall, or pitying gave
The cheap indulgence of a grave.

3.

See on our heads each neighbour Foe
Reproach and fierce derifion throw;
See, Lord, and fay how long thine ire
Shall blaze with unextinguifh'd fire,
How long thy Flock are doom'd to prove
The fad fufpenfion of thy Love.

4.

On Nations who thy Laws difown,
Nor yet, with humbled heart, have known
Thy Pow'r to fear, thy Name invoke,
On Thefe, great God, inflict thy ftroke;
On Thefe,—who *Jacob's* ftrength devour,
And ruin on his Dwelling pour.

5.

O let not our tranfgreffions paft
Within thy breaft remember'd laft,
But hafte, while helplefs thus we grieve,
Thy long-loft People to relieve,
And *Ifrael's* trefpafs purg'd away
Thy boundlefs clemency difplay.

6.

Bleſt Saviour ! Let thy pow'r divine
Conſpicuous in our reſcue ſhine ;
Say, why ſhould the reproaching Foe
His triumphs build on *Judah*'s woe,
And aſk, while thus thy ſcourge we bear,
"Where's now your God, ye Outcaſts, where?"

7.

Behold, behold thy Servants ſlain ;
Nor let their loud-tongued blood in vain
The vengeance of thine arm demand,
But give us o'er each hoſtile Land
To ſee thy Wrath terrific riſe,
And Folly's impious Brood chaſtiſe.

8.

O hear the wretched Captive's groan ;
The Souls whom Death hasm ark'd his own
Propitious ſave ; the ceaſeleſs wrongs,
By hands profane, and daring tongues,
Repeated, in thy balance weigh,
And ſev'nfold to thy foes repay.

9.

So ſhall the Flock acknowledg'd thine
To Thee in grateful homage join,
To Thee their loudeſt accents raiſe,
With thankful voices ſing thy praiſe ;
And, long as *Iſrael* boaſts a name,
From ſire to ſon tranſmit thy fame.

PSALM

PSALM LXXX.

1.

SHEPHERD of *Ifrael*, bow thine ear;
O Thou our pray'r indulgent hear,
Who *Jofeph*'s pafture haft prepar'd,
His Guide by day, by night his Guard.

2.

Betwixt the Cherubs feated high,
Glad with thy beams our longing eye :
Thine aid, great God, intreated give,
And teach our fainting hope to live.

3.

With All who from *Manaffes* claim
Their birth, and All of *Ephraim*'s name,
Each hoftile pow'r by Thee o'erthrown,
Let *Benjamin* thy prefence own;

4.

Leader of Hofts, Almighty Lord !
Extend thy fuccours oft implor'd ;
Turn us again, thy face difplay,
And grief and fear fhall fly away.

5.

How long fhall *Ifrael*'s Offspring fee
Thy wrath (while thus with bended knee
Their fupplicating hands they fpread,)
Smoke unextinguifh'd o'er their head ?

6.

Her food the bread of tears, her draught
With forrow's largeft mixture fraught,
Sad *Sion* fees deriding foes
Her fons, their deftin'd prey, inclofe.

T 3   7. Leader

7.

Leader of Hosts, Almighty Lord !
Extend thy succours oft implor'd ;
Turn us again, thy face display,
And grief and fear shall fly away.

8.

Each pow'r in adverse league combin'd,
To just excision first consign'd,
Behold a Vine from *Egypt*'s Land,
Transplanted by thy fost'ring hand :

9.

Behold in *Canaan*'s shores, her bed
By Thee prepar'd, her root outspread
Far as the utmost coast extends ;
While o'er the Hills her shade ascends.

10.

Her branches tow'ring to the skies
With healthful stem conspicuous rise,
And round the Cedar's loftiest boughs
Her cov'ring veil intwin'd she throws.

11.

Long cherish'd by thy care she stood ;
Here, verging tow'rd th' *Assyrian* Flood,
In circuit wide the earth she crown'd,
And, There, the Ocean mark'd her bound.

12.

But now, in sad reverse, (Ah ! why ?)
By Thee o'erthrown the fences lie,
The fruit expos'd beside the way,
To each rapacious hand a prey.

13. The

13.

The favage Boar with reftlefs toil
Uproots it from the loofen'd foil,
And ev'ry Monfter of the wood
Crops from the branch his obvious food.

14.

Leader of Hofts, and *Ifrael*'s Lord!
Return : Thy fuccours oft implor'd
Extend : from Heav'n's high feat incline
Thy eyes, and vifit this thy Vine.

15.

Behold the offspring of thy hand,
The Plant, which Thou hadft bid to ftand,
And ftrengthen'd by thy pow'r defy
Each ftorm that rends the wintry fky :

16.

The gath'ring flames its trunk furround,
Its ruin'd honours ftrew the ground.
Beneath the terrors of thine eye
We tremble, Lord, we faint, we die.

17.

O let the Man whom, arm'd with might,
Thy hand ordains our caufe to right,
By Thee, great God, fupported ftand;
And fave, O fave, a finking Land.

18.

So ne'er fhall Sin our fouls enflave;
O fnatch us from th' expecting grave,
And ev'ry knee to Thee fhall bend,
Thy praife from ev'ry tongue afcend.

19. Leader

19.

Leader of Hofts, Almighty Lord !
Extend thy fuccours oft implor'd ;
Turn us again, thy face difplay,
And grief and fear fhall fly away.

P S A L M   LXXXI.

1.

TO God our Strength exalt the fong,
To *Jacob*'s Lord the note prolong ;
Prepare, prepare with tuneful art
Your fhares of harmony to part :

2.

Come, take the Hymn, the timbrel ring,
Praife on the harp your heav'nly King ;
Strike into life the trembling wire,
With loudeft blafts the trump infpire ;

3.

For fee the Moon with recent horn
Lead joyous on the feftal Morn,
Whofe hallow'd mirth to *Ifrael*'s Tribes
Thy Mandate, mightieft Lord, prefcribes.

4.

Its juft obfervance *Jofeph* learn'd,
When, pleas'd, with parting ftep he fpurn'd
The ruthlefs foil, along whofe fhore
A voice he heard unknown before.

5.

Thus fpake th' Almighty—I, his God,
I from his fhoulders took the load ;
I from the clay his toiling hands
Releas'd, and burft his ftubborn bands.

6. O Thou,

6.

O Thou, the voice of whofe diftrefs
From out the thunder's dark recefs,
Propitious to thy pray'r, I heard;
In whofe defence my arm I rear'd;

7.

Whofe faith my light inflictions tried
Near *Meribah*'s contentious tide,
O *Ifrael!*—with attentive ear
Thy Maker's juft injunction hear.

8.

Let none thy homage claim but Me,
Nor bow to foreign Gods the knee;
Jehovah only be thy Dread;
Thy footfteps He from *Egypt* led;

9.

He gracious bids thee wide extend
Thy lap, while down his gifts defcend,
And ftreaming copious from on high
Yield to thy wifh the full fupply.

10.

Thus fpake my Voice, but fpake in vain;
Th' obdurate Race, with fierce difdain,
Refolv'd their error to purfue,
Back from my yoke their neck withdrew.

11.

No more their frenzy I reftrain,
But give their wild defires the rein,
And leave them, guidelefs, to fulfil
The dictates of a headlong Will.

12. O had

12.

O had my People in their breaſt,
By heav'nly Diſcipline impreſs'd,
The leſſons of my Love retain'd,
And trod the path by Me ordain'd !

13.

When forth to War thy troops were led,
Myſelf, O *Iſrael*, at their head
Had met the Battle on its way,
Thy Guide to Time's remoteſt day ;—

14.

Each humbled foe had own'd thy pow'r,
To eaſe thy want, its pureſt flour.
Th' augmented harveſt had beſtow'd,
And honey from the rock had flow'd.

P S A L M LXXXII.

1.

WHile, cloth'd with pow'r divine, their bar
Earth's Lords have fix'd, a mightier far
Amidſt the Conſiſtory ſtands,
And juſtice from their lips demands.

2.

How long ſhall your unequal ſcale
Thus bid the impious cauſe prevail ?
Why are your thoughts by Falſehood ſway'd,
And not in Reaſon's balance weigh'd ?

3. Let

3.

Let Law the Orphan's claim fecure;
Lend to the helplefs and the poor
Your willing ear; affert their right,
And fave them from oppreffive might.

4.

In vain I call: Their ftubborn mind
To blackeft darknefs is refign'd,
While Earth the dire confufion feels,
And, groaning, to her centre reels.

5.

Gods Ye were nam'd; Earth's tribes in You
The Sons of Heav'n's high Monarch view;
But Death your frailty fhall betray,
And mix with vulgar mould your clay.

6.

Rife, mightieft King, to judgment rife,
Th' oppress'd redeem, the proud chaftife,
Till Man's whole offspring Thee alone
Their Lord and juft Poffeffor own.

PSALM   LXXXIII.

I.

MY God, no longer filent ftand;
No longer let thy pow'rful hand
Withhold its oft-requefted aid,
While thus thy foes our peace invade;

2.

While flufh'd with hope the impious Band
In mingled tumult round us ftand,
Exulting in our forrows rife,
And brave with lifted head the fkies.

3. Behold

3.

Behold them, Lord, their arts employ,
The Heav'n-rais'd People to deftroy,
The Souls, whom with thy favour crown'd
Thy fecret prefence wraps around.

4.

" Come, (thus, by lawlefs fury led,
" Aloud they cry,) deftruction fpread
" Along their defolated fhore,
" Till *Ifrael*'s name be heard no more."

5.

Their leagues, their plans, with frantic aim,
Againft Omnipotence they frame ;
And, fir'd to rage, with fierce alarms
The headlong Nations rufh to arms.

6.

The tents of *Edom* o'er the plain
Here vomit forth their impious train,
While with the Sons of *Ifmael*'s line
The harnefs'd *Agaræans* join.

7.

Here *Gebal, Moab, Ammon* ftand,
With vengeance arm'd th' unconquer'd band
Of *Amalek* in clofe array
The triumphs of their heart betray.

8.

See, fearlefs, with imperial *Tyre*
Philiftia's habitants confpire ;
See *Affur* draw the hoftile blade,
And lend to *Lot*'s vile race his aid.

9. But

9.

But give them, Lord, thine Arm to feel,
That Arm that made fierce *Midian* reel,
And to th' expecting Mother's pride
Her *Sifera*'s return denied ;—

10.

That *Jabin*'s warlike troops fubdu'd
Near ancient *Kifon*'s purpled flood,
While *Endor Ifrael*'s foes beheld
Enrich with flaughter'd heaps her field.

11.

As *Oreb*, and as *Zeeb* o'erthrown,
Beneath thy terrors let them groan ;
And feel that vengeance which thy fword
On *Zebah* and *Zalmunna* pour'd.

12.

Such let their Princes, Lord, endure,
Who vaunting to their arms infure
The Land by holy Patriarchs trod,
The Heritage of *Jacob*'s God ;

13.

Such let their Princes ever find ;
As thiftle-down before the wind,
As chaff, as ftubble, let them fly,
That driv'n in air obfcure the fky.

14.

Swift as the fiery deluge ftrays,
And wraps the foreft in its blaze,
Or, furious, onward as it pours,
The mountain's fhaggy wafte devours,—

U   15. Purfue

15.

Pursue them, mightiest Lord, pursue,
And let thy vengeance, to their view
Presented, whelm their souls in dread,
And burst in tempests o'er their head.

16.

With wild confusion clothe their cheek,
And teach them, Lord, thy Name to seek,
While ruin, death, and shame, they see
To each ordain'd that errs from Thee.

17.

" *Jehovah*," shall the Rebels cry,
" *Jehovah* only reigns on high,
" And o'er the Earth from day to day
" Asserts his everlasting Sway."

P S A L M   LXXXIV.

1.

HOW sweet thy Dwellings, Lord, how
fair !
What Peace, what Bliss, inhabit there !
With ardent hope, with strong desire,
My heart, my flesh, to Thee aspire ;
I burn to tread thy Courts, and Thee,
My God, the living God, to see.

2.

Eternal King, within thy Dome
The Sparrow finds her peaceful home ;
With her the Dove, a licens'd Guest,
Assiduous tends her infant nest,

And

And to thy Altar's fure defence
Commits th' unfeather'd innocence.

3.

Bleft, who, like thefe, from day to day
To praife Thee in thy Temple ftay;
Bleft, who, their ftrength on Thee reclin'd,
Thy Seat explore with conftant mind,
And, *Salem*'s diftant tow'rs in view,
With active zeal their way purfue:

4.

Secure the thirfty Vale they tread,
While, call'd from out their fandy bed,
As grateful fhow'rs from Heav'n diftill'd
Which frefheft, kindlieft moifture yield,
The copious fprings their fteps beguile,
And bid the chearlefs Defert fmile.

5.

From ftage to ftage advancing ftill,
Behold them reach fair *Sion*'s hill,
And proftrate at her hallow'd fhrine,
Adore the Majefty divine,
Where thy refulgent glory fpreads
Its pureft fplendors o'er their heads.

6.

O Thou, whom Heav'n's high Hofts revere
God of our Fathers, bow thine ear:
Look down, our only Hope! look down;
Behold us, but without a frown;
And let thy beams, in mercy fhed,
Stream copious on th' anointed head.

U 2   7. One

7.

One day if in thy Courts I dwell,
That day a thousand shall excel ;
Far happier lot on Thee to wait,
And guard th' approaches of thy gate,
Than with the impious sons of Pride
In rich pavilions to abide. .

8.

Thou, Lord, art *Israel's* Sun and Shield ;
Thy Love shall grace and glory yield,
Nor e'er permit the pious train
Thy gifts to ask, and ask in vain.
Blest, who in confidence of pray'r
To Thee, great God, resign their care.

P S A L M   LXXXV.

1.

OUR eyes, great God, have seen thy grace
   Its beams effuse on *Jacob's* race,
Loose from their chains the captive Band,
And call them to their native land.

2.

Thy Mercy, Lord, their woes has heal'd,
Their trespass hid, their pardon seal'd,
Check'd in mid course thy dreadful ire,
And bid its kindled flames expire.

3.

O grant us still thy Love to share ;
God of our health ! accept the pray'r,
That seeks thy clemency to win,
And cleanse, O cleanse us from our sin.

4. How

4.

How long fhall *Jacob*'s offspring prove
The fad fufpenfion of thy Love;
Say, fhall thy Wrath perpetual burn;
And wilt thou ne'er, appeas'd, return?

5.

Wilt thou thy quick'ning force impart,
And wake to mirth each grateful heart,
While *Ifrael*'s refcu'd Tribes in Thee
Their Blifs and full Salvation fee?

6.

No longer, heav'nly Sire, delay
Thy wonted Mercy to difplay,
But let thy All-difpofing Will
Thy People's ftedfaft hope fulfil.

7.

Rev'rent I wait God's high Decree;
What fhall he fpeak, but peace, to Thee
O *Ifrael*; and to each who learns
His Law, nor back to fin returns?

8.

Behold, ye Souls that own his fear,
Behold your wifh'd Redemption near;
See Glory make our Land her feat,
There Verity and Mercy meet.

9.

With mutual ftep advancing There
Shall Peace and Juftice, heav'nly Pair,
To lafting compact onward move,
Seal'd by the kifs of facred Love.

10. Truth

10.

Truth from thy furrows, Earth, shall spring,
And Righteousness on healing wing
From Heav'n descend, while God our toil
Shall crown, and bless our happy soil.

11.

She, as on earth thy feet shall tread,
Shall march direct, with lifted head
Preceding, and with duteous care
'Thy path, eternal King, prepare.

PSALM LXXXVI.

1.

LORD! to my wants thy ear incline;
  Behold me, as with grief I pine;
My hope confirm, and guard from ill
A soul subjected to thy Will.

2.

From rising to declining day
To Thee with fervent lip I pray;
Propitious, to thy servant's heart
Thy chearing influence impart:

3.

To Thee, to Thee I vent my care;
I know thee, Lord, nor slow to spare,
Nor weak to vindicate from harm
The Souls with pure devotion warm.

4.

My days with sorrow clouded o'er,
Thy wonted succours I implore:
Regard me, gracious; nor forbear
The voice of my request to hear.

5. What

5.

What pow'r, great God, fhall boaft a name
Like Thine ; like Thee our homage claim ?
Or who, among the feats divine,
Difplay fuch wond'rous Works as thine ?

6.

Behold, their Maker taught to own,
Earth's future Sons before thy Throne
In *Sion* fuppliant kneel, and raife
To *Ifrael*'s God their joyful Lays.

7.

Eternal Excellence ! Thy hand
At will fhall Nature's pow'rs command ;
Thy wonders, through her confines wide,
She fpeaks, nor owns a God befide.

8.

O give me, Lord, thy paths to tread,
And, while thy Truth my fteps fhall lead,
(The faithful Guide by Thee affign'd,)
Train to thy fear my willing mind.

9.

My heart, by facred zeal impell'd,
To Thee the grateful fong fhall yield ;
My Tongue, the witnefs of thy Fame,
Thy boundlefs Glory fhall proclaim.

10.

Long as I breathe the vital air
Thy Love my loudeft praife fhall fhare,
Whofe aid my foul with health has crown'd,
And fnatch'd me from the pit profound.

11.

Thou feeſt, my God, the Sons of Pride,
In leagues of violence allied,
(Thy fear behind them thrown) my way
Surround, and mark me for their prey:

12.

But well my great Preſerver knows
To weigh and to relieve my woes ;
Suſtain'd by his Almighty aid,
What danger can my Soul invade ?

13.

Long is thy patience, ſlow thine ire ;
Eternal Mercy, mightieſt Sire,
Thy word (on that my truſt I build ;)
And unrepenting Truth have ſeal'd.

14.

My griefs with tend'reſt pity view,
With ſtrength thy Servant's heart renew,
And inſtant from th' expecting grave
The Offspring of thy Handmaid ſave.

15.

O grant me, Lord, ſome fav'ring ſign,
Some pledge that may beſpeak me Thine,
That, ſtung with ſhame, my foes may ſee
What Aid, what Bliſs, I boaſt in Thee.

PSALM LXXXVII.

1.

FIX'D is thy baſe : throughout its coaſts
No city *Jacob*'s region boaſts,
Whoſe gates, O *Sion*, ſhare, like thine,
The favour of the hand divine.

2. Thee

2.

Thee God the Manfion of his reft,
And Seat of Empire has confefs'd,
While thus aloud to lateft days
His heav'nly Edict fpeaks thy praife ;

3.

Amidft the Souls that own my fway,
And learn my precepts to obey,
Thy Sons, O *Nile*, fhall find a place,
And *Babylon*'s accepted Race ;

4.

Nor thine, O *Tyre*, nor, *Midian*, thine,
Nor whom *Philiftia*'s bounds confine,
Excluded from my thought fhall ftand,
But mix with *Sion*'s facred Band.

5.

Each tenant of the peopled Earth
Shall claim from Her his happy birth :
Aliens no more, within her Seat
Behold th' united Myriads meet :

6.

Joyous they tread her bleft Abode,
The *Ifrael* and the Heirs of God :
That God, whofe pow'r upholds her State,
And feals to endlefs time her date.

7.

When on the page, whofe wide extent
Shall *Adam*'s num'rous Line prefent,
Each Kindred, Family, and Tribe,
Th' eternal Cenfor fhall infcribe,—

8. His

8.

His hand th' adopted Names fhall there
Thy Natives, *Solyma*, declare,
And bid them with thy Sons refide,
In concord's ftricteft bands allied.

9.

Hark, how the trump, and tuneful tongue,
The facred Jubilee prolong,
To notes of loudeft triumph rife,
And echo to the diftant fkies:

10.

While I (thy Maker, God, and King,)
I, *Salem*, bid the living Spring
Amid thee yield its copious ftore,
And crown with health thy happy fhore.

PSALM   LXXXVIII.

1.

GOD of my health! To Thee by day,
  To Thee by night, aloud I pray:
O bend thine ear, and let my cries
Accepted to thy throne arife.

2.

Satiate of griefs, with downward feet
I feek the hollow grave's retreat,
And, ftrengthlefs, mingle with the train
That fill its melancholy reign.

3.

A Gueft familiar of the Dead,
Lo, in the duft I make my bed,
As One, on whom thy ftroke its aim
Directs, and blots from Earth his name.

4. As,

4.

As, loſt to ev'ry human eye,
Deep in the loweſt pit I lie,
Thy wrath incumbent whelms me o'er,
And all thy billows round me roar.

5.

No friendly feet approach me nigh,
But backward all abhorrent fly ;
With horror ſtruck, the ſight forego,
And ſhun th' infection of my woe.

6.

While, in my priſon faſt immur'd,
My eye with ſorrow's miſt obſcur'd,
With ceaſeleſs moan my ſuppliant hand
To Thee, great Monarch, I expand.

7.

Shall, whom the bands of death infold,
The wonders of thy pow'r behold,
And, ſtarting from the tomb, thy Name
In hymns of joyful praiſe proclaim ?

8.

Shall echo on thy Mercies dwell
Amid the dark ſepulchral cell ?
Or through Deſtruction's vaults profound
Thy Truth, eternal God, reſound ?

9.

Shall regions that exclude the day
Thy miracles to view diſplay,
And pale Oblivion's confines drear
The records of thy Juſtice hear ?

10. To

10.

To Thee I call; to Thee in pray'r
At earlieſt dawn diſcloſe my care:
Lord! why haſt Thou my ſoul repell'd?
Why thus·thy quick'ning beams withheld?

11.

Ere yet to manly years I grew,
My fainting heart thy terrors knew,
And through ſucceeding life ſuſtains
A long viciſſitude of pains.

12.

Beneath thy heavy hand I groan;
Woes heap'd on woes come rolling on,
And o'er me hang, ordain'd by Thee,
Tremendous.as a ſwelling ſea.

13.

Each Friend, that wont my board to ſhare,
Each kind Conſoler of my care,
As round I look, my ſight evades,
And ſeeks concealment's thickeſt ſhades.

PSALM LXXXIX.

1.

MY grateful tongue, immortal King,
Thy Mercy ſhall for ever ſing,
My verſe to time's remoteſt day
Thy Truth in ſacred notes diſplay.

2.

That Mercy (thus thy Voice mine ear
Beſpeaks,) on firmeſt baſe I rear;
That Truth in Heav'n my lips command
From age to age confirm'd to ſtand.

3. My

3.

My Love to *Jeſſe*'s Son reveal'd
Th' irrevocable Oath has ſeal'd ;
Th' irrevocable Oath is ſworn,
Nought ſhall my ſteady purpoſe turn.

4.

Bleſt Object of my choice! Thy Line,
Protected by the Hand divine,
In long deſcent thy Throne ſhall heir,
Nor rolling years their pow'r impair.

5.

Thy Acts, great God, Heav'n's lofty Seat
With awful wonder ſhall repeat ;
Aſſembled Saints their voice ſhall raiſe,
And ev'ry tongue proclaim thy praiſe.

6.

O ſay, what ſtrength ſhall vie with Thine ?
What Name among the Seats divine,
Of equal excellence poſſeſs'd,
Thy ſov'reignty, great God, conteſt ?

7.

Ye Tribes that form his choſen Choir,
Let *Iſrael*'s God your fear inſpire,
Ye Natives of each neighb'ring ſhore,
With proſtrate hearts his pow'r adore.

8.

Thee, Lord, Heav'n's Hoſts their Leader own;
Thee Might unbounded, Thee alone,
With endleſs majeſty has crown'd,
And faith unſullied veſts thee round.

X   9. 'Tis

9.

'Tis thine the Ocean's rage to guide,
And calm at will its swelling tide:
From Thee the deep-inflicted wound,
Her guilt's just portion, *Egypt* found;

10.

When, rang'd in fight, the lawless Band
Thy pow'r, presumptuous, durst withstand,
Each foe thine Arm beheld with dread,
And back in wild confusion fled.

11.

The Heav'n above, and Earth below,
Thee, Lord, their great Possessor know;
By Thee this Orb to being rose,
And All that Nature's bounds inclose.

12.

While *Tabor*'s brow, with ev'ning red,
And Eastern *Hermon*'s unshorn head,
Wide through their echoing groves thy name
In songs of grateful joy proclaim ;—

13.

From Thee amid th'ethereal space
The North and South assume their place;
Strong is thine Arm; thy stedfast Will
Thy Hands with sure effect fulfil;

14.

While Justice, 'mid th' ethereal plain,
And Equity thy Throne sustain,
And white-rob'd Truth and Mercy fair
Thy steps precede, thy path prepare.

15. O,

15.

O, Bleſt the Tribes, whoſe willing ear
Awakes the feſtal ſhout to hear;
Who thankful ſee, where'er they tread,
Thy fav'ring beams around them ſpread.

16.

How ſhall they joy from day to day
Thy boundleſs Mercy to diſplay,
Thy Righteouſneſs, indulgent Lord,
With holy confidence record.

17.

By bleſt experience taught to know
What bleſſings from thy Bounty flow!
Thy Strength their fureſt help they deem,
Thy Grace their dignity ſupreme!

18.

Behold, ye Saints, behold a Shield
In *Iſrael's* aid by God upheld;
Behold exalted to the Throne
A King, whom He has ſeal'd his own.

19.

Thy Viſions, Lord, from Heav'n reveal'd,
The raptur'd Prophet has beheld;
And thus thy Voice in awful ſtrains
The purpoſe of thy Love explains.

20.

To One ſelected from thy Line
Thy ſafety, *Jacob*, I conſign,
And, cloth'd with ſtrength, before thy eyes
High o'er his Equals bid him riſe.

 21. See

21.

See *David*, prompt my will t' obey :
On Him th' important charge I lay;
And copious on his favour'd head
The consecrating unction shed.

22.

My hand shall hold him faft ; my care
From each affault, from ev'ry fnare,
Shall guard him; nigh me shall he ftand
Safe from each proud Oppreffor's hand.

23.

When hoftile Crouds his wrath provoke;
With certain and refiftlefs ftroke
My Arm shall crush the impious train,
And load with flaughter'd heaps the plain.

24.

On Mercy and on Truth divine
Behold him (nor in vain) recline
His truft, and, by my ftrength upborne,
Aloft, exulting, lift the horn ;

25.

While (fuch my Will) o'er fubject Lands
In wide extent are ftretch'd his hands;
Beneath his left the Ocean rolls,
His right th' *Affyrian* Flood controuls.

26.

Thou art my Father, (thus my Name
His lips, inftinct with grateful flame,
Aloud shall hail ;) My God in Thee,
And Rock of fure defence, I fee.

:   27. Him

27.

Him, pleas'd, my Firstborn I avow,
Bid mightiest Kings before him bow,
And Blessings to his reach expand,
Insur'd by Compact's sacred band.

28.

Transfer'd by Me from Sire to Son,
To Heav'n's extremest date his Throne
Shall last; if to my Laws his line,
With grateful zeal, their steps incline:

29.

But should their hearts reject my sway,
Fond in forbidden paths to stray,
My rod their trespass shall pursue,
My scourge their stubborn will subdue.

30.

Yet never, never, shall my Love
From Him its steady beams remove;
Ne'er shall my Truth forget to guard
The promise by my lips declar'd.

31.

To *David*, once, (nor need I more,)
Once by my Sanctity I swore,
That, cherish'd by my care, his Race
Thy Throne, O *Judah*, long shall grace;

32.

Long as the Sun, with welcome ray,
Shall warmth and life to Earth convey,
Or Thou, O Moon, in circuit wide
The witness of my Compact glide.

33.

Yet Ah! repuls'd, contemn'd, by Thee,
Th' Anointed of thy hand we fee
No more thy plighted mercy fhare,
But, doom'd thy wrath, juft God, to bear.

34.

With countlefs woes he ftrives : His Crown
Low in the duft by Thee is thrown;
No more his Forts afcend on high,
But, fall'n, in heapy ruins lie;

35.

No more his Walls the War exclude;
But paffers-by with infult rude
His rights invade, and Nations round
His ear with keen reproaches wound.

36.

Behold while rang'd in clofe array
Infulting hofts around him ftay,
Their band by Thine uprais'd, each foe
Aims at his head the deathful blow;

37.

With ficrceft joy their bofom burns,
While back with edge rebated turns
His fword, and, thy fupport withheld,
His vanquifh'd legions quit the field.

38.

His pow'r extinct, his luftre gone,
On earth, fubverted, lies his Throne :
Age on his Youth has ftoln ; and fhame
With thickeft cloud obfcures his fame.

39. How

39.

How long shall I, with anguish torn,
Thy face, my God, averted mourn?
How long behold, in dire amaze,
Thy wrath with flames inceffant blaze?

40.

O weigh within thy thought my State!
How frail my life! how short its date!
Why is thine Art employ'd in vain,
Or Man created but to pain?

41.

O leave not, Lord, my doubtful Mind
To sad inquietude resign'd,
While thus through varied scenes of woe
With hast'ning step to death we go.

42.

For who shall boaft, of human frame,
Exemption from his doom to claim,
Or, arm'd with native might, withftand
The Sepulchre's rapacious hand?

43.

Say, where is now the Love, O where,
Which erft thy lips to *David* fware?
That Love, by Truth eternal feal'd,
Again to view, great Father, yield:

44.

O think what wrongs thy Servants bear,
Wrongs pour'd on Me in largeft fhare,
As deep within my filent breaft
Each offer'd infult I digeft.

45. Elate

45.

Elate with pow'r, the nations round
My Ear with keen reproaches wound,
And impious Crouds his fteps revile,
Whom Thou haft touch'd with facred oil.

46.

O wife in all thy Works! thy Name
Let Man's whole Race aloud proclaim,
And, grateful, through the length of days,
In ceafelefs fongs repeat thy praife.

PSALM XC.

1.

THEE, Lord, their dwelling, Thee alone
From earlieft age thy People own:
Thee, Lord, with fulleft confidence
They boaft their Refuge and Defence.

2.

Ere yet the Mountains rofe to birth,
Ere yet their form the Heav'ns and Earth
Affum'd, Thou cloth'd in light divine
Haft fhone; and fhalt for ever fhine.

3.

Thou to the Sons of human kind
In fhort extenfion haft affign'd
Their term, and bid them, at its end,
Low to their native duft defcend.

4.

To Thee as Yefterday appears
The profpect of a thoufand Years;
And Ages, roll'd fucceffive on,
Quick as the circling Watch are gone.

5. As

5.

As plants that drink the nightly fhow'r,
Refrefh'd by fleep's irriguous pow'r
At morn they flourifh: Ev'ning nigh,
Cropt like the plant, they fade and die.

6.

Thy hand with unremitted force
In mid progreffion ftops our courfe,
While ftorms of vengeance round us roll,
And whelm in dread our confcious foul.

7.

Thy eyes our inmoft guilt can read;
Thy prefence, Lord, on each mifdeed,
That ftudious fhuns the fight of day,
Refiftlefs darts its fearching ray.

8.

See, faft as words diffolv'd in air,
While crimes on crimes thy Juftice dare,
Our days in rapid flight confume,
And bear us onward to the tomb.

9.

Its date to fev'nty years confin'd,
If aught of life remain behind,
If Nature yet a ten years' day
Indulge us, ere her debt we pay,—

10.

Our ftrength but weaknefs then we know,
And added Age but lengthen'd Woe;
Stripp'd of our pride, we clofe our fpan,
And vanifh from the eye of Man.

11. O,

11.

O, who thy terrors juftly weighs?
Who to thy pow'r fubmiffive pays
The homage due? Thy vengeance drear
They feel proportion'd to their fear.

12.

Teach us, kind Lord, O teach us Thou
To count life's moments as they flow,
And, while its end our thoughts furvey,
By Wifdom's line to guide our way.

13.

Return, All-potent Lord, return:
How long fhall we thy abfence mourn?
Return, and let thy wonted Love
With fpeedieft aid our griefs remove:

14.

Thy Mercy, to our Souls reveal'd,
Satiety of blifs fhall yield,
And, while thy breath our life prolongs,
With grateful mirth infpire our tongues:

15.

That Mercy, mightieft Lord, difplay;
And bid at length fome happier day
Compenfate with its joys the years
Confign'd to forrow, groans, and tears.

16.

Author of Good, thy Work mature;
Let *Ifrael's* Tribes, in Thee fecure,
From age to age the Bleffings trace
Intail'd on their diftinguifh'd Race.

17. Q

17.

O let thy Majefty divine
On us in perfect beauty fhine,
And ftreaming copious o'er our head
Its mildeft beams around us fpread :

18.

And while, new Scenes of hope to view
Difclos'd, our labour we purfue,
O may thy hand with full fuccefs
That hope confirm, that labour blefs.

P S A L M XCI.

1.

WHO makes Omnipotence his Aid,
    Who refts beneath *Jehovah*'s fhade,
And joyful cries, " My God in Thee
" My Fortrefs and my Hope I fee,"—

2.

How bleft that Man!—Thy Maker's care
Shall fnatch thee from the hunter's fnare :
When fick'ning Nature's pow'rs fhall fail,
No fatal ftroke fhall Thee affail :

3.

His wings around thee fhall be fpread,
His pinions guard thy favour'd head :
His Truth, thy all-protecting fhield,
From hoftile rage a fhelter yield.

4.

Hail, favour'd Man! nor terror pale
By night fhall o'er thy foul prevail,
Nor fhaft, that aims its flight by day,
Thy guiltlefs bofom fhall difmay;

§   5. Nor

5.

Nor Plague, that with gigantic ſtride
In darkneſs walks its circuit wide,
Nor ſultry blaſt, whoſe dreaded breath
Taints the meridian air with death.

6.

Though thouſands by thy ſide are ſlain,
And myriads round thee preſs the plain,
No dart ſhall thy deſtruction dare,
Or wound whom God has bid to ſpare.

7.

Behold him on each impious head
The fulneſs of his vengeance ſhed :
Thy foes before thine eyes o'erthrown,
Still ſhalt thou paſs in triumph on ;

8.

And, ſince thy heart, to God reſign'd,
In him its refuge boaſts to find,
No dangers ſhall thy path await,
Or touch thine interdicted gate.

9.

While, round thee plac'd, th' Angelic Train
Thy ſteps with tend'reſt care ſuſtain,
Safe ſhalt thou walk through ways unknown,
Nor ſtrike thy foot againſt the ſtone.

10.

Go, fearleſs on the Dragon tread,
And preſs the proſtrate Lion's head :
Behold the Tyrant of the wood
In vain with youthful ſtrength indu'd ;

11. Behold

11.

Behold the Serpent (in his veins
Though half the poiſon of the plains
Be lodg'd,) before thee vanquiſh'd lie,
And cloſe in death his languid eye.

12.

Thy duteous Zeal, thy filial Love,
I mark, and all thy Acts approve:
For this, thy head aloft I rear,
And bow to thy requeſts my ear.

13.

Thy fears, thy ſorrows I attend,
Thy God, thy Guardian, and thy Friend;
Thy years prolong, and to thy heart
My health-diſpenſing grace impart.

PSALM XCII.

1.

HOW bleſt the taſk, with fervent heart
To ſummon from the tuneful Art
Its ſuccours, and thy Name record,
O Thou whom Nature owns her Lord!

2.

Thy boundleſs Mercies, heav'nly King,
At morning's earlieſt hour to ſing,
And, rapt in praiſe, thy Truth to tell,
When night's dark ſhades around us dwell.

3.

While with the ten-ſtring'd inſtrument
The pſaltry's meaſur'd ſtrains conſent,
And o'er the harp each liquid note
With ſolemn ſound is taught to float.

4.

How have thy Acts my wakeful breaſt
With rapt'rous gratitude impreſs'd !
How joys my tongue, with holy flame
Inſpir'd, thy Wonders to proclaim !

5.

With what delight, great God, I trace
Each Act of thy ſtupendous grace !
Great are the works thy hand has wrought,
And deep beyond all ſearch thy Thought.

6.

Thy Acts the minds of brutiſh mould
With unregarding eye behold,
And, ſtrangers to thy wiſe deſign,
In erring cenſure madly join;—

7.

Nor know, that, when the impious Band,
Freſh as the flow'r, conſpicuous ſtand,
Mature for death their heads they rear,
And ſwift deſtruction waits them near.

8.

But Thou, above the ſtarry plain,
In endleſs Majeſty ſhalt reign :
And downward from th' ethereal height,
O'er ſubject worlds extend thy might.

9.

Thy foes, eternal God, thy foes
In death's long ſleep their eyes ſhall cloſe,
And all, whoſe hearts thy pow'r defy,
In wide diſperſion backward fly :

While

10.

While I, by heav'nly Might upborne,
Strong as the Oryx lift the horn;
  Ando'er my head in copious show'rs
Thy Oil its richest fragrance pours.

11.

When factious Crouds against me rise,
With scenes of triumph Thou my eyes
Shalt satiate, and their full defeat
My ears with happiest tidings greet.

12.

Fair as amidst their native bed
The stately Palms their branches spread,
Or Cedars, tow'ring to the skies,
On *Lebanon*'s broad summit rise;

13.

Within thy Courts the Just shall stand
And, nourish'd by thy fost'ring hand,
Blest Objects of thy constant care,
The bounties of thy Love shall share.

14.

Their fruits, each blast by Thee repell'd,
To latest age they still shall yield
In large increase, through life's whole round
With health and youthful verdure crown'd.

15.

Thy Goodness shall their lips record,
(God of my strength!) thy ev'ry Word
InTruth's unvarying balance weigh'd,
Thy ev'ry Act by Justice sway'd.

PSALM XCIII.

1.

THE Lord th' eternal fcepter rears,
   And Nature's pow'r obfervant hears
    Whate'er his Will enjoins :
His head with pureft fplendors crown'd,
With Majefty he vefts him round,
And girds with ftrength his loins.

2.

Encircled by th' ethereal fpace,
And fix'd by Him on firmeft bafe,
    The Earth's vaft Orb appears :
.From earlieft age, great God, thy Throne
Aloft in Heav'n prepar'd has fhone ;
    Nor numbers Time thy years.

3.

A fcene of horror ftrikes my eyes ;
The Floods, my God, the Floods arife,
    And lift their voice on high :
What pow'r fhall curb the headlong tide ?
What bid the fwelling waves fubfide,
    And clear the ftormy fky ?

4.

Thee o'er all height exalted, Thee
The Deeps revere ; at thy Decree
    The Waves their rage refign :
Fix'd are the Laws by Thee ordain'd ;
And Truth and Sanctity unftain'd
    Adorn thy awful fhrine.

PSALM

PSALM XCIV.

1.

THOU God, with vengeance arm'd,
     appear;
Thou God, with vengeance arm'd, whose fear
The Earth (for Thee her Judge she knows,)
Submissive owns, thy pow'r disclose.

2.

O instant from thy seat arise,
Each bold transgressor to chastise;
Let Justice to the Sons of pride
Thy stroke with aim unerring guide.

3.

How long shall impious Crouds, how long,
With haughtiest insult arm their tongue?
How long in bitt'rest gall each word
Infuse, and boast their conqu'ring sword?

4.

Thy Flock, great God, their fury own;
Beneath their stroke thy People groan:
And long thy heritage have borne
Their keen reproach and hostile scorn.

5

Their hands remorseless, to the tomb
The Widow and the Stranger doom;
Nor innocence nor tend'rest age
Can shield the Orphan from their rage.

     6. " Ne'er

6.

" Ne'er fhall our deeds in Heav'n be known,
" Or reach (they cry,) the diftant Throne
" Or *Ifrael*'s Lord."—Ye fools and blind!
Return, and feek a better mind.

7.

Say when fhall Wifdom's light ferene
Your Souls from error's chidhood wean ?
Who knew to plant the ear, fhall HE
Not hear ? Who form'd the eye, not fee?

8.

Shall aught of guilt his fearch evade,
Who bids the Nations he has made,
Inform'd by his paternal care,
The gifts of various Science fhare,—

9.

Who Reafon in the bofom pours,
Its growth improves, its fruit matures,
Each counfel of the human brain
Weighs in his fcale, and ftamps it vain?

10.

O, Bleft the man, for ever bleft,
Whofe faithful heart by thee imprefs'd,
Eternal Teacher, from thy Laws
The leffons of his conduct draws ;

11.

Who fhelter'd from the evil day
Its diftant dangers fhall furvey,
And wait till Thou the pit prepare
For each whofe crimes thy vengeance dare.

12.

Ne'er from the Children of his Love
Shall Heav'n's high Lord his care remove,
Or to the foes of *Israel's* Line
His purchas'd Heritage refign:

13.

For Judgement fhall its feat affume,
Triumphant; while its equal doom
Each heart to Virtue's caufe a friend
With confcious tranfport fhall attend.

14.

Say, who with Me will plight the hand,
With Me the fons of guilt withftand?
Had God his aiding pow'r withheld,
How had my foul in filence dwell'd!

15.

But when my foot with fault'ring tread
Suggefted to my thought a dread,
Thy Love, its fpeedieft care applied,
Forbade my dubious fteps to flide.

16.

While deepeft woe my bofom tries,
And thoughts with thoughts conflicting rife,
Thy comforts, Lord, my foul fuftain,
And calm my fears, and footh my pain.

17.

Shall proud Oppreffion's lawlefs Chair
In thy Alliance find a fhare,
Whofe Mandates to the impious Tribe
Their tafks of cruelty prefcribe?

18. See

18.

See willing Myriads, at its word
Affembled, grafp the hoftile fword,
In guiltlefs blood their thirft allay,
And mark the Righteous for their prey.

19.

But God, my refuge and my fhield,
Firm on himfelf my truft fhall build;
To him, my foul, for help repair,
Who makes the faithful heart his care.

20.

That Lord, whom *Ifrael's* Sons adore,
Their fin fhall in their lap reftore,
Their fteps with certain vengeance trace,
And root from earth th' offending Race.

PSALM XCV.

1.

O Come, and to th' eternal King
New fongs of triumph let us fing;
With holy tranfport Him alone
The ftrength of our Salvation own ;—

2.

Admitted to his prefence pay
The tribute of the grateful lay,
And, while his Acts our mirth infpire,
Wake to his praife the vocal lyre.

3.

Extended wide beyond all bound,
Beyond all height, his pow'r is found,
Nor Lord, with Him, nor Gods befide
The honours of his Throne divide.

4. Earth's

4.

Earth's ſtores, throughout its inmoſt frame,
He, great Proprietor, ſhall claim;
Your Range, ye cloud-tranſcending Hills,
His pow'r commands, his preſence fills.

5.

Inrich'd by his prolific hand,
In Him the All-productive Land,
In Him the Sea, that rounds its ſhore,
Their Maker and their Lord adore.

6.

O come, and let your knees with mine
To Him in lowlieſt homage join;
To Him, for He your pray'rs will hear,
To Him your ſuppliant voices rear.

7.

In Him your God, your Father, ſee,
The People of his paſture Ye,
The Flock that guided by his care
The bleſſings of his bounty ſhare.

8.

O *Judah*, if in this thy day
My Will thou purpoſe to obey,
Steel not thy breaſt to truths divine,
As erſt the Fathers of thy line;—

9.

Whoſe Bands th' incloſing Deſert ſaw,
Rebellious to the Heav'n-taught Law,
With mad preſumption from my hand
The ſignals of my pow'r demand;

10. Their

10.

Their eyes, the wiſh'd for ſight obtain;
Indulg'd, require it yet again;
Such their demand a heart betray'd
Diſtruſtful of my promis'd aid.

11.

Through forty years the circling ſun
Beheld their date of mercy run,
As, griev'd, I ſtrove, but ſtrove in vain,
Their growing frenzy to reſtrain:

12.

Behold a Race, at length I cried,
Whoſe heart from Me has ſwerv'd aſide,
(By Error's pow'r ſubdu'd,) nor known
That Wiſdom's paths and Mine are one.

13.

My Oath, for by Myſelf I ſwear,
My kindled anger ſhall declare,
And bar them from my Reſt, decreed
To faithful *Abraham*'s choſen Seed.

PSALM XCVI.

1.

SING to the Lord ſome new-taught Song;
Earth, to his praiſe the note prolong:
With rapt'rous zeal, with holy flame
Inſpir'd, his benefits proclaim.

2.

Bleſs, bleſs his Name; from day to day
Let His Salvation prompt the lay,
Till Realms remote his Acts have known,
And Man's whole Race his Wonders own.

3. Great

3.

Great is the Lord, and great his Praife:
What God like Him our fear can raife?
Not fuch as Heathen Lands afford,
Created firft, and then ador'd:

4.

Creation Him its Lord avow'd,
When erft the arch of Heav'n he bow'd;
And Light and Majefty divine
With fadelefs fplendor grace his fhrine.

5.

Let ev'ry People, ev'ry Tribe,
Pow'r, glory, ftrength, to Him afcribe:
Let fartheft realms converted join
In homage to the name divine.

6.

Yield to that Name the honours due;
Oft to his Courts your way purfue
With folemn ftep, and joyful bring
The off'ring to your heav'nly King.

7.

Before the Beauty of his fhrine,
Ye Saints, in low proftration join:
Ye Natives of each diftant fhore,
His Pow'r revere; his Name adore.

8.

O tell to All whom Earth fuftains,
O tell them, that *Jehovah* reigns,
That, fix'd by His Almighty hand,
Its pond'rous Orb unmov'd fhall ftand,

9. O tell

9.

O tell to all whom earth suſtains,
O tell them, that *Jehovah* reigns,
And All who iſſue from its womb
Receive from Him th' unerring doom.

10.

Exult, ye Heav'n's; exult, O Earth;
And, partner in the ſacred mirth,
Let Ocean in its fulneſs riſe,
And thunder to the diſtant ſkies.

11.

Rich in his gifts, ye Fields, rejoice;
While in his praiſe the Woods their voice
Exalt, and hail with lowly nod
The preſence of th' approaching God.

12.

He comes, in awful pomp array'd,
He comes, to judge the World he made.
Truth ſhall with Him the cauſe decide,
And Equity his ſentence guide.

P S A L M   XCVII.

1.

TO God belongs th' eternal Sway;
    Let Earth with joy his Will obey
Exult, ye Iſles that crown the Main,
Bleſt in his mild auſpicious Reign.

2.

The ſtation'd Clouds around him meet,
And Darkneſs rolls beneath his feet;
While Equity and Truth combine
To rear aloft his awful ſhrine.

3. Before

3.

Before him walks the wafting Fire;
Wrapt in the blaft his foes expire;
While Earth, convuls'd, in dire difmay,
Beholds the forky lightnings play,—

4.

And down, like wax before the flame,
Down flows the Mountain's folid frame,
That late, ambitious, met the fky;
For God, the World's great Lord, is nigh.

5.

His righteous Acts the Heav'ns difplay,
His fame from pole to pole convey,
And bid the Majefty divine
To ev'ry eye confpicuous fhine.

6.

Shame to the Wretch that wood and ftones
The Objects of his homage owns,
And frantic to the Creature pays
The Maker's interverted praife.

7.

Ye Gods, his fov'reign Might avow,
And rev'rent at his footftool bow;
Submiffive at the hallow'd Shrine
Adore the Majefty divine.

8.

Well-pleas'd thy Counfels, Lord, to hear,
Imperial *Salem* bows the ear;
And *Judah*'s happy Daughters fing
The Mercies of th' eternal King.

Z   9. Thou

9.

Thou, Lord, in Majefty ferene
Exalted o'er the Earth art feen:
What Pow'r, great God, fhall boaft a Name
Like Thine? Like Thee our homage claim?

10.

Ye Souls with Love divine imprefs'd;
Juft to its precepts, Sin deteft;
Averfe from each injurious art,
Let evil from your thoughts depart:

11.

Each fear deliver'd to the wind,
In God your certain refuge find,
Whofe pow'r protects the pious Band,
Tho' Myriads, leagu'd, againft them ftand.

12.

To You, ye Good, to You alone
The feeds of heav'nly light are fown,
That wake within the human breaft
Joys ne'er by human tongue exprefs'd.

13.

O crown'd with Mercies from above,
To God your grateful zeal approve:
His Sanctity revere; his Name
In hymns of loudeft praife proclaim.

P S A L M   XCVIII.

1.

SING to the God whom we adore;
O fing, in lays unheard before,
The Mercies fhown us from above,
The Wonders of redeeming Love:

I   His

His powerful Hand Salvation fends,
And Conqueft on his Arm attends.

2.

His Juftice through the World has fhin'd;
His Truth, with endlefs Mercy join'd,
Now feals the promife of his Grace
To faithful *Abraham*'s chofen Race;
And Earth, to juft obedience aw'd,
Has own'd her Saviour and her God.

3.

Ye diftant Realms, your voice employ
In fhouts of gratitude and joy :
Let hymns of rapture fwell each throat ;
Call from the harp th' according note ;
On the fhrill trump your mirth prolong,
And found the cornet to the fong.

4.

To Him who claims th' eternal fway,
To Him the vocal tribute pay :
Him let the hoarfe-refounding Tide,
With All that in its depths refide,
Praife, thank, and blefs, in loudeft ftrains ;
Him Earth, and All whom Earth fuftains.

5.

Ye Floods, triumphant clap the hand ;
Ye cloud-topt hills, exulting ftand ;
See, thron'd aloft in awful ftate,
While Man's whole Race his fentence wait,
The Judge fupreme his fcale affume ;
And Equity directs the Doom.

PSALM XCIX.

1.

JEHOVAH reigns : Ye Nations own,
With proſtrate hearts, his ſway :
Betwixt the Cherubs ſtands his Throne ;
Earth ! tremble and obey.

2.

His Rule, in *Sion* long confeſt,
O'er All extends ; his Name
Shall hallow with its fear each breaſt,
Each tongue with zeal inflame.

3.

Thy Pow'r with Equity allied
Through time's long courſe has ſtood :
Thy Judgements *Jacob*, Lord, has tried,
And knows them juſt and good.

4.

Let Each, with humble joy elate,
Before thy footſtool bow ;
Thee, ceaſeleſs, praiſe : For who ſo great,
So holy, Lord, as Thou ?

5.

By God with ſacred honours crown'd,
See *Moſes, Aaron* ſee,
And *Samuel,* ever faithful found,
To Him incline the knee.

6.

To Him the favour'd Three aloud
The frequent Vow prefer'd,
And inſtant from the pillar'd cloud
His awful Anſwer heard.

7. With

7.

With wakeful zeal their bosoms burn'd;
　　Observant of his Will,
With joy the heav'nly precept learn'd,
　　And hasten'd to fulfil.

8.

To Thee, great God, their ev'ry pray'r
　　In full acceptance rose:
Thy hand their weakness knew to spare,
　　And, pitying, heal'd their woes.

9.

Yet could thy Wrath, when Sin had dar'd
　　Their erring breast to stain,
Deal to their guilt its just reward,
　　And vindicate thy Reign.

10.

Let Each, with humble joy elate,
　　On *Sion*'s Mountain bow;
Thee, ceaseless, praise: For who so great,
　　So holy, Lord, as Thou?

P S A L M   C.

1.

YE Tribes of Earth, in God rejoice,
　His presence hail with thankful voice;
To Him your willing homage pay,
And wake the tributary lay.

2.

Submissive to his Will, in Him
Behold the God of Gods supreme;
Nor Lords with Him, nor Gods beside
The Honours of his Throne divide.

Z 3　　　3. With

3.

With conscious wonder oft survey'd,
He, not Ourselves, our frame has made :
The subjects of his pow'r we stand,
The sheep that own his guiding hand.

4.

O, enter then his gates with praise,
To Him your loudest accents raise,
With grateful hearts his Love proclaim,
And bless, O bless, his awful Name.

5.

For Truth in Him and Mercy live :
That Truth shall time itself survive ;
That Mercy through the length of days
Unclouded pour its healing rays.

P S A L M CI.

I.

MERCY, Judgement, now my tongue
Makes the subject of its Song :
Lord ! to whom then shall I sing,
But to Thee, th' eternal King ?

2.

Wisdom shall my footsteps guide,
Nor permit my feet to slide,
Or from thy All-perfect Way,
Lost in paths of Sin to stray.

3.

O Come, O come, celestial Guest,
Let my roof with Thee be blest ?
Let thy Beams effulgent play,
And within my Mansion stay ?

4. Lo !

4.

Lo! my heart with ftudious care
For thy prefence I prepare,
And my Dwelling's full extent
Spotlefs to thy view prefent.

5.

Ne'er fhall my prefumptuous hand
Dare to break thy juft Command;
Ne'er within me fhalt thou find
Aught that fpeaks a faithlefs mind.

6.

Serv'd by none who ferve not Thee,
Let me not the Impious fee;
Let the wretch of froward heart
From my gate repuls'd depart;

7.

Let the Man of lofty eye,
Scornful mien, and ftomach high,
And the Tongue to flander bred,
Learn my heavieft wrath to dread.

8.

Come, ye faithful, juft and good,
Eager for the bright abode,
Come, ye pure in heart, O come,
Sure with me to find a home.

9.

Pleas'd I fee the pious Band
Round my throne attendant ftand,
And in facred homage join
To their own great Lord and mine.

10. Hence

10.

Hence ye Children of deceit,
From my threshold turn your feet:
Let the soul that dares a lye
Inftant from my prefence fly.

11.

Soon, O *Judah*, fhall my hand
Root th' offenders from thy Land;
Soon my guilt-avenging rod
Purge the City of my God.

P S A L M   CII.

1.

HEAR, Lord, my pray'r, and let my cries
Accepted to thy Throne arife:
O turn not Thou thy face away,
Nor longer my relief delay;

2.

Lord, mark my forrows from on high,
And pitying to my call reply;
Faft as the mounting fmoke decays,
On times light pinion flit my days:

3.

My bones the hearth's fierce heat fuftain;
My heart the herbage of the plain
Refembles, o'er whofe leaves have paft
The fervors of the fouthern blaft.

4.

For ah! forgetful of my food,
Inceffant o'er my griefs I brood,
While ftruggling groans their weight proclaim,
And wafte with toil my languid frame.

5. Not

5.

Not the wide Defert's confines drear
Laments of louder accent hear,
When midft the folitary gloom
The Birds of Night their plaints refume;

6.

When, 'midft its fens, with difmal note
The Pelican diftends her throat,
Or to the winds in lengthen'd ftrains
The felf-fequeftring Owl complains;

7.

Nor vents its fifter-bird a moan
So deep, when on the roof alone
She fits; whofe woes, like mine, affright
The filence of the tedious night.

8.

From Morn, till Eve extend its veil,
Reproaches keen my ears affail;
And, leagu'd by mutual oaths, my foes
With fierce intent my fteps inclofe.

9.

See afhes, fcatter'd o'er my head,
Mix, undiftinguifh'd, with my bread;
By Languor, Care, and Grief opprefs'd,
With groans perpetual heaves my breaft.

10.

See mingled tears my cup fupply;
Since firft thy wrathful Arm on high
Caught me amaz'd, and fwiftly round
Reverting hurl'd me on the ground.

11. As

11.

As fades the ſhadow of the ſun,
With quick decline my moments run,
My life, juſt verging to its cloſe,
With rapid courſe unhecded flows.

12.

My form is waſted, and my face,
Its vernal bloom and youthful grace
Extingüiſh'd, withers on the eye,
As plants beneath a hoſtile ſky.

13.

But Thou, Bleſt Guard of *Iſrael*'s fold,
Shalt ages ſee on ages roll'd,
And, thron'd above, to endleſs days
Extend thy honour, name, and praiſe.

14.

O riſe, (th' appointed hour is come;)
Riſe, mightieſt Lord, thy Charge aſſume;
And let ſad *Sion*'s ſeat no more
The abſence of thine aid deplore.

15.

How lovely to thy Servants' eyes,
How lovely ev'n in ruin lies
Her hallow'd Wall, her ſacred Shrine,
The Seat of Majeſty divine!

16.

Thy ſervants, Lord, a penſive Throng,
Walk her defenceleſs ſtreets along,
And, as her ſcatter'd waſtes appear,
Drop on her duſt the pitying tear.

17. How,

17.

How, Lord, fhall each from day to day,
The terrors of thy wrath difplay!
How fhall thy Name, great Sire, its dread
Through Earth's awaken'd regions fpread!

18.

How fhall her Kings with deep difmay
Thy boundlefs Majefty furvey,
When *Salem*'s ftructures from their fall
Thy hand, propitious, fhall recal.

19.

While down th' eternal Glory pours,
Incircles with its blaze her tow'rs,
And fpeaks thy favour (oft implor'd,)
To *Ifrael*'s exil'd Tribes reftor'd!

20.

Thy Acts the faithful pen fhall trace,
And Myriads of the human Race,
Yet ftrangers to the birth, thy fame
In Songs of loudeft note proclaim.

21.

For He, beneath whofe facred feat
The ftarry Orbs their courfe repeat,
Th' eternal Ruler of the fky,
Has caft on Earth his equal eye.

22.

He deigns the injur'd caufe to own,
To hear the helplefs Captive's groan,
The Souls to death confign'd to fave,
And fnatch them from the greedy grave.

23. For

23.

For this, through Sion's ample bound
Jehovah's Name shall oft resound;
Thy shouts, distinguish'd Salem, raise,
And wake thy tongue to hymns of praise:

24.

See to thy Courts the Nations flow,
His just dominion taught to know,
And, Each with Thee in compact join'd,
Their hearts to his obedience bind:

25.

'Twas He, whose unresisted force
In mid progression stop'd my course;
My healthful vigour reft away;
And hasten'd to its eve my day.

26.

Spare, mightiest Lord! nor thus, I cried,
My brittle chain of years divide,
O Thou, of Life th' exhaustless Spring,
Invisible, Immortal King!

27.

Thy hand the Earth's foundation laid,
Thy hand the Heav'n aloft display'd,
Ere yet along the vast profound
The restless Months began their round:

28.

That Earth, that Heav'n's stupendous frame,
Corruption with permitted claim
Shall seize: But Thou, from Age secure,
Shalt self-existent still endure.

29. These,

29.

These, as the labours of the loom,
Shall time with gradual force confume;
Till Thou again thy Hand apply,
And fold them up, and lay them by;

30.

Thou, Lord, whofe hand their texture fpun,
When Time its ftated courfe has run,
Shalt brighter Scenes difclofe to view,
And Nature's varied face renew.

31.

But varyings Thou haft none: Thy rays
With undiminifh'd luftre blaze;
Thy years fhall circumfcription fpurn,
And back upon themfelves return.

32.

Thee, Lord, their fure Protector, Thee
Thy Saints their ftrong Support fhall fee;
And, rang'd in long fucceffion, fhare
The gifts of thy paternal Care.

PSALM CIII.

1.

MY Soul, throughout thine inmoft frame,
Blefs, blefs the great *Jehovah's* Name;
Ceafe not with ftudious thought to trace
The Acts of his ftupendous Grace.

2.

He blots from Heav'n's record thy fin,
And, though thy paffions war within,
Affuafive calms their furious ftrife,
And refcues from the pit thy life;

A a   3. He

3.

He bids his bleſſings round thee riſe;
Thy ev'ry wiſh with Good ſupplies;
Thy years renews in their decline;
And makes the Eagle's vigour thine.

4.

'Tis God's, the friendleſs and the poor
From proud Oppreſſion to ſecure,
Their wants attentive to perceive,
And, ever faithful, to relieve.

5.

His ways to *Moſes* ſtood reveal'd;
Thou, *Iſrael*, haſt his Works beheld,
His breaſt with mercy fraught haſt known,
To anger ſlow, to pity prone.

6.

He ne'er with erring mortals knew
A ceaſeleſs conteſt to purſue,
But, when their crimes his vengeance raiſe,
His wrath in mid effuſion ſtays.

7.

If e'er our treſpaſs he chaſtiſe,
Not to its weight proportion'd riſe
The juſt corrections of his hand,
But bounded by his Mercy ſtand:

8.

That Mercy to the ſtarry pole
Extends; and, far as from his goal
The Sun in daily circuit roves,
The humbled ſinner's guilt removes.

9. What

What fondneſs for his infant Care,
A Father's boſom learns to ſhare,
Such from th' eternal Monarch claim
The Souls that rev'rent own his Name.

For well his eye our texture knows,
Sees that the duſt's light grains compoſe
Our frame; and marks the days of Man
Contracted to a narrow ſpan;

How ſhort, how tranſient is its date!
As flow'rs, that in their vig'rous ſtate
Exalted, now the field adorn,
And now by paſſing ſtorms are torn:

Behold the rip'ning herb decay,
Each flow'r, its vigour reft away,
At once its vernal pride reſigns,
And with'ring on the earth reclines:

In ſwift decay behold it waſte,
Nor knows the ſoil, whoſe bed it grac'd,
To witneſs to th' inquirer's view
Where late the ſhort-liv'd wonder grew

But Thy Compaſſions, Lord, the Juſt
From age to age with ſtedfaſt truſt
Shall own, and, fill'd with holy flame,
Thy care and tenderneſs proclaim:

15. Thy

15.

Thy Righteousness their favour'd Race,
In long descent, shall joy to trace,
While pleas'd thy Compact they fulfil,
And frame to thy Decrees their will.

16.

His Seat above th' empyreal plain
Our God has fix'd; his equal Reign
Creation's utmost bounds confess,
And, blest in him, their Maker bless.

17.

O magnify your heav'nly King,
His praise, ye tribes angelic, sing,
Who, cloth'd with might, his word obey,
And wing, as He directs, your way.

18.

Him praise, ye bright ethereal Band,
That rang'd beneath his banner stand,
And Ye who round his Throne of State
With duteous zeal ministrant wait.

19.

Ye Works of God, where'er his sway.
Extends, your Maker's fame display;
Nor Thou, my Soul, forget to sing
The Mercies of th' eternal King.

PSALM CIV.

1.

AWAKE, my Soul, to hymns of praise;
To God the song of triumph raise,
And thankful bless th' almighty Lord,
The God in ev'ry act ador'd.

2. O

2.

O cloth'd with Majesty divine,
What pomp, what glory, Lord, are thine
Light forms thy robe, and round thy head
The Heav'ns their ample curtain spread.

3.

Thou know'st amid the fluid space
The strong-compacted beams to place,
That proof to waiting Ages lie,
And prop the chambers of the sky.

4.

Behold, aloft, the King of Kings,
Borne on the Wind's expanded wings,
(His Chariot by the Clouds supplied,)
Through Heav'n's wide realms triumphant
    ride.

5.

Around him rang'd in awful state
Th' assembled Storms ministrant wait;
And Flames, attentive to fulfil
The dictates of his mighty Will.

6.

To Him the all-prolific earth,
From Chaos call'd, ascribes her birth,
And fix'd by his Almighty hand
Has stood, and shall for ages stand.

7.

He spake; and o'er each Mountain's head
The Deep its watry mantle spread:
He spake; and from the whelming flood
Again their tops emergent stood;

8. Now

8.

Now faſt adown their bending ſide
With refluent ſtream the Currents glide:
Aw'd by his ſtern rebuke they fly,
While peals of thunder rend the ſky;

9.

In mingled tumult backward led,
They haſte to their appointed bed,
And, taught their deſtin'd bounds to know,
No more th' affrighted Earth o'erflow.

10.

The ſprings, the rivulets (their courſe
By Nature's ever-copious ſource
Supplied,) refreſh the hilly plain,
And life in all its forms ſuſtain.

11.

Here ſtooping o'er the river's brink
The herds and flocks promiſcuous drink;
There, 'mid the barren deſert nurs'd,
The Wild-Aſs cools his burning thirſt;

12.

While faſt beſide the murm'ring ſpring
The feather'd minſtrels ſit and ſing,
And ſhelter'd in the branches ſhun
The fervors of the mid-day ſun.

13.

His ſhow'rs with verdure crown the hills
The earth with various fruits he fills:
Preventive of their wants, his aid
Yields to the Brute the ſpringing blade;

z 4   14. For

14.

For Man, chief object of his care,
His hands the toothful herb prepare,
The glad'ning wine, refreshing oil;
And bread that strings his nerves for toil.

15.

By Him with genial moisture fed,
The Trees their shades luxuriant spread;
The Cedars, virtue'd by his hand,
On *Lebanon's* high summit stand.

16.

They weave their social boughs, design'd
A refuge for th'aerial kind:
While on the Fir-tree's spiry top
The vagrant Stork is seen to stop.

17.

See from the hills the Goats depend,
Or bounding from the cliff descend:
The lesser tribes, in furry pride
Array'd, the rock's dark caverns hide.

18.

Her way by Him prescrib'd, the Moon
Our seasons marks, and knows her own;
And, taught by Him, the Orb of day
Slopes in the West his parting ray.

19.

Now Night from Ocean's bed ascends,
And o'er the earth her wings extends;
While favour'd by the friendly gloom
The sylvan race licentious roam:

20.

The Lions chief, with hideous roar,
From God their needful food implore,
And eager for the wanted prey
Along the echoing Desert stray;

21.

Till now, as Morn approaches nigh,
Back to their cavern'd haunts they fly,
Where, satiate with the bloody feast,
The lordly savage sinks to rest;

22.

His care sufficient to the day,
Man to his labour takes his way,
His task at earliest dawn begun,
And ended with the setting sun.

23.

Eternal Ruler of the Skies,
How various are thy Works, how wise;
How great the Wonders thou hast wrought,
And deep beyond all search of thought!

24.

Nor Earth alone beholds her shores
Inrich'd from thy exhaustless stores;
Alike, throughout their liquid reign,
Th' extended Seas thy gifts contain:

25.

Beneath, unnumber'd reptiles swarm,
Of diff'rent size, of diff'rent form;
Above, the ships enormous glide,
Incumbent on the burthen'd tide;—

26. And

26.

And oft, the rolling waves between,
The huge Leviathan is seen,
There privileg'd by Thee to stray,
And wanton o'er the watry way.

27.

Thy care, great God, sustains them All,
By hunger urg'd, on Thee they call,
And reap from thy extended hand,
Whate'er their various wants demand.

28.

If Thou thy face but turn away,
Their troubled looks their grief betray;
If Thou the vital air deny,
Behold them sicken, faint, and die!

29.

His breath resign'd, on Earth's low bed
Behold the Mortal rest his head;
Dust to its kindred dust returns,
And Earth her ruin'd offspring mourns:

30.

But soon thy breath her loss supplies,
She sees a new-born race arise,
And, o'er her regions scatter'd wide,
The blessings of thy hand divide.

31.

Thy Glory, fearless of decline,
Thy Glory, Lord, shall ever shine,
Thy Works in changeless order lie,
And glad their great Creator's eye.

32. Earth

Earth at thy look shall trembling stand,
Conscious of sov'reign pow'r at hand,
And, touch'd by Thee, Almighty Sire,
The cloud-topt Hills in smoke aspire.

To God in ceaseless strains my tongue
Shall meditate the grateful song,
And, long as breath informs my frame,
The wonders of his Love proclaim.

Assur'd that his paternal ear
With full regard my voice will hear,
His Acts shall be its constant theme,
His Favour my delight supreme.

Behold his wrath on Sinners shed;
Behold them number'd with the dead:
And, struck by his resistless hand,
In heaps promiscuous strew the land!

But Thou, my Soul, the hymn of praise
In loudest notes triumphant raise;
And let consenting Nations join
To bless with Me the Name divine.

PSALM CV.

COME, celebrate your God and King;
Awake the song, awake the string;
With awful rev'rence own his name;
His pow'r invoke, his praise proclaim.

2. Aloud

2.

Aloud declare, through ev'ry Land,
The Wonders of his mighty hand;
And let his Name your thought employ;
His Name, fit theme of highest joy.

3.

Such joy may each for ever share,
Whose steps to *Salem's* Fane repair;
O frequent seek that blest Abode,
O seek the face of *Jacob's* God.

4.

The Acts of Heav'n's Almighty Lord
Let *Israel's* thankful Sons record;
Ye Seed of *Abraham*, his Friend,
With joy to his Commands attend.

5.

To You his presence stands confest;
His judgments Earth's wide Realms attest:
His Promise kind, and wise Decree,
Though Man forget, yet will not He;

6.

The Oath confirm'd through periods past,
And doom'd to latest times to last,
To *Terah's* Son, to *Isaac*, made,
And thus to *Jacob's* hands convey'd:

7.

" Arise, thou favour'd of thy God,
" And claim the Gift by Him bestow'd:
" Behold thy Sons their wide command
" Extend o'er *Canaan's* fertile Land."

8. But

8.

But when ? or how ? Their number view ;
(It afks no toil ;) a helplefs Few,
And Strangers there, doom'd long to roam,
And feek through diftant climes a home.

9.

Yet, privileg'd by Him from wrong,
Secure the Exiles march along :
Kings hear his dread reproof, nor dare
To hurt whom God has bid to fpare.

10.

" Touch, touch not Thefe ; for on their heads
" My hand the facred unction fheds :
" Your eyes in Them my Prophets fee ;
" And what they fpeak, they fpeak from Me."

11.

He calls ; and on the cultur'd ground
Life's needful ftaff no more is found,
While Drought, incumbent o'er the plain,
Checks in mid growth the rip'ning grain.

12.

Yet Mercy ftill his Wrath outran ;
Thy fhores, O *Nile*, receive the Man,
Ordain'd the chofen Race to fave,
Thy future Lord, though now thy Slave.

13.

What though, his feet in fetters bound,
His foul th' afflicting irons wound,
Though various griefs around him wait
Through kindred envy, wrath, and hate ;—

14. Yet,

14.

Yet, *Joseph*, patient bear thy lot!
Thy lips, with heav'nly science fraught,
Shall soon the mystic Dream explain;
That ends thy woes, and breaks thy chain.

15.

The Monarch bids; the prison door
Detains the injur'd Saint no more;
But through succeeding Life he gains
A full exemption from his pains.

16.

New honours now his wrongs repair;
The regal Palace to his care
Its wealth consigns; and *Egypt's* land
Bows to her Captive's wise command.

17.

Ev'n Princes own'd with rev'rent awe
The dictates of his will their Law,
And Senates on his youthful tongue
In silent wonder list'ning hung.

18.

He sends; and lo, oppress'd with years
Jacob on *Mizraim's* Coast appears;
Th' illustrious Pilgrim's wearied feet
In *Egypt* fix their last retreat.

19.

With large increase his Line is bless,
And *Zoan* in th' adopted Guest
With hostile eye beholds up-grown
A strength superior to her own.

B b   20. See

20.

See hence the woes on *Egypt* pour'd !
(But·Thou, O Monarch, fhouldft thy word
Abfolve, nor thus with impious rod
Opprefs the Servants of thy God.)

21.

See *Mofes*, pleading, ftretch the hand ;
See *Aaron* lift the facred wand,
And lead th' invited vengeance on
In fcenes to Nature's Laws unknown.

22.

But O, what terrors, *Cham*, are thine,
While quick on thy devoted Line,
Far as thy utmoft coafts extend,
Thou feeft the various peft defcend !

23.

If Fear their ftubborn hearts may melt,
Let Darknefs, Darknefs to be felt,
Inclofe their Land, and o'er their head
Its melancholy mantle fpread.

24.

Thus, thus th' Almighty Monarch fpake ;
As forth the awful accents brake, .
Darknefs the high beheft obey'd,
And round them wrapt its thickeft fhade.

25.

The Heav'n·ftruck *Nile*'s extended flood
Now rolls a current black with blood :
While breathlefs on their oozy bed
In heaps the finny tribes are fpread.

26. The

26.

The loathsome Frog a num'rous Birth,
Springs instant from the teeming earth,
Nor walls that guard a Monarch's rest
Know to exclude the hideous guest.

27.

He bids; and through the darken'd air
In troops th' assembling Flies repair,
And swarms of Reptiles scatter'd wide,
Rebuke the faithless Tyrant's pride

28.

In league against them now conspire
The rushing Hail, and bick'ring Fire:
And, instant by the tempest torn,
Their ruin'd shades the forests mourn:

29.

No more array'd in native green
The fig-tree and the vine are seen,
No more with flow'ring honours crown'd,
But useless load th' incumber'd ground

30.

He bids; and join'd in close array
Th' embattled Locusts take their way:
Before them plains with verdure grac'd
Appear; behind a barren waste:

31.

While the dun Beetle through the sky
With eager speed is seen to fly,
And, partner in the offer'd spoil,
Consumes th' astonish'd planter's toil.

32.

Now to the grave with anguifh torn,
Each Mother yields her eldeft-born ;
And *Egypt's* land, along its fhores,
The firft-fruits of its ftrength deplores.

33.

Now, *Ifrael*, fhines the day to Thee
That bids thy captive Sons go free :
Rife, quickly rife ; for in their ear
Thy Sons the voice of Freedom hear :

34.

The wealth of their relenting foes
Earth's fov'reign Lord on Them beftows
And bids them leave the hoftile foil,
Each ftrong for travel, ftrong for toil.

35.

As now their deftin'd path they tread,
Egypt, yet pale with recent dread,
Exulting fees the facred Band
With parting footfteps prefs her ftrand.

36.

Fxpanded wide above their heads
The fhadowing Cloud its curtain fpreads ;
Before them walks th' embodied Fire,
And bids the fhades of night retire.

37.

His hand indulgent from on high
Yields to their wants the wifh'd fupply ;
Quails on their appetite beftow'd,
And Bread ethereal, give them food ;

38. While

38.

While, at his word, from out the rock
Th' imprifon'd ftreams luxuriant broke,
And onward pour'd with lengthen'd train,
Ran murm'ring o'er the thirfty plain.

39.

Such Mercies, All-indulgent Lord,
Thy changelefs promifes afford,
Such Bleffings thy remembrance kind
Of *Abraham*'s ever faithful mind.

40.

Redeem'd from ftern Oppreffion's feat,
With grateful joy their bofoms beat;
With fuch as ev'ry heart o'erflows
When refcu'd from its cruel foes;

41.

Joy, yet enlarg'd, when *Canaan*'s Land
Refigns her fcepter to their hand,
And bids them reap from off her foil
The harveft of another's toil.

42.

Behold the Love to *Ifrael* fhown,
That We, great God, thy pow'r might own,
And each with ftedfaft heart fulfil
The dictates of thy mighty Will.

43.

Awake the fong, awake the ftring,
And thankful praife th' immortal King,
And, faithful Heralds to his fame,
To diftant Lands his praife proclaim.

PSALM CVI. *Hallelujah.*

1.

LET songs of joy to God ascend,
Whose Love nor limit knows nor end.
But O, what tongue in equal lay
His acts can speak, his praise display?

2.

Thrice happy who with stedfast will
The dictates of his Law fulfil!
With These, thy chosen Flock, assign'd
May I my lot for ever find:

3.

O grant me, Lord, with These to prove
The pow'r of thy redeeming Love,
The grace thy Saints are blest to know
That Grace to me benignant shew.

4.

Too faithful followers of our Sires,
Our Life with theirs, great God, conspires.
Thy wrath on *Judah's* Realm to call,
And teach thy terrors where to fall.

5.

O say, thou *Erythræan* Main,
(Thy Waves beheld the rebel Train;)
How soon Oblivion could efface
Each act of God's stupendous Grace,—

6.

How soon efface each act his hand
Perform'd in *Cham's* affrighted land:
Yet, still, that Man his pow'r might own,
Conspicuous in their aid it shone:

7. Aw'd

7.

Aw'd by his voice the briny Flood
In gath'ring heaps fuspended ftood,
While, fafe as o'er the fandy wafte,
Th' admiring troops betwixt them paft :

8.

Soon as they reach the adverfe ftrand
Th' impetuous wave the hoftile Band
O'erwhelms ; nor one exempted Man
Back with the dreadful tidings ran.

9.

Convinc'd they now (What could they lefs ?)
His words the words of truth confefs,
Yield to his Name th' extorted praife,
And fongs of grateful triumph raife ;

10.

But foon rebellious as before
(His Works remember'd now no more,)
To Times by Them prefcrib'd confine
The counfels of the Will divine.

11.

By lawlefs appetite impell'd,
As o'er the Wild their courfe they held,
Fierce rife their Bands, in evil hour,
And challenge to the proof his Pow'r :

12.

That pow'r (while ev'ry eager eye
Rafhly demands the quick fupply)
Difpleas'd the wifh'd for ill fhall grant
And fatiate their imagin'd want :

13 That

13.

That pow'r alone their outrage fell
From Thee, O *Moses*, could repel,
And uncontested rev'rence claim
To confecrated *Aaron*'s name.

14.

Wide, difcontinuous, yawn'd the ground,
And *Dathan* in the dark profound,
With proud *Abiram*'s frantic Train,
Receiving inftant, clos'd again;

15.

The Almighty Lord, with wrath inflam'd
His vengeance dire at *Ifrael* aim'd,
His Fires impetuous, roll'd along,
Wrapt in the blaze th' apoftate Throng.

16.

But *Horeb!* What is wrought on Thee?
Blufh, confcious Earth, O blufh to fee
A figure from the grazing herd
To God, the living God, prefer'd:

17.

That God, their Glory late confeft;
But Ah! within their thanklefs breaft
No longer now recorded ftand
The wonders of his faving hand;

18.

No more with gratitude imprefs'd
His Miracles their hearts atteft
In vain on *Egypt* fhown, in vain
Repeated on the bord'ring Main :

19. See

19.

See, as in awful threatnings heard,
Eternal Juftice gives the word,
The fummon'd Storms the heav'nly Throne
Surround, impatient to be gone:

20.

But *Mofes* in the breach appears,
And, as his fuppliant voice he rears,
Averts, yet waiting on the wing,
The vengeance of th' Almighty King.

21.

As now in near approach they ftand
To promis'd, *Canaan*'s fertile Land,
That promife, feal'd by Truth divine,
They doubt, and at the gift repine:

22.

From tent to tent the murmur runs,
While each the heav'nly counfel fhuns,
That bids them fafe in Him confide,
Their God, their Guardian and their Guide.

23.

Their guilt mature for vengeance found,
Th' uplifted fword, in act to wound,
Hangs imminent; and myriads flain
In heaps promifcuous load the plain.

24.

The conqu'ring Foe through unknown ways
The fcatter'd Fugitives conveys;
Secluded from their promis'd home,
In foreign countries long they roam.

25. Their

25.

Their names *Bel-phegor*'s fanes behold
Amidft his Votaries enroll'd,
While pleas'd, the impious board they fpread,
And eat the off'rings of the Dead.

26.

New crimes new chaftifements provoke;
And forth the Peft wide-wafting broke,
Unfeen the furious onfet gave,
And fwept them to the crouded grave;

27.

Till, *Phineas*, thy prevenient care
Purg'd from its taint the deathful air:
The pious deed to lateft days
Shall confecrate the Hero's praife.

28.

Nor *Meribah*'s yet thirfty ground
Unconfcious of their guilt is found;
Till, fummon'd from the rock, the wave
Her plain in full effufion lave.

29.

Nor He, who often mildly ftrove
To draw them with the cords of Love;
Not *Mofes*, Leader of their Bands,
From touch of blame exempted ftands:

30.

While murmurs heard on ev'ry fide,
And loud reproach, his patience tried,
Refentment quick his bofom ftung,
And words unweigh'd efcap'd his tongue.

31. The

31.

The Nations round, with error blind,
To juſt exciſion long deſign'd,
Rebellious to their God they ſpare,
Nor ſhun the heathen rite to ſhare.

32.

Proſtrate they fall to ſculptur'd ſtone,
And frenzy's deepeſt influence own,
To *Dæmons* rear'd their altars ſtand,
And ſcenes of blood pollute the Land.

33.

While with untrembling hands the Sires
Their Son, their Daughter, to the fires
A Victim yield, and, of their cry
Regardleſs, ſee their offspring die.

34.

To images, to lifeleſs Gods
(Such, *Canaan*, ſhame thy dire abodes ;)
Streams on the knife the filial gore,
And, guiltleſs, ſtains th' unhallow'd floor.

35.

What, *Iſrael*, now ſhall waſh thee clean,
While Leſſons of inventive Sin
Have prompted thy adult'rous heart
Thus from thy Maker to depart ?

36.

Fierce o'er thy head his anger burns ;
From his own Heritage he turns,
Abhorrent : now let *Jacob*'s foes
At will th' abandon'd race incloſe.

37. Behold

37.

Behold them by oppreſſion torn,
And fix'd the mark of hoſtile ſcorn,
With flatt'ring Lip their homage pay,
And trembling own tyrannic ſway.

38.

Oft they were ſav'd, and oft again
Rebellious ſpurn'd his equal Reign,
Again their ruin'd ſtate deplor'd,
And bow'd beneath a foreign Lord.

39.

Yet He with pity from on high,
True to his Compact, heard their cry,
His hand in their Defence he rear'd,
And gracious in their cauſe appear'd.

40.

He ſaw them drag the ſervile chain,
And, ſtudious to relieve their pain,
Compaſſion's tend'reſt ſenſe impreſs'd
On the ſtern Victor's iron breaſt.

41.

O ſtill our Father, ſtill our Friend,
To _Iſrael's_ woes, great God attend :
From diſtant climes, and hoſtile lands,
Collect once more our ſcatter'd Bands ;

42.

That _Sion_ with delighted ear
The hallow'd ſtrains again may hear ;
Thy Name the ſubject of each ſong,
Thy Praiſe the boaſt of ev'ry tongue.

8

43. O

43.

'O thankful hail th' Almighty Lord,
The God by *Jacob*'s Sons ador'd:
His fame, ere Time its courfe began,
O'er Heav'n's wide region echoing ran;

44.

To Him through endlefs ages raife
One fong of oft-repeated praife ;
And let confenting Nations join
To blefs with Us the Pow'r divine.

Hallelujah.

PSALM CVII.

1.

TO God above from All below
Let hymns of praife afcend
Whofe Bleffings unexhaufted flow,
Whofe Mercy knows no end.

2.

But chief by Thofe his name be bleft,
To whom his aid he gave ;
Beheld them by the Foe opprefs'd,
And reach'd his arm to fave.

3.

To Eaft, to Weft, to South, to North,
Condemn'd awhile to roam,
His hand in pity brought them forth,
And call'd the Wand'rers home.

C c 4. Behold

4.

Behold them o'er the Defert ftray,
    A helplefs, hopelefs, Train:
Some City, where their fteps to ftay,
    They feek, but feek in vain.

5.

Ah! what fhall chear their fainting mind,
    Or what their woes affuage,
To thirft's afflictive pain confign'd,
    And famine's fierceft rage?

6.

Diftrefs'd, to God they make their pray'r:
    He guides, directs their feet;
And, fafe in his protecting care,
    They reach their deftin'd feat.

7.

O then that All would blefs his Name,
    Whofe Mercy thus they prove,
And pleas'd from age to age proclaim
    The wonders of his Love.

8.

That Love, whofe gifts with thankful breaft
    The Sons of want divide,
And find their ev'ry grief redrefs'd,
    Their ev'ry wifh fupplied.

9.

Thefe erft he bade th' Avenger's hand
    In Death's dark fhades detain;
And added to the iron band
    Affliction's heavier chain.

10. Such

10.

Such is the Doom to thofe affign'd,
    Who, frantic, durft withftand
The Counfels of th' Almighty Mind,
    And fpurn his juft Command.

11.

O'erwhelm'd with deepeft woe they lie,
    And finking to the grave :
No pitying ear attends their cry ;
    No hand is nigh to fave.

12.

Diftrefs'd, to God they make their pray'r;
    He, inftant, near them ftands,
Difpells the gloom of black Defpair,
    And breaks their ftubborn bands.

13.

O then that All would blefs his Name,
    Whofe Mercy thus they prove,
And pleas'd from age to age proclaim
    The wonders of his Love ;

14.

That Love, that oft its fuccour gives,
    The Captive's woes to heal,
The gates of brafs in funder cleaves,
    And burfts the bars of fteel.

15.

Beneath his terrors bid to groan,
    Behold the impious Band
The fruits of Folly reap, and own
    The Juftice of his hand.

    16. Eftrang'd

16.

Eſtrang'd from food, their languid ſoul
    The needful meal foregoes:
Life feels its current faintly roll,
    And haſtens to its cloſe,

17.

Diſtreſs'd, to God they make their pray'r;
    And Nature, joyous, ſees
His Word her ruin'd ſtrength repair,
    Her fierceſt tortures eaſe,

18.

O then that All would bleſs his Name,
    Whoſe Mercy thus they prove,
And pleas'd from age to age proclaim
    The wonders of his Love:

19.

That Realms of various tongue would ſing
    His Acts in frequent lays,
And yield to Heav'n's eternal King
    The ſacrifice of praiſe.

20.

Who o'er the Waves from ſhore to ſhore
    The gifts of Commerce bear,
The wonders of the Deep explore,
    And own that God is there.

21.

By Theſe his Works are ſeen; his Ways
    By Theſe are underſtood:
He ſpeaks the word; the Storm obeys,
    And riſing lifts the Flood,

22. Now

22.

Now high as Heav'n the Bark afcends,
  Now feeks the depth below:
Each heart beneath the terror bends;
  And melts with inward woe.

23.

As gorg'd with wine, in wild amaze
  They reel from fide to fide:
Nor Hope furvives, their fouls to raife,
  Nor Reafon wakes to guide.

24.

Diftrefs'd, to God they make their pray'r;
  Obedient to his Will,
The Storms that rag'd their rage forbear,
  The Seas that roar'd are ftill.

25.

Each grief, each fear, at once refign'd,
  They fee their labour o'er;
Then led by Him their haven find,
  And touch the wifh'd for fhore.

26.

O then that All would blefs his Name,
  Whofe Mercy thus they prove,
And pleas'd from age to age proclaim
  The wonders of his Love:

27.

That *Salem* in her facred fhrine
  His praife with thankful tongue
Would utter; while her Elders join
  To fwell the feftal fong.

28.

He bids; and lo a burning Waſte;
    Where roll'd the floods before;
And, touch'd by the deſcending blaſt,
    The ſprings are ſeen no more.

29.

Sad witneſs of ſome dire offence,
    Behold the fertile ſoil
No more its wonted gifts diſpenſe,
    But mock the tiller's toil.

30.

He bids; and o'er the Deſert wide
    The liquid Lake is ſpread:
New ſprings the thirſty earth divide,
    And murm'ring lift the head.

31.

There Myriads, late with hunger wan,
    By Him aſſembled, meet;
There pleas'd the future City plan,
    And fix their ſure Retreat:

32.

And now they ſow the foodful grain;
    The tender vine they rear;
Now waves the harveſt o'er the plain,
    And plenty crowns the year.

33.

Bleſt in his care, the Sires with joy
    A num'rous race behold;
Nor dares Diſeaſe their herds annoy,
    Or waſte the peopled fold.

34. Anon,

34.

Anon, if, sunk with heaviest woe,
    They feel oppression's pow'r;
If civil rage, or conqu'ring foe,
    Their boasted strength devour;

35.

Though, humbled from their state, awhile
    Their Princes feel his rod,
And wander o'er a barren soil,
    By human step untrod,

36.

His hand affords the wish'd release;
    Collects their scatter'd train;
And bids them like the flocks increase,
    That fill the verdant plain.

37.

Such Truths his Servants shall attest,
    And, joyful, wake the song;
While shame the impious shall invest,
    And chain their speechless tongue.

38.

His Works attentive while it sees,
    The Heav'n-instructed Mind
Shall own, how equal his Decrees,
    His Providence how kind.

PSALM CVIII.

1.

MY heart is fix'd, eternal Sire;
    My heart is fix'd: To Thee aspire
My Thoughts, and dictate to my lays
An argument of endless praise.

2. To

2.

To Thee, great God, my joyous tongue
Preluding forms the grateful fong:
That tongue, whofe higheft praife fhall be
The pow'r it boafts of praifing Thee.

3.

Awake, my lute, and new-ftrung lyre;
Inftinct, myfelf, with holy fire
I wake; and lo, the dawning Sun
Already hears the ftrain begun.

4.

From Me affembling Crouds fhall burn
The triumphs of thy Love to learn,
And, rapt with zeal, the Nations round
Catch from my lips the facred found.

5.

Lo! to the clouds thy Truth extends;
And heav'n's ftupendous height tranfcends,
Far as to Earth's extremeft bound
In all thy Works is Mercy found.

6.

Inthron'd thyfelf above the fkies,
O, bid thy fulleft Glory rife,
And to the earth with cloudlefs ray
The wonders of thy pow'r difplay.

7.

The Juft, bleft Objects of thy Love,
Defend propitious from above:
Let Me with Them thy Mercy fhare,
And hear, O hear, my ceafelefs pray'r.

8. God's

8.

God's Truth fhall ne'er forget to guard
The promife by his lips declar'd;
And what th' Almighty Monarch wills,
My ready hand with joy fulfills.:

9.

Behold me *Sichem*'s plain divide;
My line, to *Succoth*'s vale applied,
Its bound defcribes; Thee mine I fee,
O *Gilead*, and, *Manaffes*, Thee.

10.

Thou, *Ephraim*, art my ftrong defence,
Thou, *Judah*, fhalt my Law difpenfe:
A diff'rent lot fhall *Moab* find,
A Vafe to vileft ufe affign'd;.

11.

A doom like his fhall *Edom* meet,.
And wipe the duft from off my feet.
Philiftia fhall her tribute bring,
And own in Me her future King..

12.

Who, as our troops in clofe array
To *Edom*'s forts direct their way,
Arm'd with refiftlefs ftrength fhall bid
Her gates unfold, her bolts recede?

13.

Behold us, Lord, opprefs'd with woe,.
As exil'd from thy care we go:
Shall *Ifrael*'s hofts, thy aid withheld,.
Still unfuccefsful take the field?

14. Our

14.

Our hope, on Man repos'd in vain,
O let thy ftrength, great God, fuftain:
And let us on thy help reclin'd
In Thee our firm Protector find.

15.

Thus arm'd, each adverfe pow'r we dare,
And dauntlefs meet the rufhing war,
While from thy fword our foes retire,
Or trampled in the duft expire.

P S A L M   CIX.

1.

GOD of my praife, thy filence break;
Thy timelieft aid my woes befpeak,
While tongues to falfehood train'd prepare
To wrap me in the deathful fnare:

2.

Now words of deepeft art they try;
Now hoftile threats around me fly;
And Crouds, inflam'd with caufelefs rage,
Wars, fierceft wars, againft me wage.

3.

While thus with Enmity profeft
My Fame they wound, my Peace moleft,
While ftedfaft Hate my Love repays,
To Thee my Soul inceffant prays:

4.

But O! what anguifh rends my mind,
What keen regret I condemn'd to find
(As gifts on gifts my hands beftow,)
In each expected friend a foe.

5. On

5.

On Him whofe heart, with malice fraught,
Againft my peace has bent its thought,
Thus let thy Juftice, Lord, by Me
Aloud proclaim its fix'd Decree.

6.

Arraign'd at ftern Oppreffion's bar,
Some dread accufer let him fhare,
That, planted on his right, may ftand,
And vengeance from his Judge demand:

7.

Nor let his deprecation win
The wifh'd for pardon to his fin,
But witnefs of his guilt become,
And feal, beyond reverfe, his doom.

8.

Let death's accelerated day
To worthier hands his Charge convey,
His roof a weeping Widow fee,
Her Orphans hanging at her knee;

9.

While as from Morn to Eve they roam,
(Some ruin'd cell their cafual home,)
Let thefe, by pinching hunger led,
Seek at the rich man's gate their bread.

10.

His wealth let fell Extortion fpoil;
The gather'd harveft of his toil
Let Rapine's greedy hand furprize,
While Each his woes unpitying eyes;

8
11. And

And let his ʌ ɪ ſuccour near,
Corrected, leſſon in thy fear
This Age; and, one ſucceſſion o'er,
Be ſeen by human eye no more.

12.

Let what of ſin his Sires have done, ·
What guilt his Mother's heart has known,
In Heav'n be noted, and their Crime
Recorded ſtand to endleſs Time.

13.

Let Wrath and Horror at thy word
Quick on th' abandon'd offſpring pour'd,
(The meaſure of their ſins fulfill'd)
Their name to juſt extinction yield.

14.

Such vengeance on the miſcreant reſt,
Who, when with heavieſt woes oppreſs'd
The helpleſs innocent he view'd,
With murth'rous hate his ſoul purſu'd.

15.

In Curſes (for in them his heart
Delighted,) let him bear his part,
Dread Spectacle! a foe profeſt
To Bleſſing, and himſelf unbleſt.

16.

Himſelf he veils in curſings dire,
That, ſprung from Hell-enkindled fire;
Like water ſhall his bowels rend,
Like oil into his bones deſcend:

17. Faſt

17.

'Faſt as his veſture to his ſide
Still let them cleave, by Thee applied,
And, o'er his loyns for ever bound,
In painful cincture wrap him round.

18.

Such recompence my Foe ſhall claim;
Such All who blaſt with lies my fame;
But let thy Grace on Me beſtow'd
Thy Name exalt, immortal God.

19.

Thy Love (how ſweet that Love!) reveal,
And ſtretch the hànd my heart to heal,
That fainting pours th' inceſſant groan,
And ſorrows deepeſt wounds has known.

20.

To Life's laſt verge, impell'd by woe,
Faſt as the flitting ſhade I go;
Chac'd as the Locuſt ſee me roam,
My ſtrength by hunger's force o'ercome.

21.

While thus within my waſted frame
Sinks, half extinct, the vital flame,
Reproaching foes, around me ſpread,
With haughtieſt triumph ſhake the head.

22.

Thy wonted Clemency beſtow;
And give them, mightieſt Lord, to know
Thy Care extended to my aid,
Thy Pow'r in their repulſe diſplay'd.

D d   23. Though

23.

Though curs'd by Them, yet blefs me Thou
O teach their ftubborn hearts to bow ;
And let their rage by Thee fupprefs'd
With grateful tranfport fill my breaft.

24.

On each who calls himfelf my foe
Let fhame its thickeft mantle throw ;
Let black difgrace their name o'erfpread,
Who aim their curfes at my head :

25.

While I, amid th' affembled Throng,
Raife to my God the ceafelefs fong,
Who, conftant at his fide, the Poor
From lawlefs judgment fhall fecure.

P S A L M CX.

I.

THE Almighty Lord, beneath whofe feat
The ftarry Orbs their courfe repeat,
In awful Majefty array'd,
Thus to my Lord *Meffiah*—faid—

2.

Come feat thee at my own right hand,
Till, at my word, the hoftile Band,
As low with proftrate necks they lie,
A footftool to thy fteps fupply.

3.

Thy God from *Sion*'s lofty tow'r
Shall bid Thee ftretch the rod of pow'r ;
Victorious o'er the rebel train,
Arife, and vindicate thy reign.

9   4. Behold

4.

Behold the long-expected day,
When willing Crouds their homage pay ;
To Thee their facred off'rings bring,
And hail their Saviour and their King.

5.

Thy future Offspring view, a Birth
More num'rous than the Dews, on earth
(Beneath the twilight's dubious gloom)
Diffus'd from Morn's prolific womb.

6.

Th' irrevocable Oath is fworn :
" My Beft-belov'd, my eldeft-born,
" Charg'd with th' eternal Priefthood fee,
" And rank'd, *Melchizedec*, with Thee."

7.

Thine arm th' anointed Prince fhall fhield,
Thou, Lord, befide him tread the field,
While Kings fhall feel th' inflicted wound,
And hardieft Warriors prefs the ground.

8.

His Name the fubject World fhall awe,
His fword to diftant Lands give law ;
By him their fcepter'd Chiefs are flain,
And heaps of carnage load the plain.

9.

The Streams, that glide along the way,
Shall to his heart new ftrength convey,
And bid him, 'mid the fcene of dread,
Secure of conqueft, lift the head.

P S A L M CXI. *Hallelujah.*

1.

MY Soul with sacred zeal inspir'd,
  Shall wake to God the thankful strain,
In secret with his Saints retir'd,
And 'midst fair *Sion*'s crouded fane.

2.

Great are his Works : With studious aim
Each faithful heart those Works has trac'd ;
His Act shall highest honour claim,
His Equity for ever last.

3.

His Wonders to the grateful sense
In sweet memorial stand confest ;
For boundless grace his hands dispense,
And tend'rest pity warms his breast.

4.

His Love the Souls to Him allied
With food of heav'nly growth has fill'd;
Nor suffers from his thought to slide
The Promise to his People seal'd.

5.

Thy Pow'r that People, Lord, have known,
Blest Heirs of *Canaan*'s fertile Land:
Thy Precept Truth and Justice own,
And bid thy Deeds reverseless stand.

6.

Salvation from our God descends ;
His Faith shall *Israel*'s bliss insure ;
Majestic Awe his Name attends,
And Sanctity from blemish pure.

7. His.

7.

His fear th' obedient heart refines,
And Wisdom's path to view displays:
In brightest beams array'd it shines,
And prompts each tongue with endless praise.

PSALM CXII. *Hallelujah.*

1.

HOw blest the Man, his God who fears!
Thy Precept, on his Thoughts imprefs'd,
Eternal King, his Spirit chears,
And peace perpetual fills his breast.

2.

His Sons the reins of pow'r shall hold;
Transmissive Blessings on their Line
Be pour'd, his treasures swell with gold,
His Righteousnefs for ever shine.

3.

How to thy Saints, just, kind, and good,
Has light amidst the gloom upsprung !
Their hands have ampleft gifts bestow'd,
And fair Discretion guides their tongue.

4.

Secure from fall the Just shall stand,
Nor e'er from thy remembrance slide :
No rumour'd ills his fear demand;
Whose hopes in Thee, great God, reside.

5.

Without a dread (Thy strength his trust,)
He meets the battle on its way,
Nor turns, till prostrate in the dust
His eyes the vaunting Foe survey.

D d 3   6. Inrich'd

6.

Inrich'd by what he gives, his hands
Deal to the fons of want his bread;
His Innocence unfullied ftands;
And lafting honours crown his head.

7.

His blifs Tranfgreffors fhall behold,
And grind their teeth, and inly groan,
Their impious toil by Thee controul'd,
Their ev'ry wifh by Thee o'erthrown.

PSALM CXIII. *Hallelujah.*

1.

YE faithful Servants of your God,
On Him be all your praife beftow'd;
Through time's extended courfe his Name.
Shall praife, and thanks, and homage, claim.

2.

Its circuit from the Eaft begun,
To fartheft Weft his fame fhall run,
His glory. Earth's wide Realms o'erflow,
Nor higheft Heav'ns its limit know.

3.

Great is the Lord, and great his Praife;
What God like Him our Thoughts can raife?
O whom to Him fhall Mortals dare,
To equal, whom to Him compare?

4. He

4.

He fits aloft, o'er Gods a God,
Eternity his dread Abode,
Yet ftoops to view, and, view'd, records
The fcenes that Earth's low feat affords;.

5.

He from the duft uplifts the Poor,
And gives the abject and obfcure,
The dunghill for a throne exchang'd,
To fit with mightieft Monarchs rang'd.

6.

'Tis His the barren houfe to blefs;
His gift let each the Babes confefs,
That, long to her requeft denied,
The joyful Mother's care divide..

Hallelujah.

PSALM CXIV.

1.

WHEN *Jacob's* Sons through paths
       unknown
From *Egypt* took their way,
In *Judah's* Tribe his prefence fhone,
   And *Ifrael* own'd his fway.

2.

Old Ocean faw them as they came;
   He faw, and backward fled:
Recoiling *Jordan* turn'd his ftream,
   And fought his fountain-head.

3. The

3.

The Mountains feel the fudden fhock;
 As rams, from off the ground
They fpring: As younglings of the flock;
 The Hills affrighted bound.

4.

Thou, Ocean, fay, why, as they came,
 Thy billows backward fled:
And what, O *Jordan*, urg'd thy ftream
 To feek its fountain-head?

5.

Ye Mountains, whence the fudden fhock?
 Why leap ye from the ground
As rams? As younglings of the flock,
 Say why, O Hills, ye bound.

6.

Earth, inftant, to thy loweft bafe
 Convuls'd, avow thy fear,
While Heav'n's high Lord reveals his face,
 While *Jacob*'s God is near:

7.

Diffolv'd beneath whofe potent ftroke
 The flint a torrent gave;
Who fpake; and from the yielding rock
 Gufh'd forth the bidden wave.

P S A L M   CXV.

1.

O Let not Us, thou God of Hofts,
 O let not Us, with frantic beafts,
The merit and the glory claim,
Due only to thy hallow'd name.

2. To

2.

To Thee, great God, to Thee alone,
Thy Truth and Grace, to *Ifrael* known,
Shall ceafelefs honour yield, and raife
Each heart to Love, each tongue to Praife.

3.

Why fhould the heathen tribes demand,
" Where's now the God of *Ifrael's* Land?"
In Heav'n our God has fix'd his throne,
That Lord whofe Will and Act are one.

4.

Not fuch the Gods whom Ye adore,
That, once a mafs of fhapelefs ore,
Now crown'd with furtive honours ftand,
The creatures of the Artift's hand;

5.

Mouths have they, not for fpeech defign'd;
And ears and eyes, yet deaf and blind;
Their noftrils, as along the fane
It breathes, the incenfe greets in vain:

6.

Their hands th' imprinted kifs ne'er feel,
While fuppliant crouds before them kneel;
Their feet have never ftep effay'd;
Their throat has never found convey'd:

7.

Unvifited by Wifdom's ray
Their breaft: nor lefs infenfate They,
Who made their mimic forms, or, made,
With fruitlefs pray'r invoke their aid.

8. Ye

8.

Ye happier Sons of *Israel's* Line,
Conducted by the Light divine,
On God your firm reliance build ;
Him own your refuge, Him your shield.

9.

Ye, who from vested *Aaron* trace
The honours of your chosen Race,
On God your firm reliance build ;
Him own your refuge, Him your shield.

10.

Ye Souls, with pure devotion warm,
Whose Lives to his Decrees conform,
On God your firm reliance build ;
Him own your refuge, Him your shield.

11.

Behold, his beams around us shine :
He, *Jacob*, He shall bless thy Line,
You, who from vested *Aaron* trace
The honours of your chosen Race.

12.

And You, with pure devotion warm,
Whose Lives to his Decrees conform,
From Him whose hand the scepter guides,
To Him who in the cot resides.

13.

To You, to Yours, till time shall end,
His Love its blessings shall extend,
Heirs of the changeless promise giv'n
By Him who form'd the Earth and Heav'n ;

14. That

14.

That Heav'n, within whofe awful bound
Himfelf, with brighteft glory crown'd,
His Seat has rear'd ; while *Adam's* Sons
The Earth (his Gift) its tenants owns.

15.

Not Thofe whom death has fnatch'd away
The debt of hallow'd praife fhall pay,
Or wake his wonders to difclofe,
But filent in the duft repofe :

16.

'Tis Ours, who ftill thofe wonders view,
The grateful labour to purfue ;
Nor ever fhall our lips decline
To crown with hymns the Name divine.
Hallelujah.

PSALM CXVI.

1.

HOW glows with grateful Love my breaft?
For God the voice of my requeft
Accepts, and, while my hands I rear,
Bows to my plaint the willing ear :
For this, to Life's extremeft hour,
My lips to Him the pray'r fhall pour.

2.

While Death its fnares around me threw,
The grave, its horrors to my view
Prefenting, prefs'd with heavieft grief,
From Thee, great God, I fought relief :
" O fave me, heav'nly Sire, I cried,
" And turn th' impending ftroke afide."

3. Great

3.

Great is our God, beyond all bound
His Providence and Pow'r are found;
Juft, good, and kind, is *Ifrael's* Lord,
His breaft with tend'reft pity ftor'd,
And prompt his Arm, when Ills invade,
The guilelefs and the meek to aid.

4.

His Mercies, 'midft thy deepeft woe,
By bleft experience taught to know,
Turn, turn thee to thy reft, my Soul;
For He who fits above the pole
(Tremendous Name) has o'er thy head
The fulnefs of his bounty fhed.

5.

Thou, mightieft Father, Thou wert nigh,
To fave my foul from death, mine eye
From tears, to guard from lapfe my feet,
And bid me in this earthly Seat
(Life's wide dominion) ftill refide,
To Thee in filial fear allied.

6.

To God my heart refign'd its care;
To Him my tongue addrefs'd its pray'r:
While, ftruck with terrors as I ftood,
A fea of forrows round me flow'd,
" No more, my Soul, no more, I cried,
" In Man's fallacious aid confide."

7.

O, what requital at my hand
Shall Mercies, Lord, like Thine, demand?

By

By Thee from each diſtreſs enlarg'd,
The Cup with benediction charg'd
I take, and, touch'd with holy flame,
Invoke my great Deliv'rer's name.

8.

Ev'n now, before th' aſſembled Train,
Ev'n now, within thy ſacred Fane,
(That Fane, whoſe Walls, on firmeſt baſe
Uprear'd, fair *Salem*'s confines grace,)
Behold me at thine altar bow,
And, pleas'd, abſolve my offer'd vow.

9.

Who Thy Decrees, great God, obey,
Secure on Thee their hope ſhall ſtay;
Nor Fraud nor Rapine's iron hand
Shall dare to touch the pious Band,
For ſacred is their blood, and high
Its price in thy paternal eye.

10.

In Me thy Servant, Lord, in Me
The Offspring of thy Handmaid ſee,
Releas'd by thee, from day to day
The ſacrifice of praiſe to pay
I joy, and, touch'd with holy flame,
Invoke my great Deliv'rer's Name.

11.

Ev'n now, before th' aſſembled Train,
Ev'n now within thy ſacred Fane,
(That Fane, whoſe walls, on firmeſt baſe
Uprear'd, fair *Salem*'s confines grace,)

E e   Behold

Behold me at thine altar bow,
And, pleas'd, abſolve my offer'd vow.

Hallelujah.

PSALM CXVII.

I.

LET thy various Realms, O Earth,
Praiſes yield to Heav'n's high Lord;
Praiſe him All of human birth,
And his wondrous Acts record.

2.

See his Mercy o'er our Land
Spread its ever-healing wing,
And his Truth through ages ſtand;
Praiſe, O praiſe, th' eternal King.

PSALM CXVIII.

I.

LIFT your voice, and thankful ſing
Praiſes to your heav'nly King;
For his Mercies far extend,
And his Bounty knows no end.

2.

Iſrael, thy Creator bleſs,
And with joyous tongue confeſs,
That his Mercies far extend,
And his Bounty knows no end.

3.

Aaron, let thy choſen Line
Grateful in th' avowal join,
That his Mercies far extend,
And his Bounty knows no end.

5

4. Ye

4.

Ye who make his Will your care,
With affenting voice declare,
That his Mercies far extend,
And his Bounty knows no end.

5.

To my plaint propitious, He
Bade my captive Soul go free;
He fhall in my caufe appear;
Let not Man excite my fear.

6.

He amid my Helpers ftands;
Struck by Him, th' oppofing Bands
Inftant from before mine eye
Back in wild retreat fhall fly.

7.

O, how fafe the Man, whofe mind
Refts on *Jacob*'s God reclin'd !
Safer far then they who truft
On the help of breathing duft.

8.

O how fafe the Man, whofe mind
Refts on *Jacob*'s God reclin'd !
Safer far than they who deem
Kings on Earth their pow'r fupreme.

9.

Gather'd from each diftant Coaft
Round me prefs'd th' embattled Hoft;
But my Arm, by God upheld,
Strew'd with flaughter'd heaps the field.

E e 2 10. Round

10.

Round me, thirsting for my blood,
Round me adverse myriads stood;
But my Arm, by God upheld,
Strew'd with slaughter'd heaps the field.

11.

Round me, see! as Bees they dwell,
Bees, that, issuing from their cell,
Mix in swarms, and on the wing
Arm'd with fury onward spring:

12.

See their rage at once expire
Like the thorn-enkindled fire;
While my Arm, by God upheld,
Strews with slaughter'd heaps the field.

13.

Soon thy stroke, relentless Foe,
Soon thy stroke had laid me low,
Had not God's supporting hand
Bid my fault'ring feet to stand.

14.

He my Strength, and he my Song,
Lo! my days I yet prolong,
And, each hostile force o'erthrown,
Him my great Salvation own.

15.

Shouts of health and hymns of praise
Wisdom's faithful followers raise,
While amid their peaceful Seat
Thus the ear their accents greet:

16. "O

16.

" O how ſtrong the hand divine !
" O what wonders, Lord, are thine !"
See that hand, from Heav'n reveal'd,
Wonders yet on wonders yield.

17.

Vaunt thy terrors, Death, no more ;
He whom *Iſrael*'s Sons adore,
He, each danger chac'd away,
Bids me ſtill his Acts diſplay.

18.

He indulgent, juſt, and kind,
Trials to my lot aſſign'd,
Yet amidſt the doubtful ſtrife
Reſcu'd from the ſword my life.

19.

Ope the gates of Righteouſneſs ;
Let my feet have full acceſs ;
There I'll praiſe my Saviour's Name,
And his boundleſs Love proclaim.

20.

Here the hallow'd gate behold ;
See its valves at once unfold,
Pleas'd t' admit the choſen Train,
Pure from Sin's infectious ſtain.

21.

Thee, the God inthron'd above,
Thee my lips ſhall ſing, whoſe Love
To my voice attention gave,
Prompt to hear, and ſtrong to ſave,

E e 3   22. See

22.

See the Stone, that, caſt aſide
By the Builders' erring pride,
In the Dome aſſumes its place,
Own'd the Angle's nobleſt grace.

23.

Thou the Work, great God, haſt wrought ;
In its ſcenes our wond'ring Thought
Joys thy clemency to trace,
Seal'd to *Jacob*'s favour'd Race.

24.

Lit by thy auſpicious ray
Downward ſtreams the wiſh'd-for Day,
Big with Acts that ſhall ſuggeſt
Endleſs mirth to *Iſrael*'s breaſt.

25.

Save, O ſave, eternal Lord,
And thy proſp'ring aid afford:
Bleſt the Man, who, ſent by God,
Viſits *Salem*'s lov'd abode.

26.

Come, ye Saints, and in his Train
Tread with licens'd ſtep her Fane,
While from out her ſacred Tow'r
Bleſſings on your head we pour.

27.

Safe in *Iſrael*'s Lord confide ;
He is God, and none beſide ;
See his fav'ring beams ariſe
To his People's longing eyes.

28. Fair,

28.

Fair, and innocent of fpot,
Let the victim Lamb be brought,
And befide his Altar ftand,
Fetter'd in the writhen band.

29.

Thee, my God, in lengthen'd lays,
Thee my raptur'd lips fhall praife ;
Thee, my God, aloud proclaim,
Zealous to exalt thy fame.

30.

Lift your voice, and thankful fing
Praifes to your heav'nly King ;
For his Mercies far extend,
And his Bounty knows no end.

PSALM CXIX.

ALEPH.

1.

HOW bleft, who Thee, great God, obey,
And ftedfaft walk th' all-perfect way !
How bleft, whofe hearts with will intire
Thy prefence feek, Almighty Sire ;
Whofe feet thy guidance own ; whofe mind
Has each nefarious act declin'd.

2.

Thy voice has charg'd us to fulfil
The dictates of thy heav'nly Will ;
Such, Lord, thy charge ; and O may I
Attentive to the tafk apply,

Truft

Truſt in thy Aid, thy Works record,
And 'mark the Precepts of thy Word.

3.

My ſteps conform'd to thy Decrees,
Nor ſhame nor dread my Soul ſhall ſeize ;
Thy Precepts on my mind impreſs'd
Shall ſwell with joy my faithful breaſt, .
Thy Juſtice prompt my tongue to raiſe
The ſong of gratitude and praiſe.

4.

Thy Law my love ſhall claim : Do Thou
Thy ear to my petition bow ;
O treat me not with cold diſdain,
Let not my Vows return in vain,
Nor leave me, helpleſs and forlorn,
The abſence of thy grace to mourn.

B E T H.

1.

HOW, early wiſe, ſhall Youth, O ſay,
In Innocence direct its way ?
Thy Word its ſteps, to Thee reſign'd,
The ever faithful Guide ſhall find.

2.

Hail, beſt Inſtructor ! Thee my Thought
With full deſire, great God, has ſought ;
O let me not, by Error's ſway
Impell'd, from thy direction ſtray.

3.

Thy Precept, in my breaſt conceal'd,
From Sin's aſſault my heart ſhall ſhield :
Bleſt is thy Name, eternal Lord !
O write within my mind thy Word :

4. That

4.

That Word, whofe rules from day to day
My lips with grateful zeal difplay;
Thefe, my beſt wealth, my treafur'd ſtore
I keep, and view them o'er and o'er.

5.

Thy Dictates ſtill, my conſtant joy,
My ſoul's attention ſhall employ;
Nor aught ſhall from my ſight withdraw
Thy path, or from my thought thy Law.

·GIMEL.

1.

THY Mercy let thy Servant fee,
   Grant me to live conform'd to Thee,
And let my Soul, each miſt away,
The wonders of thy Law furvey.

2.

Behold me, abſent from my home,
Through Life's wild maze a Pilgrim roam,
Nor Thou to my deſiring eye
Thy Word's directing beams deny.

3.

With ardent zeal, with ſtrong deſire,
My thoughts to thy Decrees aſpire;
With fervent hope thy paths I tread
By Mercy and by Truth outſpread.

4.

O Thou, whofe threat the proud ſubdues,
Whofe wrath the finner's ſteps purſues,
My ſoul, of each tranfgreffion pure,
From fcorn and fierce reproach fecure.

5. While

5.

While Princes with malignant aim
Aſſembled wound my honeſt fame,
My Life, thy will its fix'd purſuit,
Shall each opprobrious tongue refute.

6.

Thy Laws my ev'ry thought controul,
While, fill'd with ſacred joy, my Soul
Its ever faithful Friends in Theſe
And inmates of its counſel ſees.

D A L E T H.

1.

L OW in the duſt my ſoul is laid;
　O reach me, Lord, thy promis'd aid;
Thou, as my heart its guilt avow'd,
Thy pitying ear, great God, haſt bow'd;
Let thy Commands my footſteps lead;
O give me, Lord, thy paths to tread;
And let me, leſſon'd in thy way,
The wonders of thy Grace ſurvey:

2.

While on my ſoul, that melts with woe,
That Grace its ſuccours ſhall beſtow,
(Such hope thy Word has bid me form;)
Let me, with holy tranſport warm,
And privileg'd thy Law to learn,
From Error's path abhorrent turn;
Averſe from each injurious art,
Let falſehood from my lips depart.

3. Truth,

3.

Truth, Lord, my fteady thoughts purfue,
Thy Judgments fix'd before my view
In full difplay : Exempt from fhame
O give me Thou by Thefe to frame
My courfe ; and mark with what delight,
(As onward Thefe my fteps invite,)
Its bands by Thee diffolv'd, my Soul
Anticipates the diftant goal.

H E.

I.

TEACH me, O teach me, Lord, thy Way;
So to my life's remoteft day,
By thy unerring Precepts led,
My willing feet its paths fhall tread.

2.

Inform'd by Thee, with facred awe
My heart fhall meditate thy Law,
And with celeftial Wifdom fill'd
To Thee its full obedience yield.

3.

Give me to know thy Words aright,
(Thy Words, my foul's fupreme delight)
That, purg'd from thirft of gold, my mind
In Them its better wealth may find.

4.

O turn from Vanity mine eye,
To Me thy quick'ning ftrength fupply,
And with thy promis'd mercy chear
A heart devoted to thy fear.

5.

O vindicate my Name from wrong,
And filence the reproachful tongue;
My dreaded fhame, great God, remove;
Thy Judgments, Lord, my thoughts approve.

6.

Thy wife Commands my breaft inflame;
O hafte, and to my inmoft frame
Permit thy Juftice to difpenfe
Its all-reviving influence.

V A U.

1.

O LET me, Lord, thy Mercy know;
   Thy promis'd health, great God, beftow;
So from my Soul, on Thee reclin'd,
Shall each reproach an anfwer find.

2.

My truft thy Judgments, mightieft Lord,
Support; O let not then thy Word
(Thy Word, by Truth eternal feal'd)
Be ever from my lips withheld:

3.

That Word to Life's extremeft ftage
My juft remembrance fhall engage,
My Soul to thy Decrees incline,
And make the paths of freedom mine.

4.

The Heav'n-taught truths that warm my breaft
My tongue to Monarchs fhall fuggeft,
And, rapt with zeal, each check difclaim
Of fervile dread, and infant fhame.

5. Thy

5.

Thy Dictates on my Thoughts impreſs'd
With ſweet delight ſhall fill my breaſt ;
Thy Law, *Jehovah*, ſtill ſhall ſhare
My ardent Love, my conſtant Care ;

6.

And, while from Thee with lifted hands
Pleas'd I receive its juſt commands,
My Life, ſubmitted to its rein,
Shall ſpeak them not receiv'd in vain.

ZAIN.

1.

THY promiſes, Almighty Sire,
  Accompliſh : Theſe my hope inſpire ;
Theſe, when oppreſs'd with ills I lie,
With vital ſtrength my ſoul ſupply ;
Nor loud reproach nor hoſtile ſcorn
My heart from thy obedience turn :
Amid my woes, through ages paſt
In long memorial backward trac'd,
Thy Judgments have my truſt upheld,
And ſorrow's heavieſt cloud diſpell'd.

2.

How trembles, Lord, my heart to ſee
The ſouls that err from thy Decree !
Long as within this ſeat of clay,
My houſe of Pilgrimage, I ſtay,
Thy Statutes are my Song ; thy Name
Wakes in my breaſt the holy flame,

F f   That

That heav'n-ward lifts my thoughtful foul,
When night's dark fhades inveft the pole.
What hopes, great God, are mine, what joy,
While thy Commands my care employ!

CHETH.

1.

MY heart's beft portion, Lord, art Thou;
To Thee my Thoughts obedience vow:
To Thee with ardent zeal I pray;
Thy promis'd mercy, Lord, difplay.

2.

While back my yet unfinifh'd race
With fcrutiny fevere I trace,
Thy Law with full delight I greet,
And turn to Thee my willing feet.

3.

With ftudious hafte I ran, I flew,
Intent thy Dictates to purfue,
Nor Thefe forget, though troops of foes
Amid their fnare my fteps inclofe.

4.

Thy juft Decrees within my breaft
Revolv'd, I quit my bed of reft,
And pleas'd, at midnight's awful hour,
In thanks to Thee my fpirit pour.

5.

I mark where'er the fouls I find
To Thy Commands, great God, inclin'd;
I mark them, and with fuch refide
In friendfhip's ftricteft bands ally'd.

6. That

6.

That Mercy, Lord, whofe beams extend
Far as to Earth's remoteft end,
That Mercy to my Soul impart,
And grave thy precepts on my heart.

TETH.

1.

MY grateful heart thy Love has known,
O Thou, whofe words and deeds are one;
O ftill that Love impart, and ftore
My Soul with thy celeftial Lore,
Whofe thought its full affent refigns
To what thy facred Will injoins.

2.

In devious paths awhile I trod,
Ere yet corrected by thy rod;
But from thy juft and perfect Law
Fair Virtue's Leffons now I draw,
And, difciplin'd, great Sire, by Thee,
Obfequious bow to thy Decree.

3.

Thy Mercies, Lord, exhauftlefs flow;
O give my Soul thy Will to know:
While Crouds, whofe hearts thy fear difclaim,
With ftudied falfehood blaft my fame,
Thee, Lord, I feek; by thy Command
My Acts, my Thoughts, directed ftand.

4.

Amidft their rage, with joyful view
My heart thy Precepts can purfue,
While folly theirs from truth withholds,
And round them wraps its thickeft folds:

Behold

Behold them, Lord, in Error loſt,
Thy Law rejeɔt with impious boaſt.

5.

Bleſt be thy hand, ſeverely kind,
Whoſe ſtroke recall'd my erring Mind,.
And urg'd me, as to Thee I turn,
Thy hallow'd Inſtitutes to learn,
And, taught their worth, to prize them more
Than heaps of *Ophir*'s richeſt ore.

J o d.

1.

THY plaſtic art, throughout my frame,
  Each limb, each nerve, great God, pro-
    claim;
O give me Thou with mind ſincere
To learn th' Inſtructions of thy Fear:

2.

So ſhall the Souls, that Fear who know,
With ſocial joy, my God, o'erflow,
And pleas'd my conſtant heart approve,
That waits, with Them, thy plighted Love.

3.

Thy Judgments praiſe eternal claim,
Wiſe, juſt, and good; with friendlieſt aim
Thy faithful hand each woe I feel
Inflicts, and wounds me but to heal.

4.

O let thy promis'd mercy ſhed
Its quick'ning effluence on my head,
And comfort to my Soul inſtil,
That loves the dictates of thy Will.

4   5. Let

5.

Let fhame th' Aggreffors proud repay,
Who feek my footfteps to betray :
Thine aid I afk, eternal Lord,
And treafure in my heart thy Word.

6.

With Me in facred friendfhip join
The fouls that to thy fear incline,
And from the well-fpring of thy Law
Exhauftlefs ftreams of knowledge draw.

7.

O never from my conftant heart
Let thy Decrees, great God, depart,
So fhall I thence, by Thee renew'd,
Guilt, and its offspring Shame, exclude.

CAPH.

1.

BEHOLD, while wearied with delay
My foul, my fight, confume away,
Thy Servant o'er th' ethereal plain
Send the long look, but fend in vain.

2.

O when, to my expecting eyes,
When fhall thy wifh'd Salvation rife,
Through ftruggling clouds its promis'd ray
Tranfmit, and o'er me pour the day ?

3.

Faft as the wine-exhaufted hide
Amid the circling fmoke is dried,
I wafte ; yet never from my heart
Shall thy Commands, great God, depart.

4.

How long fhall I my days, O fay,
In fad fucceffion roll'd furvey ;
How long to haughtieft infult yield,
Thy vengeance from my foes withheld ?

5.

The Proud, thy Precepts who defpife,
(Thy Precepts, Lord, how juft, how wife !)
With caufelefs rage their pits prepare ;
O hafte, and make my life thy care.

6.

How nigh had Conqueft crown'd their aim,
And rooted from the earth my name !
While ftill thy paths, eternal God,
With undiverted ftep I trod.

7.

O let thy Mercy to my heart
Its life-fuftaining pow'r impart ;
So fhall my Soul with facred awe,
And juft obfervance, hear thy Law.

LAMED.

1.

FIX'D in the Heav'ns, eternal Lord,
On firmeft bafis refts thy Word ;
Thy Truth, unconfcious of decay,
Sees wafting ages roll away.

2.

Pois'd on its centre by thy hand
Earth long has ftood, and yet fhall ftand :
The whole Creation, ev'ry hour,
Subfervient owns thy fov'reign Pow'r.

3. How

3.

How had I perifh'd, 'midft my woes,
But that within my bofom rofe
The joys which thy Injunctions yield,
And each invading grief difpell'd!

4.

O never, never, fhall my heart,
Forgetful, from thy Law depart,
Which, inftant, kindlieft fuccour gave,
And wrought my refcue from the grave.

5.

Behold me, Lord, behold me thine;
Thy ear to my requeft incline,
And fave a Soul whofe wakeful Thought
With fervent zeal thy Truths has fought.

6.

And though with fecret art their fnare
The impious for my Life prepare,
Thy Precepts ftill, my conftant joy
My fix'd attention fhall employ.

7.

Mine eyes Perfection's limit fee
Through Nature's Works; but thy Decree
No period, mightieft Monarch, knows,
Nor bounds of fpace its breadth inclofe.

MEM.

I.

WITH what defire, great God, I burn
Thy facred Oracles to learn!
Each day, each hour, with ftedfaft mind
Thy Truths I meditate, and find

The

The knowledge, to my foes denied,
To Me in fulleſt weight ſupplied.

2.

My Teachers, while from out thy Law
The leſſons of my life I draw,
My guidance aſk ; the Aged Me
Their Elder in diſcretion ſee,
As, onward led, with ſteady pace
The Heav'n-appointed paths I trace.

3.

O with what zeal my boſom burn'd,
With joy the heav'nly precept learn'd !
How have I kept my feet from ill,
Intent thy Mandate to fulfil,
My ear to diſcipline reſign'd,
Nor ever from its rules declin'd !

4.

In full ſatiety of joy
Abſorpt, thy Words my thought employ,
And ſweeter on my palate dwell
Than honey dropping from its cell :
My Soul, by thy Inſtruction, wiſe,
From Error's path abhorrent flies.

N u n.

1

THY Law, from *Sinai*'s mount reveal'd,
A lantern to my feet ſhall yield,
A light, whoſe beams ſhall o'er me dwell,
And night's incircling ſhades diſpel.

2. Thy

Thy Precepts (thus my tongue has sworn,
Nor aught my purpose, Lord, shall turn;)
Thy Precepts, just, and wise, and true,
My steps, unwearied, shall pursue.

3.

Beneath a weight of woes I bend;
Thy promis'd aid, my God, extend:
My lips their willing off'rings pay;
Accept them, gracious Lord, I pray.

4.

Thy Judgments to my longing eyes
Display; while dangers round me rise,
My soul just ready to resign,
To These my thoughts I still incline.

5.

No impious force, or hostile snare,
Shall alienate from These my care;
Nor e'er shall Sin my steps betray
From these in devious Paths to stray.

6.

These, while their worth my Soul inflames,
Its lasting heritage it claims,
And pleas'd the dictates of thy Will
To life's last period shall fulfil.

S A M E C H.

I.

FAR hence each Superstition vain,
   Wild offspring of the human brain;
The Truths that fill thy hallow'd page
My happier choice, great God, engage;

Safe

Safe on thy Word my truſt I build,
O Thou, my Refuge, and my Shield.

2.

Ye impious, from my ſight away;
My Soul ſhall God's beheſts obey:
O ever faithful to thy Word,
Do Thou thy vital ſtrength afford;
Thy help impart, eternal Sire,
Nor let my hope in ſhame expire.

3.

Suſtain'd by tby Almighty aid,
What danger ſhall my Soul invade?
Nor error's cloud, nor arts of ſin,
My ſoul from thy obedience win;
In vain ſhall theſe their force apply
To turn from thy Decrees mine eye.

4.

Subverted by their own deceit,
And ſpurn'd beneath thy conqu'ring feet,
Thy wrath the rebel tribes deplore;
Spurn'd,—as the droſs, that from the ore
(Amid the glowing furnace caſt)
Is ſever'd by the fiery blaſt.

5.

For this, with ardent Love thy Law
I ſeek; for this, while rev'rent Awe
And holy Horror ſhake my frame,
Thy dreaded judgments I proclaim;
And, wrapt in fear, moſt mighty Lord,
Thy pow'r, thy righteouſneſs record.

AIN.

A I N.

1.

WHILE Justice o'er my life presides,
Each act, each word, each purpose guides,
Friend of the guiltless! nigh me stand,
And save me from th' Oppressor's hand.

2.

O still thy wonted grace disclose;
Still in my quarrel interpose
Thine arm, nor let my haughty foe
Exulting triumph in my woe.

3.

My wasting eyes with earnest view
Thy promis'd health, my God, pursue:
Thy mercies to thy Servant show,
Give me each Heav'n-taught rule to know.

4.

Behold me, Lord, behold me thine,
And let thy influence on me shine,
Till, each illusion purg'd away,
My Soul thy mystic Truths survey.

5.

Thy wise Injunctions cast aside,
The sons of Insolence and Pride
With oft-repeated crimes demand
Th' unwilling vengeance from thy hand.

6.

Thy Dictates on my thought imprefs'd
With sweet delight shall fill my breast;
Not Gold like These my love shall claim,
Gold sev'n times tortur'd in the flame.

7. These,

7.

Thefe, Lord, I keep, thy Works record,
And mark the precepts of thy word,
Truft in thine aid, and, fix'd, decree
To fhun each path that leads from Thee.

P E.

1.

O HOW the Wonders of thy Law
My heart to juft obedience awe !
What ftreams of pureft knowledge yield
Thy Words in full difplay reveal'd !
By Thefe the Souls untaught before
To heights of heav'nly fcience foar.

2.

With earneft zeal, and anxious thought
Thy words my panting bofom fought ;
With thirft, with facred thirft I burn'
To Thefe my op'ning mouth I turn'd,
And from thy Precept wife and true
Its life-imparting fpirit drew :

3.

What grace thy Saints are bleft to know,
That grace on Me, great God, beftow ;
Thy Dictates to my foul convey,
And level to my fteps thy way ;
Redeem from Error's growth my mind,
Nor leave one baleful root behind.

4.

O fave me from Oppreffion's hand ;
So fhall my foul thy wife command
Obferve, and, leffon'd inthy fear,
The precepts of thy law revere :

Indulgent

Indulgent on thy ſervant ſhine,
And make the paths of knowledge mine.

5.

My tears, great God, my zeal diſcloſe,
And down the copious torrent flows,
As oft, with inward anguiſh torn,
Thy violated Laws I mourn
By guilty Souls, whoſe Love of ill
To raſh Tranſgreſſion prompts their will.

TSADDI.

1.

HAIL, Arbiter ſupreme ! thy Will
    Truth, Equity, and Juſtice ſeal ;
Truth, Juſtice, Equity, thy Voice
Preſcribes to favour'd *Iſrael*'s choice ;
Theſe while my foe preſumptuous ſpurns,
With zeal conſum'd my boſom burns.

2.

O how thy Precepts, in the fire
Long prov'd, thy ſervant's Love inſpire !
To indigence and ſcorn reſign'd,
Theſe ſtill I ſeek with ſtudious mind ;
Nor ceaſe with conſtant thought to trace
The acts of thy ſtupendous grace.

3.

Eternal Rectitude is thine ;
Truth to thy Laws adjuſts its line ;
Thy Laws, my Soul's beſt comfort found,
When pains and ſorrows wrapt me round :
Thy juſt Decrees ſhall Time ſurvive ;
Them teach me, and my Soul ſhall live.

G g   KOPH.

K o p h.

1.

O Maker, Guide, and Judge of All!
  With earneſt voice to Thee I call;
To Thee I call; propitious hear;
So ſhall the Precepts of thy fear
My Soul inform, and, Thou my aid,
My ev'ry Act by Theſe be ſway'd.

2.

Ere yet the dawn has ſtreak'd the ſky,
God of my Life, to Thee I cry;
My hope (nor ſhall that hope be vain,)
Thy ſacred promiſes ſuſtain :
On thy Decrees, great God, intent,
My Thoughts the early watch prevent.

3.

O let thy Mercy, while I pray,
My night illumine, guide my day,
Thy Word within my inmoſt frame
Awake the everliving flame,
And, inſtant, to my breaſt diſpenſe
Its all-reviving influence.

4.

Behold a Croud, from Thee eſtrang'd,
In dire alliance near me rang'd ;
But Thou, my God, art nearer ſtill :
My Soul the dictates of thy Will
Fix'd on eternal baſe has view'd,
And owns them wiſe, and juſt, and good.

R E S H.

RESH.

1.

BEHOLD my griefs ; my Soul preferve ;
For ne'er from thy direction fwerve
My thoughts : Do Thou my caufe defend ;
O let thy word its aid extend.

2.

In vain thy grace the Souls would heal,
Whofe crimes their juft rejection feal ;
Who, bold each impious deed to try,
Thy Laws oppofe, thy Pow'r defy.

3.

O let thy Mercy, Lord, (how great
That Mercy !) on thy Servant wait,
Its beams in full effufion give,
And teach my fainting heart to live.

4.

While hoftile Crouds around me ftand,
My fteps I guide by thy Command
Unvarying, and indignant fee
The Souls whofe Will has err'd from Thee.

5.

Behold what love, what full delight,
Thy Precepts in my breaft excite,
And let thy Favour o'er my head
Its vital pow'r inceffant fhed.

6.

With truth thy Word, great God, was crown'd,
Ere time began its reftlefs round :
Thy Laws through length of days extend,
Firft, midft, and laft, and without end.

Gg 2   SCHIN.

S C H I N.

1.

WHILE princely Pow'r, without a cause,
  The threat'ning sword against me draws,
My mind, to thy Commands applied,
Them fears, nor owns a fear beside.

2.

My heart with secret transport swells,
While studious on thy Word it dwells;
Nor wealthiest spoils such joy bestow,
New wrested from the prostrate foe.

3.

To Lies averse, thy Laws I love;
Thy just Decrees my Thoughts approve;
And sev'n times, each revolving day,
To Thee my grateful vows I pay.

4.

Great is the peace prepar'd for All,
Whose willing feet obey thy Call;
Great is the peace for such prepar'd,
Nor aught their footsteps shall retard.

5.

Thy health, my God, I wait, thy Will
With unremitted zeal fulfil,
And wrapt in love and filial fear
The Heav'n-descended Truths revere.

6.

Thy Truths my soul reveres: Each day,
Thy wise Instructions I obey,
Assur'd that to thy searching eyes
My life's whole path conspicuous lies.

                              T A U.

Tau.

1.

O Let my cries thy heav'nly feat
  Approach; my pray'r indulgent meet,
And give (for on thy Word relies
My hope;) O give me to be wife.

2.

Behold, (for Mercy lives in Thee;)
Behold me fuppliant bend the knee,
And let thy promis'd aid difpel
The clouds of grief that o'er me dwell.

3.

Thy facred Precepts taught to know,
How fhall my lips, great God, o'erflow
With praife, and, touch'd with holy flame,
The juftice of thy Laws proclaim!

4.

While pleas'd I bow to thy Command,
Reach, in my refcue, reach thy hand;
Do Thou, whofe Dictates warm my heart,
Thy long-expected health impart.

5.

O let my Soul, to life reftor'd,
Thy Love in lafting hymns record,
While o'er my head its beams fhall fhine,
And make thy great Salvation mine.

6.

Thine eyes in Me the Sheep behold,
Whofe feet have wander'd from the fold,
That, guidelefs, helplefs, ftrives in vain
To find its fafe retreat again;

7. Now

7.

Now liſtens, if perchance its ear
The Shepherd's well-known voice may hear,
Now, as the tempeſts round it blow,
In plaintive accent vents its woe.

8.

Great Ruler of this earthly Ball,
Do Thou my erring ſteps recall:
O ſeek thou Him who Thee has ſought,
Nor turns from thy Decrees his thought.

P S A L M CXX.

1.

TO God I cried, with anguiſh ſtung,
Nor form'd a fruitleſs pray'r.
O ſave me from the lying tongue,
And lips that would inſnare.

2.

Thou Child of Guilt, to falſehood bred,
Say, what ſhall be thine end?
See keeneſt arrows o'er thy head,
And quenchleſs coals, impend.

3.

Ah! Woe is Me, to *Meſech*'s ſeat
And *Kedar*'s tents confin'd;
Perpetual inſult doom'd to meet
From Men of reſtleſs mind.

4.

When offers mild of Peace I make,
And friendlieſt terms prepare,
My words their ſlumb'ring rage awake,
And arm them for the War.

P S A L M

PSALM CXXI.

1.

LO ! from the Hills my help defcends ;
   To Them I lift mine eyes :
My ftrength on Him alone depends,
   Who form'd the Earth and Skies.

2.

He, ever watchful, ever nigh,
   Forbids thy feet to flide ;
Nor fleep nor flumber feals the eye
   Of *Ifrael's* Guard and Guide.

3.

He at thy hand, array'd in might,
   His fhield fhall o'er thee fpread ;
Nor Sun by day, nor Moon by night,
   Shall hurt thy favour'd head.

4.

Safe fhalt thou go, and fafe return,
   While He thy Life defends,
Whofe eyes thy ev'ry ftep difcern,
   Whofe Mercy never ends.

PSALM CXXII.

1.

THE feftal Morn, my God, is come,
   That calls me to thy honour'd Dome,
Thy prefence to adore :
My feet the fummons fhall attend,
With willing ftep thy Courts afcend,
   And tread the hallow'd floor.

x   2. Ev'n

2.

Ev'n now to our tranfported eyes
Fair *Sion's* tow'rs in profpect rife ;
 Within her gates we ftand,
And, loft in wonder and delight,
Behold her happy Sons unite
 In friendfhip's firmeft band.

3.

Hither from *Judah's* utmoft end
The Heav'n-protected Tribes afcend ;
 Their off'rings hither bring;
Here, eager to atteft their joy,
In hymns of praife their tongues employ,
 And hail th' immortal King.

4.

By His Command impell'd, to Her
Contending Crouds their caufe refer ;
 While Princes from her Throne
With equal doom th' unerring Law
Difpenfe, who boaft their birth to draw
 From *Jeffe's* favour'd Son.

5.

Be Peace by Each implor'd on Thee,
O *Salem*, while with bended knee
 To *Jacob's* God we pray :
How bleft, who calls himfelf thy Friend !
Succefs his labour fhall attend,
 And fafety guard his way.

6.

O may'ft thou, free from hoftile fear,
Nor the loud voice of tumult hear,
 Nor war's wild waftes deplore :

May

May Plenty nigh thee take her ſtand,
And in thy Courts with laviſh hand
  Diſtribute all her ſtore.

7.

Seat of my Friends and Brethren, hail!
How can my tongue, O *Salem*, fail
  To bleſs thy lov'd Abode ?
How ceaſe the zeal that in me glows
Thy good to ſeek, whoſe walls incloſe
  The Manſion of my God ?

PSALM CXXIII.

1.

TO Thee, above the ſtarry ſpheres
  Inthron'd, his look thy ſuppliant rears :
As tow'rds their Lord the menial Band,
As Maidens tow'rds their Miſtreſs' hand
Obſervant caſt th' expecting eye,
So lift we ours, great God, on high,
Till Thou thy mercy ſhalt diſplay,
And chaſe theſe clouds of grief away.

2.

Enough thy People, Lord, have borne
Of inſult keen, and hoſtile ſcorn :
O let thy clemency divine
Conſpicuous in our reſcue ſhine,
And hear, in pity hear, the ſighs
From our full hearts inceſſant riſe,
While, round us rang'd, the Sons of pride
Our name revile, our woes deride.

PSALM

PSALM CXXIV.

1.

HAD God abandon'd from his care
Our caufe, when adverfe hofts to war
Uprofe; had God, may *Ifrael* fay,
Our caufe abandon'd, in the day
When o'er the plain their troops were pour'd;
Our tribes their fury had devour'd;

2.

Down we had funk; and o'er our head
The fwelling floods their waves had fpread:
Down we had funk; but bleft be God,
Whofe arm the timely help beftow'd,
And, each invader chas'd away,
Snatch'd from their jaws th' expected prey.

3.

See! as the Bird with fudden fpring
Exulting mounts upon the wing,
Juft refcu'd from the fowler's art,
So triumph We, with thankful heart,
And, fav'd by his preventing care,
Shake from our feet the broken fnare.

4.

When woes, when dangers round us rife,
On Him alone our Hope relies,
To Him our Liberty we owe,
And own his ftrength againft the foe,
Whofe hand thy center fix'd, O Earth,
And gave th' enduring Heav'ns their birth.

PSALM

PSALM CXXV.

1.

THEY, who with holy confidence,
    Truft in the Lord for their defence,
Secur'd by his protecting hand,
Shall ftedfaft as Mount Sion ftand,
That, proof to Ages, meets the fkies,
And, fix'd, each adverfe fhock defies.

2.

Behold fair *Salem*'s hallow'd ground,
By fhadowing hills encompafs'd round;
Thy prefence thus, great God, we trace
Incircling *Jacob*'s chofen Race:
Nor diftant times fhall fee thy Love
Its bleffings from thy Saints remove.

3.

Ne'er on the lot by Thefe poffefs'd
Shall impious Pow'r its fcepter reft;
Left Sin, eftablifh'd into Law,
Their hearts from thy obedience draw:
O ftill our Guardian, ftill our Friend,
Thy mercies to the Juft extend;

4.

While All, whofe heart from Wifdom's way
Through paths perverfe has lov'd to ftray,
In fuff'rings, as in guilt, allied,
Shall fee the Peace to them denied
The fulnefs of its influence fhed
On happier *Ifrael*'s favour'd head.

PSALM

PSALM CXXVI.

1.

IS this a Dream? amaz'd we cried,
⠀⠀When, led by their celeſtial Guide,
Fair *Sion*'s captive Tribes again
Beheld her late deſerted plain:
Then forth to laughter burſt each tongue,
And ſongs of loudeſt triumph ſung.

2.

The Nations round, with ſecret awe,
The mighty work admiring ſaw;
And, " Great (they cried,) the Gift beſtow'd
" On Theſe, the favour'd of their God !"
" O, great the Gift !" Our hearts rejoin,
And joyful bleſs the hand divine.

3.

Let thoſe, whoſe exile ſtill we mourn,
Beneath thy conduct, Lord, return,
Faſt as the copious torrents glide,
When, to its vacant bed their tide
Reſtoring, o'er the waſtes they run,
That burn beneath the ſouthern Sun.

4.

Let ſcenes of Hope our thought employ;
Who ſow in tears, ſhall reap in joy:
The weeping Hind, whoſe dubious hand
Now ſtrews with grain the furrow'd land,
Shall homeward ſoon exulting bear
The Bleſſings of the loaded year.

PSALM

PSALM CXXVII.

1.

A Race by God unbleſt who rear,
  A fruitleſs toil ſuſtain ;
If God to ſhield the Town forbear,
  The Watchman wakes in vain.

2.

Why riſe Ye early, late take reſt,
  And eat the bread of care ?
The balm of ſleep, his gift confeſt,
  His Children only ſhare.

3.

Know too thy Sons, that round thee ſtand,
  A gift by Him prepar'd ;
Nor arrows in the Giant's hand
  Can yield ſo ſure a guard.

4.

Bleſt, who his quiver ſtores with Theſe :
  When hoſtile troops are near,
His gate the ſtorm approaching ſees,
  Yet ſees without a fear.

PSALM CXXVIII.

1.

HOW bleſt the Souls, their God who fear,
  His Pow'r confeſs, his Law revere !
Who ſtedfaſt walk th' all perfect way,
Nor loſt in paths of folly ſtray.

2.

O happy Thou! ordained to ſhare
Thy Maker's ever conſtant care;
Thou privileg'd from want ſhalt ſtand,
And eat the labour of thy hand.

3.

The Object of thy wedded Love
Prolific as the Vine ſhall prove,
Whoſe foliage o'er thy walls diſplay'd
Spreads wide its amicable ſhade:

4.

While, as the Olive-branches fair,
Around thy board thy infant Care
Shall croud, and bid thy heart o'erflow
With joys that only Parents know.

5.

Such Bleſſings, Lord, thy hands provide
For all who make thy fear their guide,
And ſtedfaſt walk th' all perfect way,
Nor loſt in paths of folly ſtray.

6.

Hail, favour'd Man! From *Sion*'s Tow'r
Thy God on Thee his gifts ſhall ſhow'r:
Thou, thankful, to thy lateſt day
Shalt *Salem*'s proſp'ring ſtate ſurvey.

7.

With lengthen'd joy, thine aged eyes
Shall ſee thy Children's Children riſe,
And Peace her healing wings expand
O'er *Judah*'s Heav'n-diſtinguiſh'd Land.

P S A L M

PSALM CXXIX.

1.

OFT from my youth, may *Ifrael* fay,
  Oft from my youth, in clofe array
Againft me rang'd, the hoftile train
My ruin fought, but fought in vain.

2.

My back with ftripes the ploughers tore;
The lengthen'd furrows ftream'd with gore;
But Thou, juft God, haft burft their bands,
And fav'd me from their ruthlefs hands.

3.

Back let them fly in wild retreat,
Whofe rage fair *Sion*'s hallow'd feat
Purfues: Let fhame their guilt repay;
And let them like the grafs decay,—

4.

That, on the houfe-top feen to rife,
Stops in mid growth, and fades, and dies;
Nor fills the Mower's hand, nor gives
One grafp to him who binds the fheaves;

5.

Nor prompts th' obferving paffenger
To greet them with this friendly pray'r;
" May Heav'n's high Lord your labours blefs,
" And crown them with the wifh'd fuccefs."

PSALM

PSALM CXXX.

1.

TO Thee from out the Deeps I pray,
    With heaviest woes oppress'd:
Lord, let thine ears attentive weigh
    The voice of my request.

2.

If from the Sons of human birth
    Thy wrath its debt demand,
O who, throughout the peopled earth,
    Beneath that wrath shall stand?

3.

But Sin's worst wounds thy Mercy heals:
    As down its pow'rs descend,
The grateful Soul their influence feels,
    And trembles to offend.

4.

Thee, Lord, I seek, the Wise, the Just;
    My soul, by Thee upheld,
Expectant waits (thy Word its trust)
    Till Thou thy beams shalt yield.

5.

Not thus intent their longing sight
    The wearied Watchmen rear,
Not thus intent the growing light
    Observe, when morn is near.

6.

O trust in God; for Love in Him,
    And Grace abundant, reign:
He, *Jacob*, shall thy Sons redeem,
    And purge their ev'ry stain.

PSALM

PSALM CXXXI.

1.

THINE eyes, my God, nor lofty mind
    Nor haughty look in me fhall find,
Nor Earth's vain pomp attracts my view,
Nor Honour's prize my thoughts purfue.

2.

Behold me of affections mild,
Behold me humble as the Child,
That meek and filent finks to reft,
Wean'd from the tender Parent's breaft.

3.

O, fonder than that Parent, fee
'Thy Maker, *Ifrael*, cherifh Thee :
To lateft times on Him depend,
Thy Guide, thy Guardian, and thy Friend.

PSALM CXXXII.

1.

GREAT Ruler of this earthly Ball,
    Thy *David* to thy thought recall ;
O hear my voice, All-potent Sire,
Nor diftant from the pray'r retire.

2.

O think what pangs his bofom tore,
When to his God the Oath he fwore,
And thus, with various preffures bow'd,
To *Jacob*'s Lord a Manfion vow'd.

2. Be

3.

Be Witnefs, if my floor I tread,
Be Witnefs, if my couch I fpread,
If fleep thefe weary orbs fhall feal,
Or flumber o'er mine eyelids fteal,—

4.

Till to my fearch fair *Judah*'s Land
Some place prefent, whereon may ftand,
Through future age, thy fix'd Abode,
The Seat of *Jacob*'s mighty God.

5.

To Thee, O *Ephrata*, we came,
Inquifitive, and, led by fame,
The hallow'd Tabernacle found
Within the forefts ample bound.

6.

Behold us, Lord, with willing feet
The manfion of thy prefence greet,
(Each heart inflam'd with grateful zeal,)
And proftrate at thy footftool kneel.

7.

Rife, *Ifrael*'s Father, God, and Friend;
Pleas'd to thy place of reft afcend,
Thou and thine Ark, tremendous fhrine
Of Majefty and Pow'r divine.

8.

While Righteoufnefs thy Priefts arrays,
O let thy Saints their thankful lays
Prolong; and in thy *David*'s name
Let *Judah*'s King thy favour claim.

9. Thus

9.

Thus to the Prince of *Jesse* born
God the reverselefs Oath has sworn;
Thy Throne, protected by my care,
The offspring of thy loyns shall heir.

10.

Through distant times their hallow'd Line,
Long as to Me their hearts incline,
My Compact keep, my Laws obey,
Shall, uncontroul'd, extend their sway.

11.

Thy Walls, O *Sion*, to thy Lord
His destin'd residence afford;
Here will I rest, nor e'er my Love
From thy distinguish'd seat remove.

12.

Thy plenteous board my hand shall spread,
Distribute to thy Poor their bread,
Thy Priests with lasting health invest,
And wake to mirth each faithful breast.

13.

Amid thy Race, O *David*, here,
Salvation shall her standard rear,
While copious on th' anointed head
The heav'nly Lamp its beams shall shed.

14.

Thy foes with shame invelop'd o'er,
Their blasted counsels shall deplore,
And see the Crown that binds thy brow,
With unextinguish'd splendors glow.

P S A L M

PSALM CXXXIII.

1.

HOW bleſt the ſight, the joy how ſweet,
  When Brothers join'd with Brothers
      meet
  In bands of mutual Love !
Leſs ſweet the liquid fragrance, ſhed
On *Aaron*'s conſecrated head,
      Ran trickling from above,

2.

And reach'd his beard, and reach'd his veſt :
Leſs ſweet the Dews on *Hermon*'s breaſt
      Or *Sion*'s Hill deſcend :
That Hill has God with Bleſſings crow'd,
There promis'd Grace that knows no bound,
      And Life that knows no end.

PSALM CXXXIV.

1.

YE Servants of th' eternal King,
  Your grateful hymns triumphant ſing :
To You I call, the choſen Band,
Who take amid his Courts your ſtand,
While, gliding round the duſky pole,
The ſtarry Orbs in ſilence roll.

2,

Within his Temple's vaulted frame,
With lifted hands, his praiſe proclaim :
And He, may He, whoſe pow'r has made
'The Earth, and Heav'n's wide arch diſplay'd,
From ſacred *Sion* bid thee prove
The Bleſſings of his boundleſs Love.

PSALM

PSALM CXXXV. *Hallelujah.*

1.

YE faithful Servants of your God,
  To him be all your thanks beftow'd;
Through Times extended courſe, his fame
In ſongs of higheſt praiſe proclaim:

2.

Ye who, on his beheſts intent,
The Courts of *Ifrael*'s Lord frequent,
And pleas'd, within his hallow'd gate,
In regular ſucceſſion wait:

3.

Him praiſe, the everlaſting King,
And Mercy's unexhauſted ſpring;
Haſte, to his Name your voices rear;
What Name like his the heart can chear?

4.

His Love from out the num'rous Birth,
That crowns the wide-extended Earth,
Selects the Race of *Ifaac*'s Sons,
And *Jacob* his poſſeſſion owns.

5.

Thy Greatneſs, Lord, my thoughts atteſt,
With awful gratitude impreſs'd,
Nor know, among the Seats divine,
A Pow'r that ſhall contend with Thine.

6.

Tis God, whoſe All-diſpoſing Sway
The Heav'n's, the Earth, and Seas obey;
Whoſe Might through all extent extends,
Sinks through all depth, all height tranſcends—

7. From

7.

From Earth's low margin to the Skies
He bids the pregnant Vapours rife,
The Lightning's pallid fheet expands,
And glads with fhow'rs the furrow'd lands;

8.

Now from His Storehoufe built on high,
He gives th' imprifon'd Winds to fly,
And, guided by thy Will, to fweep
The furface of the foaming Deep.

9.

By His refiftlefs ftroke affail'd,
Her Eldeft-born proud *Egypt* wail'd;
Nor rag'd His fword on Man alone;
Her flocks, Her herds, its fury own.

10.

New fcenes of Dread her Land furpriz'd,
When God the haughty chief chaftis'd,
And Each who lent th' affifting hand
To execute his ftern command.

11.

From *Egypt*'s defolated fhore
Its courfe His vengeance onward bore
To diftant realms, by Juftice led;
And mightieft Kings beneath it bled:

12.

Their Monarch *Hefbon*'s Coafts deplor'd,
And *Bafan* her gigantic Lord,
While *Canaan* wept her forfeit Lands
Refign'd to *Ifrael*'s chofen Bands.

13. Thy

13.

Thy Name fhall ever live, thy Name
Shall ceafelefs Praife and Honour claim;
Thy Works, atchiev'd in ages paft,
To endlefs time remember'd laft.

14.

From Thee our Judge, we wait our doom:
Thou, Lord, the balance wilt affume,
And, prompt thy People's woes to heal,
The fentence of thy wrath repeal.

15.

Behold, on each polluted fhore
The heathen tribes their Gods adore;
Of Gold and Silver form'd, they ftand
The Creatures of the Artifts hand.

16.

Mouths have they, not for fpeech defign'd,
And Ears and Eyes, yet deaf and blind:
Their lips, by Nature's finger feal'd,
Ne'er knew the vital breath to yield:

17.

Unvifited by Wifdom's ray
Their breaft: Nor lefs infenfate They,
Who made their mimic forms, or made,
With fruitlefs pray'r invoke their aid.

18.

Ye favour'd Tribes, from *Ifrael* fprung,
Jehovah's Praife with grateful Tongue
Aloud proclaim, and thankful join
To blefs the Majefty divine.

19. Him

19.

Him bleſs, ye Sons of *Aaron*'s race;
Ye who your birth from *Levi* trace,
And All whoſe heart His Laws delight,
In thanks to Him your ſongs unite.

20.

Let *Sion* with enraptur'd ear
His fame throughout her precinᵈts hear,
Who 'midſt her walls, eternal Gueſt,
Has fix'd the Manſion of his reſt.

Hallelujah.

PSALM CXXXVI.

1.

LIFT your voice, and thankful ſing
Praiſes to your heav'nly King;
For his Bleſſings far extend,
And his Mercy knows no end.

2.

Be the Lord your only theme,
Who of Gods is God ſupreme;
For his Bleſſings, &c.

3.

He to whom All Lords beſide
Bow the knee, and vail their pride;
For his Bleſſings, &c.

4.

Who aſſerts his juſt Command
By the Wonders of his hand;
For his, &c.

5. He

I

5.

He, whofe Wifdom, thron'd on high,
Built the Manfions of the fky ;
  For his, &c.

6.

He, who bade the watry Deep
Under Earth's foundation fleep ;
  For his, &c.

7.

And the Orbs that gild the pole
Through the boundlefs Æther roll ;
  For his, &c.

8.

Thee, O Sun, whofe pow'rful ray
Rules the Empire of the Day;
  For his, &c.

9.

You, O Moon and Stars, whofe light
Breaks the horrors of the Night ;
  For his, &c.

10.

When his vengeful wrath he fhed,
Egypt mourn'd her Firftborn dead ;
  For his, &c.

11.

Thence by Him from bondage freed
March'd all *Ifrael*'s chofen feed;
  For his, &c.

12.

While his mighty hand he rear'd,
And his outftretch'd arm appear'd ;
  For his, &c.

13.

Aw'd by Him, from fide to fide,
Lo, th' obedient Deeps divide;
　　For his, &c.

14.

At his word the billows ftay,
Part, and give his People way;
　　For his, &c.

15.

At his word again they clofe
O'er the head of *Jacob*'s foes;
　　For his, &c.

16.

Safe in his Almighty aid
Ifrael o'er the Defert ftray'd;
　　For his, &c.

17.

Kings, unable to withftand,
Felt the vengeance of his hand;
　　For his, &c.

18.

Chiefs for hardieft deeds renown'd
Proftrate fell, and bit the ground;
　　For his, &c.

19.

Sihon fierce, who forth to fight
Led the harnefs'd *Amorite*;
　　For his, &c.

20.

Mightieft *Og*, beneath whofe fway
Bafan's fertile region lay;
　　For his, &c.

21.

These he slew, and from their hands
Took the forfeit of their Lands;
 For his, &c.

22.

Lands, which erst by promise due,
Sons of *Jacob*, fell to You;
 For his, &c.

23.

On our sorrows from on high
He with pity cast an eye;
 For his, &c.

24.

In our battles o'er each head
He the shield of safety spread;
 For his, &c.

25.

He with food sustains, O Earth,
All who claim from Thee their birth;
 For his, &c.

26.

Lift your voice, and thankful sing
Praise to Heav'n's eternal King;
 For his Blessings far extend,
 And his Mercy knows no end.

P S A L M CXXXVII.

1.

WHERE *Babylon*'s proud water flows,
 We sate and wept, while in us rose
The dear remembrance of thy name,
O fair, O lost *Jerusalem!*

Our filent harps the willows bore,
Whofe branches fhade th' extended fhore,

2.

In haughty triumph thus the Foe
Infulting aggravates our woe :
" Come, tune to mirth your fullen tongue ;
" Rife, *Hebrew* flaves, and give the fong ;
" Such ftrains as wont your fane to fill
" On captive *Sion*'s boafted Hill."

3.

· How fhall we yield to the demand ?
How, exiles in a heathen Land,
Prefume the heav'n-taught fong to raife,
And defecrate the hallow'd lays ?
Shall *Ifrael*'s vanquifh'd Tribes employ
Their mournful voice in hymns of joy ?

4.

If *Sion* from my breaft depart,
Forget my hand its tuneful art :
Faft to my palate cleave my tongue,
If, when I form my fprightlieft fong,
Aught to my mirth fupply a theme,
But Thou, O lov'd *Jerufalem*.

5.

'Think, Lord, O think, when *Sion* lay
Abandon'd to the dreadful day,
How, as thy heavieft wrath fhe tried,
" Down, down, exulting *Edom* cried,
" Down let the hated City fall,
" And level to the duft her wall."

6. Daughter

6.

Daughter of *Babylon*, that woe,
Deprefs'd, confum'd, thyfelf fhalt know,
Which We, dire Murth'refs, found from Thee:
And Bleft the Man whom God's Decree
Ordains to lead the flaughter on,
And dafh thine Infants on the ftone.

PSALM CXXXVIII.

1.

THEE, Lord, my harp's awaken'd ftrings
Shall praife, and to the ear of Kings,
Whofe pow'rs thy facred imprefs bear,
The ardor of my zeal declare.

2.

In low proftration, tow'rd thy fhrine,
His knees thy Servant fhall incline,
And thankful teach the rapt'rous lay
Thy Faith and Mercy to difplay.

3.

Thy Sanctity all height tranfcends;
Thy word eternal Truth attends;
Thy Pow'r, while Thee my pray'r addrefs'd,
Has fill'd with Heav'n-born ftrength my
    breaft.

4.

Earth's Lords, by thy inftructions led,
With *Ifrael's* fons thy path fhall tread,
And, joyous, as they march along,
Thy Glory chaunt in grateful fong.

5.

Inthron'd above the loftieft fky,
Thou deign'ft the Humble to defcry,
And, from thy diftant feat, deride
The frantic boafts of human pride.

6.

When hoftile troops excite my fear,
Thy quick'ning Grace my heart fhall chear,
Thy hand compofe their furious ftrife,
And refcue from the fword my life.

7.

What blifs thy promife bids me fhare,
Hafte, Lord, to yield; nor from thy care
(O ever faithful, wife and good,)
The creature of thy hands exclude.

PSALM CXXXIX.

1.

THOU, Lord, haft fearch'd me out;
  thine eyes
Mark when I fit, and when I rife;
By Thee my future thoughts are read;
Thou, round my path, and round my bed,
Attendeft vigilant; each word,
Ere yet I fpeak, by Thee is heard.

2.

Life's maze, before my view outfpread,
Within thy prefence wrapt I tread,
And touch'd with confcious horror ftand
Beneath the fhadow of thy hand;
Such knowledge, Lord, how deep! in vain
I feek its fummit to attain.

3. Where

3.

Where fhall I fhun thy wakeful eye,
Or whither from thy Spirit fly?
Aloft to Heav'n my courfe I bear;
In vain; for Thou, my God, art there:
If prone to Hell my feet defcend,
Thou ftill my footfteps fhalt attend.

4.

If now, on fwifteft wings upborne,
I feek the regions of the Morn,
Or hafte me to the weftern Steep,
Where Eve fits brooding o'er the Deep,
Thy hand the fugitive fhall ftay,
And dictate to my fteps their way.

5.

Perchance within its thickeft veil
The Darknefs fhall my head conceal;
But, inftant, Thou haft chas'd away
The gloom, and round me pour'd the day:
Darknefs, great God, to Thee there's none;
Darknefs and Light to Thee are one.

6.

My reins, my fabrick's ev'ry part,
The wonders of thy plaftic art
Proclaim, and prompt my willing tongue
To meditate the grateful fong:
With deepeft awe my Thought their frame
Surveys:—"I tremble that I am."

7.

While yet a ftranger to the day
Within the burthen'd womb I lay,

My

My bones, familiar to thy view,
By juſt degrees to firmneſs grew:
Thy pow'r my lineaments began,
To ſhapes preſcribed the texture ran.

8.

Day to ſucceeding day conſign'd
Th' unfiniſh'd Birth ; thy mighty Mind
Each limb, each nerve, ere yet they were,
Contemplated diſtinct and clear ;
Thoſe nerves thy curious finger ſpun,
Thoſe limbs it faſhion'd one by one ;—

9.

And, as thy pen in fair deſign
Trac'd on thy book each ſhadowy line,
Thy Handmaid Nature read them there,
And made the growing work her care,
Conform'd it to th' unerring plan,
And gradual wrought me into Man.

10.

With what delight, great God, I trace
The Acts of thy ſtupendous Grace!
To count them, were to count the ſand
That lies upon the ſea-beat ſtrand :
When from my temples ſleep retires,
Thy preſence, Lord, my heart inſpires.

11.

Shall impious Men thy will withſtand,
Nor feel the vengeance of thy hand?
Shall not thy wrath terrific riſe,
The bold tranſgreſſors to chaſtiſe?
Hence, Murth'rers, hence, nor near me ſtay;
Ye Sons of Violence, away.

12. When

12.

When lawlefs Crouds with infult vain
Thy Works revile, thy Name profane,
Can I unmov'd thofe infults fee,
Nor hate the Wretch that hateth Thee?
Indignant, in thy Caufe I join,
And all thy foes, my God, are mine.

13.

Searcher of hearts, my thoughts review;
With kind feverity purfue
Through each difguife thy Servant's mind,
Nor leave one ftain of guilt behind:
Guide through th' eternal path my feet,
And bring me to thy blifsful Seat.

PSALM CXL.

1.

MY impious foes, great God, repel;
Their rage by pow'r fuperior quell;
Do thou fubdue the adverfe band,
That, leagu'd in guilt, againft me ftand.

2.

They toil, on fierce contention bent,
New arts of mifchief to invent;
Whet, as the Afp, their tongues, and dip
In Death's worft gall their venom'd lip.

3.

O fave me from the hand of Wrong,
And backward turn the frantic Throng,
That, pleas'd, in dire alliance meet,
And tempt to fatal lapfe my feet.

4. The

4.

The murth'rous trap, th' intwining fnare,
The Sons of Violence prepare,
And guileful, onward as I tread,
Befide my path their net outfpread.

5.

Thou art my God; to Thee on high
Thus proftrate at thy throne I cry ;
O let my pray'r by Thee be heard,
From undiffembling lips prefer'd :

6.

Strength of my health, indulgent Lord,
Thy Arm unfeen each adverfe fword,
As o'er the field the battle burn'd,
Preventive from my head has turn'd.

7.

O let not the remorfelefs Band
(Each counfel by thy profp'ring hand
Accomplifh'd, and each wifh fupplied,)
Their conquefts boaft with growing pride :

8.

Do Thou, vindictive, on their heads
(While round the hoftile circle fpreads,
Intent my guiltlefs Soul to flay,)
The mifchief of their lips repay.

9.

Let rufhing flames their fin chaftife ;
Prone tow'rd the pit (no more to rife,)
Let each with fault'ring footfteps bend,
And headlong to its depths defcend.

10. The

10.

The tongue to Wifdom unfubdu'd
From blifs its Owner fhall exclude :
Detraction in the Earth's domain
No lafting heritage fhall gain.

11.

The feet to violence inclin'd,
Deftruction, following faft behind,
Shall hunt, and with unwearied pace
Thro' fin's dark maze their path fhall trace.

12.

My heart has known Thee, Lord, prepar'd
The helplefs and the poor to guard,
To fave them from Oppreffion's jaws,
And vindicate their injur'd caufe.

13

The Souls fubjected to thy fear
To Thee the thankful voice fhall rear,
And, ftudious of thy juft Command,
Within thy fight accepted ftand.

P S A L M   CXLI.

1.

TO Thee I call; O hafte thee near;
    My voice, great God, indulgent hear;
With grateful odour to the fkies
As incenfe let my pray'r arife,
And let my hands, uplifted high,
With full acceptance meet thine eye,
As Victims on thine altar laid,
When Eve extends its deep'ning fhade.

2. O

2.

O let my mouth to guilt be barr'd,
And o'er its portal plant a guard;
Turn, turn from fin's purfuit my will,
Nor let th' artificers of ill
In Me the wifh'd affociate greet,
Or fee me to their path my feet
Incline, and, caught in Error's fnare,
Their feaftful board luxurious fhare.

3.

Let Virtue's Friends, feverely kind,
With welcome chaftifement my mind
Correct, and by their precepts won
Let me each error learn to fhun;
But give not thefe, great God, to fhed
The balm of flatt'ry o'er my head,
Left fudden from thy wrath I feel
The ftroke, that none fhall know to heal.

4.

The pray'r, that from my lips proceeds,
My juft abhorrence of their deeds
Shall fpeak; nor Thou that pray'r defpife,
But, while before their ftartled eyes
From rocky heights their Chiefs are thrown,
Incline their ftubborn hearts to own .
How fweet my words, and, taught thy fear,
The leffons of thy truth to hear.

5.

The beafts, the birds that wing the air
Thy flaughter'd faints infatiate tear,
Behold the grave's wide mouth difplay'd,
Our bones in heaps before it laid,

I

As

As when beneath the Woodman's ſtroke
From the tall Aſh or ſpreading Oak
The branches fall, and ſcatter'd round
In wild diſorder ſtrew the ground.

6.

Father of All ! to Thee mine eyes
I lift : on Thee my hope relies:
Do Thou, as 'mid the toils I tread
By Men of impious heart outſpread,
My danger (nor regardleſs,) ſee,
And let me, while by thy decree
Wrapt in the ſnare themſelves I view,
With ſtep ſecure my path purſue.

P S A L M   CXLII.

1.

TO God I cry; to Him my pray'r
    Addreſs; to Him my heart its care
Shall pour, and to his ear diſcloſe,
In ſad recital, all its woes :
To Him (for He the pray'r can hear)
To Him my ſuppliant voice I rear.

2.

To Thee, great God, to Thee alone,
The traces of my paths are known ;
Thy ſearching eyes, with ſteady view,
Through ſorrow's gloom my ſteps purſue,
And ſee my foes athwart my way
The cover'd ſnare inſidious lay.

3.

I turn'd me, anxious, on the right,
I turn'd, and round me caſt my ſight

K k   With

With fruitlefs fearch; no friend was nigh,
Th' expected fuccour to fupply,
With lenient tongue my griefs to chear,
Or pitying drop the focial tear.

4.

Forlorn of help, Thee, mightieft Lord,
My Soul with humble truft implor'd:
In Thee, All-bounteous God, I cried,
In Thee alone my hopes refide;
O while beneath my woes I bend,
To me thy kindlieft fuccour lend.

5.

While life along my veins fhall ftream,
Its portion Thee and blifs fupreme
My heart fhall own: O gracious hear,
While worn with griefs my voice I rear,
And let my foe's fuperior might
Thy pity to my aid excite.

6.

Do Thou my prifon doors unbar;
So fhall my tongue thy Love declare
In hymns of praife, while, joy'd in Me
Th' event of pious Hope to fee,
The Souls that own thy juft Command
With thankful wonder round me ftand.

P S A L M   CXLIII.

I.

THINE ear, my God, propitious lend;
O ever juft and true, extend
Thy pity, while to Thee I pray,
Nor fcrutinize with ftrict furvey

Thy

Thy fervant's Acts; for who, O who,
Shall pure of guilt approach thy view?

2.

Thou feeft the Foe with furious ftrife
My foul purfue; to earth my life
He treads, and in the horrid gloom,
(As thofe who 'mid the filent tomb
Through ages fleep,) from human eye
Secluded far, has bid me lie.

3.

I feel my vital ftrength depart,
And wild amazement fills my heart:
But, backward borne to periods paft,
Thy Mercies, Lord, my thoughts have trac'd;
And in my breaft recorded ftand
The wonders of thy mighty hand.

4.

Aloft my fuppliant palms I fpread;
Nor more the glebe, its moifture fled,
Longs the defcending fhow'r to fee,
Than thirfts my wearied foul for Thee:
O hide not, Lord, thy face, but fave
Thy fervant from the yawning grave.

5.

O let the hour that wakes the day
Thy Mercy to my ear convey:
While (for on Thee my hope depends)
In fervent thought my mind afcends,
Expectant, tow'rd thy heav'nly Seat,
Train to the paths of Truth my feet.

K k 2 6. To

6.

To Thee, my refuge, Lord, I fly;
Do Thou the deaths that wait me nigh
Repel.   My will to thine (for Thou,
Thou, art my God) corrective bow,
And give me, by thy Spirit led,
The Land of Righteousness to tread.

7.

Thy wonted mercy, Lord, impart,
O quicken with thy grace my heart,
And let thy Justice interpose,
My sorrows to relieve, my foes
To crush, and from their rage remove
A Soul devoted to thy Love.

P S A L M   CXLIV.

1.

BLEST be the Lord my strength, whose
aids,
When lawless force my peace invades,
My fingers for their task prepare,
And discipline my hands to War:

2.

My hope, my shield, my strongest tow'r,
The Friend that in the dang'rous hour
My life protects, and bids each land
Subjected own my just command.

3.

Lord, what is Man, that in thy care
His humble lot should find a share?
Or what the Son of Man, that THOU
Thus to his wants thine ear shouldst bow?

4. What

4.

What are his days? (a fpan their line;)
Or what his age compar'd with thine?
Himfelf, when in the balance weigh'd,
A Nothing, and his Life a fhade.

5.

Defcend, from Heav'n's vaft height defcend:
Its wide-fpread arch beneath thee bend:
Touch the proud hills, eternal Sire;
And fee them quick in fmoke afpire!

6.

Let fierceft lightnings through the air
Now rufhing now reverting tear
Thy ftubborn foes; and, edg'd with flame,
Swift at their heads thy arrows aim.

7.

Stretch to my aid thine arm, and fave
My life from the devouring wave;
Back let the vengeful foe retire,
Whofe lips, whofe hands, in fraud confpire.

8.

So fhall my finger's artful ftroke
The harp and tenftring'd lute provoke
New ftrains t' attempt, and with my tongue
In fweet divifion form the fong.

9.

Guardian of Kings! thy fav'ring might
Thy *David* through the thickeft fight
With watchful care vouchfafes to guide,
And turns each threat'ning fword afide.

 10. Stretch

10.

Stretch to my Aid thine arm, and save
My life from the devouring wave;
Back let the vengeful foe retire,
Whose lips, whose hands, in fraud conspire.

11.

So, nurs'd beneath indulgent skies,
Our Sons with full increase shall rise,
Like youngling plants in order rang'd,
Of healthful stem, and leaf unchang'd—

12.

Our Daughters as the column fair,
That, fashion'd by the Artist's care,
Claims in the regal Dome a place,
The polish'd angle's noblest grace.

13.

So shall the hind exulting bear
The blessings of the loaded year,
And the rich harvest's gather'd store
Load with its heap th' extended floor,

14.

Our Oxen strong for toil behold!
The teeming Mothers of the fold
See, scatter'd o'er the rural scene,
Their thousands and their myriads yean.

15.

No more our Streets the cries of fear
Or shouts of violence shall hear:
Thou, Lord, the tumults shalt assuage
Of hostile force, and civil rage.

16. O

16.

O happy We, while thus our Race
The fignals of thy Love fhall grace!
O bleft the People, that in Thee
Their God and faithful Guardian fee!

PSALM CXLV.

1.

THEE will I blefs, my God and King,
  Nor ceafe thy wondrous Acts to fing :
From earlieft morn to lateft eve
Thy praifes on my tongue fhall live ;
To Thee my harp fhall wake each ftring,
Nor ceafe thy wondrous Acts to fing.

2.

Great is our God : In vain our praife
His Excellence in equal lays
Would celebrate ; in vain the Mind
Its height its depth effays to find :
Age to fucceding age thy Might
Shall fpeak, thy Works, bleft Lord, recite.

3.

My tongue thy glory fhall proclaim,
The faithful witnefs of thy fame,
Bid Contemplation's inmoft thought
Survey the wonders thou haft wrought,
And with affenting myriads join
To blefs the Majefty divine.

4.

Thy dreaded pow'r fhall each rehearfe,
Thy Greatnefs fhall my thankful verfe
       Infpire,

Inſpire, thy Righteouſneſs and Love
Our hearts inflame, our ſongs improve :
Thee good and kind ſhall Mortals own,
To anger ſlow, to pity prone.

5.

Far as Creation's bounds extend,
Thy Mercies, heav'nly Lord, deſcend ;
One chorus of perpetual praiſe
To Thee thy various works ſhall raiſe,
Thy Saints to Thee in hymns impart
The tranſports of a grateful heart,—

6.

The ſplendors of thy Kingdom tell,
Delighted on thy wonders dwell,
And bid the Worlds wide realms admire
The glories of th' Almighty Sire,
Whoſe Throne ſhall Nature's wreck ſurvive
Whoſe Pow'r through endleſs Ages live. .

7.

Thy Promiſe Truth eternal guides,
And Mercy o'er each Act preſides :
The feet whoſe ſteps to lapſe incline
With faithful care thy Arm divine
Shall prop ; the ſpirit bow'd with woe
Thy All-ſupporting aid ſhall know.

8.

From Thee, great God, while ev'ry eye
Expectant waits the wiſh'd ſupply,
Their bread proportion'd to the day
Thy op'ning hands to each convey :
Thy Ways eternal Juſtice guides,
And Mercy o'er thine Act preſides :

9. Who

9.

Who aſk thine aid with heart ſincere,
Thee ever gracious, ever near,
Shall own; their pray'r, in each diſtreſs,
To Thee thy Servants, Lord, addreſs,
And find thee (verging on the grave,)
Nor ſlow to hear, nor weak to ſave.

10.

Ye Souls among his Saints inroll'd,
In God your ſure defence behold,
Who wakes your choſen Train to guard;
While Pride ſhall meet its juſt reward,
And fierce Deſtruction at his Word
Shall bathe in impious blood its ſword.

11.

Long as I breathe, my thankful tongue
To Him ſhall meditate the ſong;
My willing lips with praiſe o'erflow,
My grateful ſoul with tranſport glow;
From Man's whole Race his hallow'd Name
Shall thanks and endleſs honour claim.

PSALM CXLVI. *Hallelujah.*

1.

PRAISE, praiſe thy God, my Soul; his
Name
To Life's laſt date my thanks ſhall claim,
And, long as I exiſt, my lyre
Shall wake to ſing th' eternal Sire.

2. O

2.

O feek not, with prefumption vain,
Your hope on Princes to fuftain,
Nor truft, when threat'ning ills invade,
The ftrengthlefs prop of human aid.

3.

His breath refign'd, on earth's low bed
Behold the Mortal reft his head;
Nor farther fhall his Thoughts extend,
But with him to the grave defcend.

4.

Bleft, who their help in Thee alone,
The God to *Jacob*'s Offspring known,
Have found, and to the hand divine
In each diftrefs their care refign:

5.

That hand, that form'd the Heav'ns and Earth
And call'd the watry Deep to birth,
With All that in the ample round
Of Nature's utmoft reign is found.

6.

'Tis God's, whofe Truth, through Ages paft
Confirm'd, fhall time's extent outlaft;
'Tis His, the injur'd caufe to right,
And crufh the arm of lawlefs Might;

7.

'Tis his to loofe the Captive's chain,
With bread the hungry to fuftain,
The blind reftore, the weak uprear,
And fave the fouls that own his fear.

8. Through

8.

Through diftant regions doom'd to roam,
In Him the ftranger finds a home;
'Tis His, the Orphan's breaft to chear,
And wipe the heart-fwoln Widow's tear.

9.

The impious fouls, whofe Love of ill,
To rafh tranfgreffion prompts their will,
Who dare from his Decrees to ftray,
Shall reap the error of their way.

10.

O *Sion*, in thy God confide,
And know how fix'd his Reign, how wide;
Q'er fubject Worlds his juft Command
To endlefs age confirm'd fhall ftand.

Hallelujah.

PSALM CXLVII.

1.

O Blefs *Jehovah* : Sweet the joy,
    When tafks like thefe the voice employ;
To Him our higheft thanks belong
And Praife fits comely on our tongue.

2.

'Tis He who builds fair *Salem*'s walls,
And *Ifrael*'s exil'd fons recalls;
Yields to the contrite heart relief,
And binds its wounds, and fooths its grief:

3.

He to the ftars affigns their names,
(As, fcatter'd wide, their vivid flames
Adorn the bright ethereal plain,)
And numbers with his eye their train.

4. Great

4.

Great is our God : beyond all bound
His Pow'r, beyond all fearch is found
His Knowledge ; in his Arm the Meek
With fure fuccefs their Aid fhall feek ;

5.

That Arm, whofe unrefifted ftroke,
On Each who dares his Wrath provoke,
With fwift defcent its aim fhall guide,
And level to the duft their pride.

6.

Let ev'ry tongue, let ev'ry chord,
Exalt the Name of *Jacob*'s Lord,
Whofe hand with clouds the Heav'n obfcures,
On Earth the genial moifture pours ;

7.

He bids the herb its mantle fpread,
Luxuriant o'er the Mountain's head :
Gives to the Beafts their wonted Food,
And ftills the Raven's clam'rous Brood.

8.

If o'er the field the battle bleed,
His watchful eye the ftrengthful Steed
Regards not, nor the Chiefs whofe feet
Unmov'd the fhock of legions meet.

9.

On You, in whom his fear refides,
On You whofe heart in Him confides,
His Grace its fignals fhall beftow,
His Arm with conqueft bind your brow.

10. O

10.

O *Solyma*, his lov'd Abode,
Him praife, unceafing! Blefs thy God,
O *Sion*, who thy gates has barr'd;
Whofe various gifts thy Sons have fhar'd;

11.

His vifits teach thy grateful foil
To recompenfe the tiller's toil;
He crowns with peace thy happy plain;
Calls from thy glebe the pureft grain.

12.

His Word, from Heav'n in fwift career
Convey'd, fuggefts to Nature's ear
The Laws that regulate her frame,
And gives her ev'ry act its aim.

13.

Flak'd by his Art, the woolly fnow
Falls filent on the ground below;
By Him the froft, as afhes hoar,
Lies fprinkled earth's wide furface o'er:

14.

In harden'd fragments through the air,
While Man its rigours fhuns to bear,
His Hail defcends; in icy chains
His hand the gliding ftream detains.

15.

Till, at his Word, th' inftructed wind
With friendly breath the Wave unbind,
And bid it, onward borne, again
With liquid lapfe its courfe maintain.

L l   16. Such

16.

Such is the God, and such his Might,
Whose Precepts *Israel's* Love invite,
And to his Tribes in full display
His Life-directing truths convey.

17.

What Realm, thro' earth's extended Coasts,
His Care, like thine, O *Judah*, boasts,
Or, taught, as Thou, his fear to own,
The dictates of his Will has known?

18.

O come, your thankful voices join,
And bless the Majesty divine:
His praise, to Time's remotest day,
His pow'r in sacred notes display.

P S A L M   CXLVIII. *Hallelujah.*

1.

YE Blest Inhabitants of Heav'n,
   To God be all your praises giv'n;
O praise him from the realms that lie
Above the reach of mortal eye :
Him praise, ye Angels of his Train,
Him, All whom Heav'n's vast Hosts contain.

2.

Praise Him, thou glorious orb of light,
And Thou, pale Ruler of the night ;
Praise Him, ye Stars; His praise repeat,
Thou Heav'n of Heav'ns, his awful Seat,
And You, ye Floods, that, heap'd on high,
Press with your weight th' extended sky.

3. Let

3.

Let Thefe to God their voices rear,
Who bade them be ; and ftrait they were :
Who bids them ftand ; and ftand they fhall ;
Nor aught the Mandate fhall recall,
That, fix'd by his Almighty Mind,
To endlefs age their date affign'd.

4.

Nor let the Heav'n his praife confine ;
O All of Earth the chorus join :
Ye Whales, ye Deeps, in praife confpire,
Snow, Vapour, Hail, and bick'ring Fire,
And ev'ry Wind, and ev'ry Storm,
That duteous his behefts perform ;—

5.

Ye leffer Hills, ye Mountains high,
Ye Trees, whofe fruits Man's food fupply,
Ye Cedars, whole expanded Shade
Nor Storms nor Ages teach to fade,
Ye Beafts, that range th' uncultur'd foil,
Or patient lend to Man your toil.

6.

Praife Him, each Bird that wings the air,
Each Reptile, nurtur'd by his care ;
Ye Kings and Nations of the Earth ;
O praife him All of princely birth,
And Ye, whofe Doom, as Juftice guides,
The long-contefted caufe decides.

7.

Ye Youthful Bands and Virgin Choir,
Each lifping Babe, and hoary Sire,

Wake

Wake to his Name your grateful fongs;
To Him alone all Praife belongs;
His glory Earth's wide bounds o'erflows,
Nor higheft Heav'n its limit knows.

8.

Ye Tribes, exalted by his Arm,
You, chief, the heav'nly Theme fhall warm,
Bleft Sons of *Ifrael*'s hallow'd Land,
Who neighb'ring to his prefence ftand :
O come, your thankful voices raife,
And confecrate to Him your praife.

PSALM CXLIX. *Hallelujah.*

1.

SING to our God the new-form'd lay;
Ye Souls who his commands obey,
Affembling join your thankful tongues,
And hallow with his praife your Songs.

2.

O *Ifrael*, let thy Maker's Name
With joyous zeal thy breaft inflame,
And *Sion*'s fons exulting fing
The Mercies of their heav'nly King.

3.

Range in the dance the facred Band,
And urge the Minftrel's well-taught hand
To ftrike the loud-refounding lyre,
While timbrels in his praife confpire.

4. With

4.

With what delight, great God, behold
Thine eyes the People of thy fold!
Thy Strength the Souls of humble frame
Their ever prefent Aid proclaim.

5.

With conqueft crown'd, and rapt in joy,
Let All whom thy Decrees employ
Thy Name exalt, and thankful raife
The fong of gratitude and praife:

6.

Let all unite with willing mind,
Nor ceafe, when on their beds reclin'd,
The filent midnight's lift'ning ear
With fongs of loudeft mirth to chear.

7.

Thy Mercy let their lips record;
Give to their grafp the two-edg'd fword;
And let them, guided by thy hand,
Deal vengeance through each heathen land.

8.

Let them the guilty tribes chaftife
Whofe impious Arm thy pow'r defies;
Triumphant in the iron chain
Their Nobles and their Kings detain,—

9.

And while, infpir'd with active zeal
Thy prefcript thus their hands fulfil,
The glories wear for All prepar'd,
Whofe hearts thy juft behefts regard.

Hallelujah.

PSALM

PSALM CL. *Hallelujah.*

I.

PRAISE, O praife, the Name divine ;
  Praife it at the hallow'd Shrine ;
Let the Firmament on high
To its Maker's praife reply.

2.

Let each tongue, and let each chord
Praife the name of *Jacob*'s Lord,
Let his Acts, and Pow'r fupreme,
To your Song's fuggeft a theme.

3.

Be the harp no longer mute ;
Sound the trumpet, touch the lute ;
Wake to life each tuneful ftring ;
Bring the pipe, the timbrel bring.

4.

Let the organ in his praife
Learn its loudeft note to raife,
And the cymbal's varying found
From the vaulted roof rebound.

5.

All who vital breath enjoy,
In his praife that breath employ,
And in one great Chorus join ;
Praife, O praife, the Name divine.

GLORIA

GLORIA PATRI.

1.

IN Thee, O Heav'n, O Earth, in Thee
Be Glory to th' eternal Three;
That Glory, which through ages paſt
Was; is; and ſhall for ever laſt.

OR THIS.

2.

To Father, Son, and Spirit bleſt,
Be praiſe in Heav'n and Earth addreſs'd,
As was, and is, and yet ſhall be,
When Time its lateſt hour ſhall ſee.

OR THIS.

3.

To Father, Son, and Spirit bleſt,
Be praiſe in loudeſt notes addreſs'd,
Such praiſe as from th' Angelic Choirs,
And Saints whom zeal like theirs inſpires,
In Heav'n above and Earth below
Still flows, and ſhall for ever flow.

OR THIS.

4.

To Father, Son, and Spirit bleſt,
Be praiſe in loudeſt notes addreſs'd,
Such as the Stars of Morning ſung,
When Earth was on its balance hung,
Such praiſe as from th' Angelic Choirs,
And Saints whom zeal like theirs inſpires,
In Heav'n above and Earth below
Still flows and ſhall for ever flow.

a   ANO.

ANOTHER.

5.

All Glory to th' Eternal Three ;
Thee, Father ; Thee, O Son ; and Thee,
   The Spirit ever bleſt :
That Glory, which through ages paſt
Unchang'd has ſtood, and yet ſhall laſt,
   When time has ſunk to reſt.

ANOTHER.

6.

All Glory to th' Eternal Three,
   As was, ere Time began to roll,
As is, nor yet ſhall ceaſe to be,
   When Time has reach'd its deſtin'd goal.

ANOTHER.

7.

Be Glory to th' Eternal Three
   Aſcrib'd, and higheſt Praiſe,
As was, and is, and ſtill ſhall be
   Beyond the end of days.

ANOTHER.

8.

To th' Eternal Three be giv'n
Praiſe on Earth, and Praiſe in Heav'n ;
Such as was through Ages paſt,
Is, and ſhall for ever laſt

⁎ The *Tranſlations of the* G L O R I A
P A T R I, *here given, exhibit a Specimen of
ſix different Sorts of Metre uſed in the Verſion
or Paraphraſe of the* Pſalms.

F I N I S.

www.ingramcontent.com/pod-product-compliance
Lightning Source LLC
Chambersburg PA
CBHW021334110726
47900CB00005B/1461